DATE DUE

Holding Accountants Accountable

Founded in 1807, John Wiley & Sons is the oldest independent publishing company in the United States. With offices in North America, Europe, Asia, and Australia, Wiley is globally committed to developing and marketing print and electronic products and services for our customers' professional and personal knowledge and understanding.

The Wiley Corporate F&A series provides information, tools, and insights to corporate professionals responsible for issues affecting the profitability of their company, from accounting and finance to internal controls and performance management.

Holding Accountants Accountable

How Professional Standards Can Lead to Personal Liability

JEFFREY G. MATTHEWS

WILEY

Published by John Wiley & Sons, Inc., Hoboken, New Jersey.
Published simultaneously in Canada.

For general information on our other products and services or for technical support, please contact our Customer Care Department within the United States at (800) 762-2974, outside the United States at (317) 572-3993, or fax (317) 572-4002.

Wiley publishes in a variety of print and electronic formats and by print-on-demand. Some material included with standard print versions of this book may not be included in e-books or in print-on-demand. If this book refers to media such as a CD or DVD that is not included in the version you purchased, you may download this material at http://booksupport.wiley.com. For more information about Wiley products, visit www.wiley.com.

NOTE: Any views or opinions represented in this work are personal and belong solely to the author and those quoted or cited. They do not represent those of people, institutions or organizations that they may or may not be associated with in any professional or personal capacity, unless explicitly stated.

Library of Congress Cataloging-in-Publication Data:

Names: Matthews, Jeffrey G., 1973- author.
Title: Holding accountants accountable : how professional standards can
   lead to personal liability / Jeffrey G. Matthews.
Description: Hoboken : Wiley, 2019. | Includes index.
Identifiers: LCCN 2019025700 (print) | LCCN 2019025701 (ebook) | ISBN
   9781119597698 (hardback) | ISBN 9781119597711 (adobe pdf) | ISBN
   9781119597704 (epub)
Subjects: LCSH: Accountants—Professional ethics. | Accounting—Standards.
Classification: LCC HF5625.15 .M38 2019 (print) | LCC HF5625.15 (ebook) |
   DDC 657.02/18—dc23
LC record available at https://lccn.loc.gov/2019025700
LC ebook record available at https://lccn.loc.gov/2019025701

Cover Design: Wiley
Cover Image: © gremlin/Getty Images

Printed in the United States of America
V10014392_100319

Contents

Preface

ONE WOULD HAVE TO scorch the earth and search long and hard to find a profession more grounded in ethical principles than accounting. It goes without saying, but ethics and accounting go together like "peas and carrots," as Forrest Gump would say. However, would it surprise you to know that very few professionals face more ethical challenges than accountants face? Especially when it comes to preventing, detecting, deterring, and disclosing fraud and misconduct? It may also surprise you to know just how *easy* it is for accountants to find themselves facing ethical dilemmas whose outcomes have far-reaching implications. One single decision can be career ending, or career defining. That is where I come in.

Over the course of my 25-year career, I have faced my fair share of ethical dilemmas, death threats, retaliation, and family hardships. I have experienced first-hand the peaks and valleys associated with the life and times of a fraud fighter. I have always heard that what doesn't kill you makes you stronger. Well, brothers and sisters, I think I am about as strong as I care to be! I like to think that being raised in a small town in north Louisiana and being force-fed faith and family helped sharpen my sense of right and wrong. And although I sometimes struggled, I survived and learned valuable lessons along the way. I have also seen clients, colleagues, and family members rise and fall, their careers made and delayed over one critical decision or lapse in judgment. I feel very fortunate to have experienced my fair share of second chances, as have many others mentioned herein. I feel even more blessed that I get to share those stories with you.

I have sought to illustrate the simple concept, "What can cause an accountant to do a bad job and violate professional standards? What can happen to them if they do?" In this narrative, I share common tendencies that hinder practitioners' ability to detect, deter, and prevent fraud and misconduct, some of which could violate professional standards leading to dire consequences. I also categorize these ethical impediments in the following chapters, the headings of which ironically spell the word *fraud*:

> **F – Forgetting the Present and the Past:** Many practitioners feel that fraud could never happen to them or to their clients. However, one needs only to grab today's newspaper to address this fallacy. Professionals must stay on top of emerging trends to identify areas of weakness, or they could find themselves on the front page.
>
> **R – Relying on Others:** Often, practitioners face time and budget constraints, which require delegation to lower-level staff. If the work environment is not conducive to collaboration, inexperienced staff, combined with an overextended supervisor with limited time (or budget), can lead to a disaster. If you think reviewing working papers is expensive, try skipping the review and see what that costs!
>
> **A – Accepting, Not Verifying:** In God we trust; all others we audit. Practitioners must maintain a healthy dose of skepticism in discharging their duties. Having a habit of *accepting*, not *verifying* can put an examiner in the crosshairs of agencies that will certainly do more than just test.
>
> **U – Underestimating the Effort:** Many practitioners are given assignments with little time, budget, or direction. Sometimes, practitioners fight to "win" those very assignments, and shortcuts to the finish can ensue. Another iteration is within firms that espouse an "eat what you kill" environment that can push examiners to accept engagements they are not qualified to perform. Our profession is not to imitate *Naked and Afraid*, so examiners should stick to what they know and build an extensive referral network for situations outside their area of expertise.
>
> **D – Determining the Outcome Before the Work:** We have all heard it hundreds of times: "This is a relationship business." But we have also heard horror stories that begin with "Well, I knew this guy . . . ." or "I had these friends and . . ." This is another area ripe for abuse, in that examiners can become close to their clients and establish biases. Sometimes, the examiner may not realize there is a bias at all. Overlooking red flags while at the same time looking forward to the holiday party invite or the honey-baked ham gift basket can lead an examiner to looking for a new career.

Finally, yet importantly, I talk about the barriers accountants face in situations in which they do find fraud, but struggle to decide whether to disclose it. Sometimes accountants do their jobs so well, they find the unimaginable and unanticipated. However, the burdens and consequences the accountant may face in "doing the right thing" can sometimes weigh heavily on an already weary accountant's shoulders.

In my occasionally homespun way, I share my personal challenges and perspectives, as well as my observations of other ethical lapses that have affected our profession. I write this to show that all accountants face challenges. I also like to remind accountants that even when they feel alone, they are not. Have faith greater than fear. Accountants must be reminded that even in these trying times there are strong and honorable professionals behind them. I hope after reading this, you will someday consider me one of them.

Introduction

W HAT MAKES US WHO we are? What is at work to make us enjoy the things we enjoy, to choose our life's work, to cause us to be attracted to certain people and not to others?

We all are very complex individuals – a monumental understatement. While there is a formula for who we are becoming (which is or should be a life-long process), it is highly unpredictable, but here it is:

> Nurture (our environment) + Nature (our DNA) + Our Own Choices = Who We Are. The wild card here is our decisions – heavily influenced by the first two addends. Nevertheless, we own our choices.

In my life, it is difficult to separate the environment of my youth from the DNA my ancestors contributed to this equation. My mother's family moved into the agricultural area that would come to be known as Boeuf Prairie in the early 1800s. These settlers from Virginia, Kentucky, Tennessee, and Arkansas arrived in what was essentially a wilderness at that time. Families settling here were predominantly of Scotch-Irish and British ancestry, but had lived in America since before the Revolutionary War.

It is beyond my understanding why they would leave the mountains of Appalachia to establish a community in the hot, humid, insect- and snake-infested region of northeast Louisiana; public records would indicate that they were drawn to the fertile farmlands available in the Mississippi Delta. Nine generations later, my grandmothers, mother, uncle, and sister still live in the same parish as those early pioneers. Fortunately, air conditioning and insect repellent have improved the standard of living.

Settling near the Boeuf River was necessary to get produce to market and obtain household goods. The chief cash crop was King Cotton. Two hundred years ago, waterways were the interstates of today. Rivers provided the main routes for transportation and shipping, and New Orleans was the principal shipping point. A trip to New Orleans via steamboat was about a 20-day journey.

My great-grandfather's family, the Daileys, owned a gin near the river and had their own shipping dock, known as Dailey Landing. My father's family, the Thomases, had a landing in another part of the parish. We have records showing there were four cotton gins on our family settlement (whereas none exist today; corn and soybeans predominately grow where cotton once stood tall).

I grew up hearing stories about the Daileys of the past, my maternal grandmother's family. One of my ancestors traveled to California during the Gold Rush. However, he did not return with a fortune, and letters saved indicated he got very homesick, but his handwriting was impeccable. My great-great-great-grandfather was killed in a duel during the Civil War. My uncle, Greg Kincaid, still farms our family's "place" (actually called "The Place" for generations) and raises cattle. He has a restored shotgun house full of historical memorabilia and is a fountain of knowledge of our family's history. If you can spare an afternoon, he will tell you all about it (bring a stool and stay awhile). His hard work was recently rewarded, and he received an acknowledgment in the state historical registry for maintaining our heritage by managing a farm with an unbroken chain of family ownership of more than 150 years. In fact, our family cemetery, which is still maintained in the highest order, has tombstones that date back into the early 1800s. I hope that is my final resting place. I have a rich heritage.

The families who settled in what is now southern Franklin Parish were of the Methodist faith, and a local church was soon established. The Boeuf Prairie Methodist Church is currently the oldest church in Franklin Parish, established in 1833. Lemuel Bowden, my great-great-great-great-great-grandfather, was listed as one of the church founders, assisting in the financing and planning of the building in 1837. As a child, I enjoyed many summer Vacation Bible Schools in that church. The lovely sanctuary still holds worship services every Sunday morning.

Until the mid-1840s, the Boeuf Prairie community was part of Catahoula Parish. The church was the scene of the first parish organizational meetings, when the parish of Franklin was being established. The first grand jury and the first court were held here, until the courthouse was constructed in Winnsboro, around 1945. Apparently, no one in those days thought it politically incorrect to meet in a church to conduct government business.

By the 1940s, several Baptist families had joined the community. After attending services with the Methodists for a few years, they were able to build a church across the road from the Fort Necessity High School. My father's family attended the Baptist church, and that is where I was baptized and where my dad and his dad are buried. Although I grew up in the Baptist church, I knew all the folks from the Methodist church just as well (our attendance sometimes was determined by which one was having a potluck lunch or dinner). Both congregations had close friendships and fellowship. Church was the main source of social connection and support in that community for its first 100 years.

I know very little from my dad's side of the family. My dad's great-great-great-grandfather was a showboat entertainer from Natchez, Mississippi. My dad's great-great-grandmother told the story of our legacy to the local newspaper, the *Monroe Morning World*, on her ninetieth birthday, in May 1939. She told of the fun times, such as when her father was a young boy and was fishing on the river when a showboat passed. Being that he was a long way upstream, the boat picked him up and refused to let him leave . . . or, more likely, deep down in his heart, he wanted to stay. That was the last he saw of his people again. When he grew into manhood, the boat stopped in Natchez, and that is where he met the love of his life.

She also told of tough times, such as living through three wars in which the United States was involved. She once even cheated death. While playing in the yard, she heard a voice whisper "get on the porch." Just then, a cannonball struck the tree under which she had been playing. She saw eight of her 10 children die, and lived through spells of bad health and poverty. Yet the article described her as being fondly referred to as "Aunt Mary" and possessed "a jolly and contented spirit." She lived by the motto of her father, "Life Must Go On." Her philosophy was "to only want the simplest and be cheerful over that." I love it! Could this possibly be where I get my penchant for storytelling? Presenting? Could this be the conflict between my educational DNA, and that of a mischievous cartoon character? I digress.

My dad's father, my paternal grandfather, died of heart disease at 56. My dad's grandfather was also the exact same age when he cashed in his chips. My father had his first heart attack at 41 years old, and over the next 10 years, he had several more. He lost his spleen, half his pancreas, and a leg (to diabetes) before the last big attack sent him home a couple of months after his fifty-fourth birthday. Despite these ailments, he continued to work until he passed. One of his biggest fears was being unable to provide (being unable to use the restroom on his own was a close second). One of his brothers and both sisters also had heart attacks early in their lives, but each lived to tell about it. His youngest brother, my second uncle Greg – my lifelong mentor – not only survived, but made it out and thrived. And the world is better because of it. I would have often been lost without him. My dad's mother is also still with us, at the ripe old age of 89. Nonetheless, and all in all, I spent many nights with both great-grandmothers, a great-grandfather, and both grandfathers. Both of my grandmothers remain with me today (and have good days and bad days). I can tell you whose genes I hope have been passed on to me!

If my family valued faith in God first of all, education ran a close second. In the 1800s, there were public and some private schools (provided by the older, established families), but no high school facility. That changed in 1925; under the leadership of my great-great uncle, John L. Dailey, a beautiful two-story building was built, and 11 grades were taught for the first time at a public school in Fort Necessity. My great-grandmother, Eula Ross (Dailey), was one of six very excited girls in the first graduating class of Fort Necessity High School in the spring of 1926, and she was there for my graduation in 1991. We will get to that in moment.

I am the fourth generation in my family (on my mom's side) to obtain a four-year college degree; this was not common in the rural South where I grew up. Those in the community who did not farm typically taught school, or had long retired from doing so. In fact, I counted six teachers who actually taught both of my parents (and a couple who even spanked both my dad and me). My maternal great-grandmother and grandmother both taught English, and my paternal grandmother worked in the cafeteria. The men farmed, and for a while commercial catfish ponds doused the area. If neither of those career opportunities appealed to you, there was also the hope that you would be invited to work offshore on an oil/gas drilling rig, at least until you received your early retirement (aka back injury). My dad was an electrician on drilling rigs and was gone most of the time. When he was home, he raised and sold animals of all types. One week, he might have sold rabbits, whereas the next weekend he was dealing in miniature donkeys. I do not ever remember having a pen to corral any of them. Our animals, to many of our kin's dismay, were "free-range animals." It was a mess.

I must admit, I sometimes felt insecure about my upbringing while living my life in the world of PhDs, attorneys, judges, and Fortune 500 executives. I don't remember anyone in my white-collar world telling me their family only had enough hot water for one family member to have a hot bath, nor have I run across many people in our profession who received free lunch at school and wore homemade clothes until high school. Yet I know they are out there. And perhaps they should share, as I share with you. We'd have more in common and probably be kinder to one another. But, as I write this, I've never been more proud. I think I have made the most out of what I was given. It was a much simpler place and time.

There were two kinds of music: country and western. There were also two types of blue jeans: Sears and Roebuck. In 1985, my father purchased his first full-service gas station. It was just like Goober's Garage from *Mayberry*. From the age of 12 until 18, every free moment I had was spent pumping gas, changing oil, fixing flats, and washing cars. A lot of my experiences from the gas station are best left on the therapist's couch, but I do think some of the best life lessons I learned came from serving others in that small town.

I attended grades K–12 in this small, rural school, where my parents and maternal grandparents all graduated. I was a "spirited" child I am told. I was known to get in trouble intentionally, just so that I could be sent into the hall. I knew the spanking was coming, but I was also able to play for a few minutes before that. Since I wasn't bothered by the spankings, it was a big win! And sometimes, I got several per day (my own "cost/benefit analysis" in kindergarten).

I was 13 years old when *The Untouchables* was released in 1987. Although I did not understand many of the concepts in that film, watching Kevin Costner in the role of Eliot Ness cemented my desire to become a fraud-fighter. I had been infatuated with the idea of catching "bad guys" long before that, staying up past my bedtime to watch mob movies and read about their misdeeds and downfalls (there was always a downfall). I was fascinated by the idea of corralling the smartest of the bad guys, and those types of bad guys didn't always shoot back (at least in the movies). From that point forward, anytime someone asked me what I wanted to be when I grew up, I would answer "a Forensic Accountant." That did not earn me many friends and it certainly did not earn me a seat at the cool kids table. Think about it . . . have you ever seen a Forensic Accountant Halloween costume? Do you know a single woman who dreams of being swept off her feet by an accountant? It was hopeless.

Now, growing up in a somewhat poor, rural town of 300 people, I knew a lot of bad guys, and I'm not sure I would call any of them particulary smart. I can easily start with my dad. My dad was never accused of being particularly trustworthy, although most of his shenanigans were small, buyer-beware and get-rich-quick schemes. When I started at the gas station, I was instructed to save the plastic containers of certain types of oil, and refill them with another. When I questioned my dad as to the point, he barked at me to do what I was told, and "those containers looked better on the shelf." What I later realized was he was charging customers for premium oil, but the contents were something else. I moved to his second gas station shortly after that, and made sure we never took part in that nonsense.

I suppose he grew tired of that simplistic scheme and went on to bigger things. In 1990, while my mother was away visiting family (when Mamma traveled, all sorts of "exciting" things often took place), he staged a trip to Mexico with one of the gas station employees and a friend. He returned a few days later and claimed that his truck had been stolen. He quickly filed an insurance claim and bought a bigger and nicer rig. I noticed in the back of the gas station (by the damn oil I was supposed to be refilling) all of his "stolen" truck's contents were in a crate under a blanket. I confronted him, and asked how that was possible, and whether he was a fortuneteller, predicting the truck's taking. He would not answer me, and I knew immediately what happened. (I also remembered a year or two earlier that his van had mysteriously caught on fire, during a trip down a road he never used nor had reason to be on.) I wasn't the only one who found it odd. The sheriff's office launched an investigation. It wasn't long until the gas station employee who accompanied Daddy to Mexico got nabbed for a DWI (driving while intoxicated). He cut a deal and told the tale of what really happened in Mexico. I remember being on a lunch break, eating Popeye's Fried Chicken (love that chicken from Popeye's), when the sheriff's deputy came and picked up my dad. The deputy had the decency to wait until they were out of my sight to handcuff him. My dad pled guilty to felony insurance fraud charges and received probation. It was the talk of the town. That was the last time I was involved in any business dealings with my dad.

Despite showing much promise as a grease monkey, I was undeterred in my pursuit of a forensic accounting career. The school I mentioned combined elementary through high school grades. At our highest enrollment, K–12 totaled 323. While I was a "spirited" child throughout most of my time there, I made good grades. I entered high school with 15 people in my homeroom class. The challenge was that our school did not have, nor had it ever had, an accounting class. I could not major in accounting at the university without taking at least one of them. Our endearing business teacher, Ms. Betty Byergeon, assembled a class for me, and I had a friend who agreed to attend. And wouldn't you know it? I finished at the top of my class in accounting. I even received a small trophy at the end of the year – although I do believe that was the last time I topped any of my accounting classes.

I went to a small college in Monroe Louisiana: Northeast Louisiana University. Despite having an annual enrollment of less than 10,000 students, it felt enormous and frightened me. I remember filling my Isuzu pickup truck with dorm room furnishings and making the one-hour trek from my home to Monroe. I was ticketed for speeding within 20 minutes of leaving my house, and the first night on campus, my toolbox was stolen from the back of my truck. Welcome to the big city, country boy!

I played baseball, basketball, and tennis in high school. The university awarded me a $500-a-semester job as an intramural referee. It was a disaster. In a new place where I knew no one, *no* one wanted to hang out with the referee who cost them the game or blew a call. I did not need any other reason to be uncool! Not long after that, I took a job at the local Mexican restaurant. After a year and a half, I left the restaurant business and followed my uncle into the banking world. I met tons of people and made good money for a college student.

As my classes began to get tougher, I grew to hate accounting. The meticulous detail necessary to complete homework conflicted with my social and work schedule, and I found nothing enjoyable about it. I remember contemplating changing my major a number of times, but I had come too far. My dreams of the FBI or the IRS were fleeing, and I became resigned to being a banker. After all, I had excelled as a loan officer at one of the world's largest loan companies, and I was making $13 an hour. That was a lot of money in 1994 for someone without a degree. In addition, despite working part-time, I won many monthly origination (sales) contests and received multiple prizes that enabled me to furnish my apartment and replace some tools.

I remember asking my supervisor questions about the value of collateral we were accepting as security, which included items such as water hoses, lawn mowers, weight benches, and furniture. It became sort of a game to see what outrageous items you could add to the collateralization form. It was even more fun to call our customers when they had fallen behind, to check and see if the treadmill was still working, and to ask when I could come by and pick up their dishes. I don't ever remember seizing one single item, but those calls became the highlight of my day as I was able to defer their payments here and there and occasionally waive penalties. I could also insert some humor and encouragement into what had likely become a stressful situation for them.

Despite the comfortable living I was achieving while working 32 hours a week, I felt depressed and guilty for selling loans to people when, despite what the formulas and supporting documentation showed, I knew, deep down, they could not afford the terms. As graduation neared, the loan company offered me a full-time job, with a salary that would have placed me at the top of my graduating accounting class. It was more than a Big Four firm offered a friend of mine who graduated with a perfect 4.0. I turned it down and never looked back. I wanted to feel good about what I did for a living, and this was not the place for me.

I had not given the loan company an answer, and their offers continued to increase. I felt an enormous amount pressure and stress. While a number of big banks had expressed their interest, their offers were 30% less than the one I had with the finance company. I was truly thankful to have the opportunity, but I had worked hard putting myself through school, and I did not feel loan-sharking was my calling. I was restless. At the time, I lived in an abandoned newspaper factory that contained a makeshift loft apartment. It was not in a safe area, but it was far away from the distractions of campus, which I desperately needed to avoid if I wanted to graduate. I often biked (well, until my bike was stolen) the levies of the Ouachita River at midnight when I could not sleep. In fact, I once discovered a body on the Ouachita River bank in the wee hours one morning. I dismounted my mountain bike (another contest prize) and saw that it was indeed a body wrapped up in a blanket. I approached the body, and nudged it with my foot. My heart was racing. I nudged it again. Nothing. Keep in mind, this was long before cell phones, and my legs were too shaky to speed away on my bike. I had no clue what to do, but I needed to know for sure if it was a body, and whether it was alive or dead. So I reached down to peeled back the blanket, and that's when his hand grabbed mine. I screamed like a wild banshee. I am fairly certain I soiled myself, but considering the current company, that wasn't as embarrassing as it could have been.

I snatched my hand from his mitts, tripped over my bike, and crawled to a safe distance. I said a few choice words and quickly came to my wits. I asked him if he needed help. "Would you like a Hot Pocket or a Pop-Tart?" His response was gruff: "What I really need is some money." And I had the perfect response: "I do have some money for you. Anything in that shopping cart I can hold as collateral?" I had no doubt that I could get him approved. Shortly thereafter, my bike was stolen from the top of my car in broad daylight as I was preparing for a ride. I bet it ended up on someone's loan collateralization form.

The job interviews continued on campus: one bank after another and an occasional insurance company. I grew anxious, and I had no direction. Then, everything changed early one Thursday morning in March 1995.

In March 1995, I was sequestered to a "meeting" being held by the department head of accounting. The meeting was set for the afternoon, which conflicted with my work schedule. I sat down in a room full of graduating accounting seniors a little after noon. The department head shared that we were required to take an "aptitude test" in order to assess the accounting department's teacher competencies, and while the exam would not count for or against us as students, it was important to the department. He estimated the exam would take four hours. Ever the accountant, I quickly determined the exam would cost me nearly $100 in wages. That was a lot of money to me then, as it is now!

Much to the department head's ire, I walked my exam to the front of the room after 10 minutes. You can only imagine the exchange the two of us had, as I walked out of the room and headed to work.

Two days later, on a Thursday morning, the department head came to my morning Accounting Systems class, opened the door, pointed his finger at me, and motioned me to come with him. I panicked. I knew what it was about, and I knew he was about to punish me for exiting the exam room earlier.

I accompanied him to his office. He asked me to explain myself. I told him that I had work, and that I was not positive that I even desired a career in accounting. I went into great detail as to my plans to become an investigator for the FBI, the DOJ, or some other agency. I took him back to my early years, from Sunday school to high school. I knew my purpose.

He took a deep breath, and stated, "I thought you would say that. I just received a call from a friend of mine from the Louisiana Legislative Auditor's Office, who is also an alumnus. He is building a public corruption and forensic accounting department for the state, and is looking for a smart accountant who does not seem to fit in with the others. Someone who is not easily intimidated, but respectful. I thought of you. Would you like my recommendation?"

I cried out on the spot. And screamed "*Yes!*" To which he replied, "I thought you would say that, too." As he pulled something from his desk, he added, "But first, I need you to take this damn test."

Ha! I did, and the rest is history. I interviewed with the department and got the job. It truly was a dream come true.

If I haven't made this abundantly clear by now, I was taught to value faith, family, and education. And while I have had far more than my fair share of struggles, I have strived to pass these values on to my own children. If only they could inherit the good and leave out the bad. I have included some history of my environment to partially explain my deep connection to family roots, and why I have always had such strong ideas of right and wrong. While this background is a moral foundation that helps guide my decisions and is a stabilizing influence, it can also cause some internal conflict, both in my personal and professional life. Perhaps, through these passages, I stir something in you. Something you can draw on in times of need and when you feel challenged.

Okay, enough on all that. Why are we here? Well, during the course of my career, I have learned to embrace accounting. Similar to my heritage, the accounting profession is known for its strict standards and ethical requirements. Other than perhaps law and patient care, there are few occupations that define "acts discreditable to the profession." Considering that I have chosen a career that largely focuses on the alleged misconduct of others, I often see where good people do bad things. I see where strong practitioners are exposed in moments of weakness. In fact, I even thought of calling this book *Accountants Gone Wild*, but calmer heads prevailed.

It seems fitting to put this right here. This is a personal journey. Any views or opinions represented in this work are personal and belong solely to me. They do not represent those of people, institutions, or organizations that I may or may not be associated with in any professional or personal capacity, unless explicitly stated. Heck, I'm just glad they still claim me (and that's only on occasion). And I certainly do not intend to convey legal advice. Them lawyers charge way more than I do. Ha!

For this narrative, I have included standards from the American Institute of Certified Public Accountants (AICPA), the Association of Certified Fraud Examiners (ACFE), and the Institute of Internal Auditors (IIA). I have compiled case law and related cases. I have also obtained white-papers and interviewed those who could have easily spun this yarn. We will get to all of those, but I find the public is more aware of the AICPA, so let's start with those I frequent the most.

 ## STATEMENT ON STANDARDS FOR CONSULTING SERVICES

Most of the work I do will fall under the Statements for Consulting Services. (That will change in 2020. In July, 2019, the AICPA released new standards for those practicing forensic accounting. Among other changes, the AICPA specifically defines "investigation" and "litigation". The standards will be into effect for 2020. Nonetheless, research and watch for updates on this development.) Statements on Standards for Consulting Services are issued by the AICPA Management Consulting Services Executive Committee, the senior technical committee of the Institute designated to issue pronouncements in connection with consulting services. Council has designated the AICPA Management Consulting Services Executive Committee as a body to establish professional standards under the Compliance with Standards Rule (ET sec. 1.310.001) of the Institute's Code of Professional Conduct (code). Members should be prepared to justify departures from this statement.

Consulting services that CPAs provide to their clients have evolved from advice on accounting-related matters to a wide range of services involving diverse technical disciplines, industry knowledge, and consulting skills. Most practitioners, including those who provide audit and tax services, also provide business and management-consulting services to their clients.

Consulting services differ fundamentally from the CPA's function of attesting to the assertions of other parties. In an attest service, the practitioner expresses a conclusion about the reliability of a written assertion that is the responsibility of another party, the asserter. In a consulting service, the practitioner develops the findings, conclusions, and recommendations presented. The nature and scope of work are determined solely by the agreement between the practitioner and the client. Generally, the work is performed only for the use and benefit of the client.

The general standards of the profession are contained in the General Standards Rule of the code (ET sec. 1.300.001 and 2.300.001) and apply to all services performed by members. They are as follows:

- *Professional competence.* Undertake only those professional services that the member or the member's firm can reasonably expect to be completed with professional competence.
- *Due professional care.* Exercise due professional care in the performance of professional services.
- *Planning and supervision.* Adequately plan and supervise the performance of professional services.
- *Sufficient relevant data.* Obtain sufficient relevant data to afford a reasonable basis for conclusions or recommendations in relation to any professional services performed.

You will also read a lot about:

- *Integrity.* Integrity (ET sec. 0.300.040) is described as follows: "Integrity requires a member to be, among other things, honest and candid within the constraints of client confidentiality. Service and the public trust should not be subordinated to personal gain and advantage. Integrity can accommodate the inadvertent error and the honest difference of opinion; it cannot accommodate deceit or subordination of principle."
- *Objectivity.* Objectivity and Independence (ET sec. 0.300.050) are differentiated as follows: "Objectivity is a state of mind, a quality that lends value to a *member's* services. It is a distinguishing feature of the profession. The principle of objectivity imposes the obligation to be impartial, intellectually honest, and free of conflicts of interest. *Independence* precludes relationships that may appear to *impair* a *member's* objectivity in rendering attestation services."

■ *Conflicts of interest.* Conflict of Interest (ET sec. 1.110.010) may occur "if a *member* or the *member's firm* has a relationship with another person, entity, product, or service that, in the member's professional judgment, the client or other appropriate parties may view as impairing the *member's* objectivity."

A *member* may perform the *professional service* if he or she determines that the service can be performed with objectivity because the *threats* are not significant or can be reduced to an *acceptable level* through the application of *safeguards.*

As a Certified Fraud Examiner, I also fall under the purview of the Association of Certified Fraud Examiners. The ACFE is the world's largest anti-fraud organization and premier provider of anti-fraud training and education. Together with nearly 85,000 members, the ACFE is reducing business fraud worldwide and inspiring public confidence in the integrity and objectivity within the profession. Based in Austin, Texas, the ACFE was founded in 1988 by the preeminent fraud expert and author Dr. Joseph T. Wells, CFE, CPA. Dr. Wells's insight as an accountant-turned-FBI-agent led to the formation of a common body of knowledge known today as fraud examination.

Bruce Dorris is the ACFE president and CEO. The ACFE's objective is to reduce business fraud worldwide and inspire public confidence in the integrity and objectivity within the profession.

Mr. Dorris's travel has taken him around the globe, speaking on professional standards and ethics, which has provided him with a global perspective. Most notably, the realities of the profession vary by country and by industry. For example, some developing countries are still struggling to combat corruption in many sectors and to put solid anti-fraud frameworks in place. Consequently, the need for recognition and support between government, business, and industry is imperative to successful fraud risk management strategies.

However, the ACFE's professional standards do not vary by country; all ACFE members in every jurisdiction are held to the same high standard of ethics and professionalism. This is important because the ACFE believes that to effectively combat fraud around the globe, its members must be the change that they wish to see – that is, they must set the ethical tone and display the professional conduct necessary to truly create an environment that is contrary to the fraud and corruption they are all working to fight. While cultural norms and customs might vary across geographic lines, the hallmarks of an ethical anti-fraud professional are universal.

The one constant "language" spoken by all countries is the desire to deter and detect fraud and misconduct. Mr. Dorris recalls a recent conversation with a Certified Fraud Examiner (CFE) in the Middle East regarding a government agency partnering with the ACFE to provide education for anti-fraud professionals. It has opened a new door in the region for collaboration with business, industry and academia for anti-fraud training. Strong leadership in fighting fraud makes a huge difference in bringing all these groups together.

- In keeping with the mission to reduce the incidence of fraud and white-collar crime and to assist the membership in fraud detection and deterrence, all ACFE members must meet the rigorous criteria for admission to the Association of Certified Fraud Examiners. Thereafter, they must exemplify the highest moral and ethical standards and must agree to abide by the bylaws of the ACFE and the Code of Professional Ethics. An ACFE Member shall, at all times, demonstrate a commitment to professionalism and diligence in the performance of his or her duties.
- An ACFE Member shall not engage in any illegal or unethical conduct, or any activity which would constitute a conflict of interest.
- An ACFE Member shall, at all times, exhibit the highest level of integrity in the performance of all professional assignments and will accept only assignments for which there is reasonable expectation that the assignment will be completed with professional competence.
- An ACFE Member will comply with lawful orders of the courts and will testify to matters truthfully and without bias or prejudice.
- An ACFE Member, in conducting examinations, will obtain evidence or other documentation to establish a reasonable basis for any opinion rendered. No opinion shall be expressed regarding the guilt or innocence of any person or party.
- An ACFE Member shall not reveal any confidential information obtained during a professional engagement without proper authorization.
- An ACFE Member will reveal all material matters discovered during the course of an examination which, if omitted, could cause a distortion of the facts.
- An ACFE Member shall continually strive to increase the competence and effectiveness of professional services performed under his or her direction.[1]

---

[1]ACFE 2019 Code of Ethics, https://www.acfe.com/code-of-ethics.aspx.

Similar to the AICPA rules I mentioned earlier, the ACFE requires the same standards: (check the lettering below)

A. Integrity and Objectivity

1. Certified Fraud Examiners shall conduct themselves with integrity, knowing that public trust is founded on integrity. CFEs shall not sacrifice integrity to serve their client, their employer, or the public interest.
2. Prior to accepting the fraud examination, Certified Fraud Examiners shall investigate for actual, potential, and perceived conflicts of interest. CFEs shall disclose any such conflicts of interest to potentially affected clients or to their employers.
3. Certified Fraud Examiners shall maintain objectivity in discharging their professional responsibilities within the scope of the fraud examination.
4. Certified Fraud Examiners shall not commit acts discreditable to the ACFE or its membership, and shall always conduct themselves in the best interests of the reputation of the profession.
5. Certified Fraud Examiners shall not knowingly make a false statement when testifying under oath in a court of law or other dispute resolution forum. CFEs shall comply with lawful orders of the courts or other dispute resolution bodies. CFEs shall not commit criminal acts or knowingly induce others to do so.

B. Professional Competence

1. Certified Fraud Examiners shall be competent and shall not accept assignments where competence is lacking. In some circumstances, it may be possible to meet the requirement for professional competence by use of consultation or referral.
2. Certified Fraud Examiners shall maintain the minimum program of continuing professional education required by the Association of Certified Fraud Examiners. A commitment to professionalism combining education and experience shall continue throughout the CFE's professional career. CFEs shall continually strive to increase the competence and effectiveness of their professional services.

C. Due Professional Care

1. Certified Fraud Examiners shall exercise due professional care in the performance of their fraud examination services. Due professional care requires diligence, critical analysis, and professional skepticism in discharging professional responsibilities.
2. Conclusions shall be supported with evidence that is relevant, reliable, and sufficient.
3. Fraud examinations shall be adequately planned. Planning controls the performance of a fraud examination from inception through completion and involves developing strategies and objectives for performing the services.
4. Work performed by assistants and other professionals operating under the Certified Fraud Examiner's direction on a fraud examination shall be adequately supervised. The extent of supervision required varies depending on the complexities of the work and the qualifications of the assistants or professionals.

D. Understanding with Client or Employer

1. At the beginning of a fraud examination, Certified Fraud Examiners shall reach an understanding with those retaining them (client or employer) about the scope and limitations of the fraud examination and the responsibilities of all parties involved.
2. Whenever the scope or limitations of a fraud examination or the responsibilities of the parties change significantly, a new understanding shall be reached with the client or employer.

E. Communication with Client or Employer

1. Certified Fraud Examiners shall communicate to those who retained them (client or employer) significant findings made during the normal course of the fraud examination.

F. Confidentiality

1. Certified Fraud Examiners shall not disclose confidential or privileged information obtained during the course of a fraud examination without the express permission of a proper authority or the lawful order of a court. This requirement does not preclude professional practice or investigative body reviews as long as the reviewing organization agrees to abide by the confidentiality restrictions.[2]

What about those accountants who are neither CPAs nor CFEs? Accountants who are:

1. *Members of executive management.* We will cover those in great detail. There are many laws that pertain to those who serve in the management capacity. One that you may have heard of is the Sarbanes-Oxley Act of 2002. We will cover many more provisions that create exposures for accountants, such as:
   a. The Dodd-Frank Act
   b. The Foreign Corrupt Practices Act
   c. The UK Bribery Act
   d. The Security Exchange Acts of 1933 and 1934
   e. Various industry and professional guidance
2. *Internal auditors.* Internal auditors are often governed by the same laws as management. Internal auditors are also guided by the Institute of Internal Auditors. We will cover those pronouncements in great detail.
3. *Expert witnesses.* Accountants may also serve as expert witnesses. Those willing to endure an entirely different level of stress will not only have to familiarize themselves with the regulations and laws referenced above, but also meet Federal Rules of Evidence requirements. There are also unique requirements in some countries and districts within the United States.

Unlike other authors of textbooks, I will weave together my personal experience, as well as the experiences that many of my colleagues have shared. The cases referenced here are current. My hope is that the lessons we all learned from living through them will outlive us.

---

[2]ACFE Code of Professional Standards, https://www.acfe.com/uploadedFiles/ACFE_Website/Content/documents/rules/Code-of-Standards-2018-03-05.pdf.

I can summarize this book in a simple caption:

What causes accountants to do a bad job? And what can happen to them if they do?

Recall from the Preface that to help you grasp that concept, I chose a word we all can remember: F.R.A.U.D.:

1. F – *Forgetting the present and the past.* Accountants can believe that fraud or misconduct "will never happen to me." This book is filled with examples of those who felt that way. It can happen to you.
2. R – *Relying on others.* Accountants can also land in a minefield of peril by relying on others who do not work as diligently, or are not as knowledgeable of the implications of a job "not well-done."
3. A – *Accepting, not verifying.* Accountants can be headed for trouble if they assume that supporting documentation is accurate, relevant, and reliable without applying professional skepticism.
4. U – *Underestimating the effort.* Many practitioners are given assignments with little time, budget, or direction. Sometimes, practitioners fight to "win" those very assignments, and shortcuts to the finish can ensue. Another iteration, within firms, is espousing an "eat what you kill" environment, which can push examiners to accept engagements which they are not qualified to perform. Our profession is not to imitate *Naked and Afraid*, so examiners should stick to what they know and build an extensive referral network for situations outside their area of expertise.
5. D – *Determining the outcome before the work.* Accountants are not immune from the bias that exists in everyday lives. Taking a position or reaching an opinion based on personal beliefs or tendencies can lead accountants astray.

We conclude this study with a detailed discussion of barriers. What if an accountant does a great job, but faces obstacles that prevent them from "doing the right thing"? It happens more often than you think.

DISCUSSION POINTS

In the text I use in my class at the University of Texas at Arlington, *Fraud Examination*, the authors compile nine factors as the component of a *perfect storm* that made for a hotbed of fraud in the late 1990s and early 2000s. Element 9 was called "Educator Failures." This ninth element of the perfect storm involved several educator failures. The author shared that educators had not provided sufficient ethics training to students, and had not shared realistic ethical dilemmas in the classroom. They shared that a second failure was not teaching students about fraud. I hope this book provides plenty of both.

As we share this journey, consider the following:

- What areas in your professional career may present the most risk?
- Which of those risks are within your control? For those that aren't, who controls them?
  a. For those that you control, what is your risk mitigation plan?
  b. For those than you do not control, how do you address the risk? Have you accepted it? Transferred it? Insured it?
- Recall a time in which you or a loved one faced an ethical challenge. Hindsight being what it is:
  a. What would you do differently, if anything?
  b. What advice would you give the loved one?

CHAPTER ONE

F – Forgetting the Present and the Past

I N THIS CHAPTER, WE discuss the landscape of the global ethical environment, and then establish the professional standards that help address the dilemmas that arise out of fraud and misconduct. We compare financial statement audits and fraud investigation from the perspectives of auditors and fraud examiners.

FRAUD IN THE PRESENT AND PAST

I challenge you to grab a periodical. A newspaper (if you are still able to stomach the news). Scan it. How many articles mention fraud or misconduct? I would be willing to wager each issue has a few. I would also be willing to bet that each victim represented in the article strongly felt that "it could never happen to us." We, as accountants and auditors, are not immune. We are lulled into a false sense of security, and feel that our clients or companies "are better than that." This is very apparent in recent studies on the impact of fraud on small business. In fact, the Association of Certified Fraud Examiners 2018 Report to the Nation showed that small organizations with less than 100 employees are mostly likely to suffer from occupational fraud (28% of cases) and suffered the largest median loss (USD 200,000).

It *can* happen to you. I know, because it happened to me. I am a life-long mixed martial arts fan. While I have never had the time or the ability to fully immurse myself into the sport, I have done my fair share of sparring and training. In 2016, I was awarded several prime territories to open Ultimate Fighting Championship (UFC) Gym franchises. My first territory was near my home in Flower Mound, Texas. My second was in the Lakewood suburb just four miles east of downtown Dallas. I had the absolute best management team at my Flower Mound location. I had challenges in Dallas during the presale and our soft-opening periods. The president of the UFC Gym Corporation and others within management referred a candidate to me. Unbeknownst to the president, I had interviewed the candidate before, and declined to present him an offer. There were certain things in his background that concerned me. Nonetheless, I was in a tight spot, and regardless of the candidate's background, he had an impressive membership sales record. Upon the president's strong recommendation, I hired the candidate at a very favorable wage. And boy, did he sell!

The candidate led the region in sales nearly every period for six weeks of his employment. He terminated historic underperformers and removed other negative influences. I could not have been more pleased with the direction of the gym . . . until I received the first bank statement. I saw that no cash had been deposited. I called him immediately. He told me the cash was in the safe, and he simply had not had the time to visit the bank. He assured me it would be taken care of that day. I trusted him at his word and went back to my busy world of forensic accounting, litigation consulting, and, of course, teaching.

A few days went by and I checked the bank account again. Nothing. I placed another call. He told me he was actually on his way to the bank just that minute. "Great." I said. "Please send me a copy of the deposit slip."

"Of course!" He quipped. I heard nothing that day and saw no deposit. It was two days away from our grand opening.

The very next day, I called to confront him. A week had now passed and I had seen nothing. As he began his excuses, I stopped him immediately, asked that he meet me at the gym, and said I would make the deposit myself. He agreed . . . and called a few moments later to resign, saying "the job was simply too stressful." Well, it was about to become much more stressful for this deadbeat.

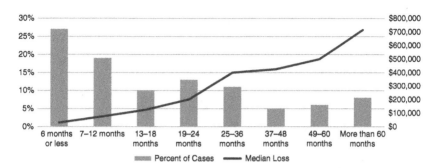

FIGURE 1.1 Duration of a fraud and median loss. *Source*: Based on data from ACFE 2018 *Report to the Nation.*

The safe was empty. No checks and no cash. We immediately began reviewing the security cameras (which are highly effective, if you are able to monitor them by the minute). We saw him regularly pocketing cash, as well as giving his girlfriend cash. I was crushed. However, considering the commissions and monetary incentive awards he forfeited, it was not a huge loss for me, and the scheme was halted after a few weeks. I turned everything over to the police, who as you can imagine were not all that enamored about pursuing my small loss. All in all, I survived, but I was embarrassed. It could have been much worse, as it generally is for so many.

While I was able to stop the fraud within a few weeks, that is not the case for most. Every two years, the Association of Certified Fraud Examiners completes a global study on occupational fraud and abuse. In their 2018 *Report to the Nation*, the ACFE found the median duration for all the fraud cases was 16 months. And obviously, as shown in Figure 1.1, the longer a fraud goes undetected, the larger the scheme will grow and the higher the loss will be.

The ACFE also examined the duration of the cases reported, based on the type of scheme involved (see Figure 1.2). Payroll schemes lasted the longest, at

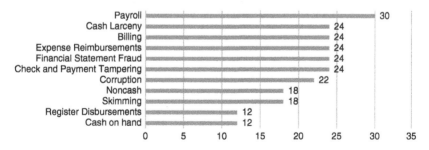

FIGURE 1.2 Duration of different occupational fraud schemes (in months). *Source*: Based on data from ACFE 2018 *Report to the Nation.*

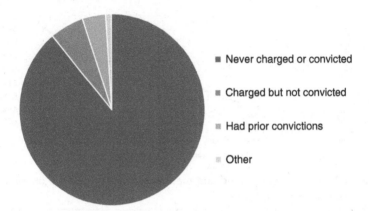

FIGURE 1.3   Percentage of perpetrators having prior fraud convictions. *Source:* Based on data from ACFE 2018 *Report to the Nation.*

30 months, whereas register disbursements, the scheme that plagued my gym, lasted six weeks. So I at least had that working for me!

And while my fraudster had prior history, another interesting fact from the 2018 *Report to the Nation* is that the vast majority of occupational fraudsters had no prior history (see Figure 1.3).

In fact, only 4% of the perpetrators in the study had previously been convicted of a fraud-related offense (see Figure 1.4). It was saddening to learn that some 40% of fraud cases are never reported to the police. However, it is understandable. Many companies fear the bad press that often accompanies a criminal or civil matter. Others simply feel it is not worth the cost or that a recovery is unlikely.

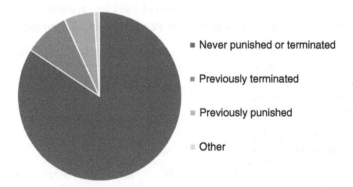

FIGURE 1.4   Percentage of perpetrators' prior employment-related disciplinary actions of fraud. *Source:* Based on data from ACFE 2018 *Report to the Nation.*

FIGURE 1.5 Comparison of fraud losses in small and large businesses. *Source:* ACFE 2018 *Report to the Nation.* © Copyright 2018 Association of Certified Fraud Examiners, Inc.

Perhaps the most provocative finding revealed in the study was the victim organizations themselves. Facts show that small organizations, those with fewer than 100 employees, experienced the greatest percentages of cases and suffered the largest median losses at $200,000, almost twice as much as the median loss larger organizations with more than 100 employees suffer. The graph in the ACFE 2018 *Report to the Nation* (see Figure 1.5) visually summarizes fraud statistics compared between small and large organizations.

I equate the disproportionate share of losses within small businesses to three common themes:

1. *Trust.* Whether the business is family-owned or a new start-up, it is entirely possible that management knows each and every employee. With that familiarity comes trust. And as we will learn, trust alone is a terrible control.
2. *Lack of resources.* Resources can consist of people and money. Small companies may find it challenging to adequately segregate critical duties, or invest in external audits (that are often not required).
3. *Lack of controls.* In addition to lacking resources, small organizations may lack the knowledge to implement adequate internal controls. It is very difficult to monitor controls that aren't there.

Additionally, I typically see more emotion when fraud is discovered at small organizations. Whereas in some cases involving fraud at large companies, perpetrators can rationalize that it is a "victimless" crime and the money wont be missed. That is not the case with small organizations. Now that you understand that fraud is happening, we will discuss your responsibilities to detect, prevent, and deter it. For the purpose of this chapter, I segregate "accountants" into three categories: (1) management, (2) external auditors, and (3) internal auditors.

 ## MANAGEMENT

When I have been called to opine on management's responsibilities, I use guidance afforded by the Financial Executives International, or FEI. FEI is a network of 10,000+ best-in-business professionals with 65+ chapters. Founded in 1931, FEI connects senior-level executives by defining the profession, exchanging ideas about best practices, educating members and others, and working with government to improve the general economy.

FEI's mission includes significant efforts to promote ethical conduct in the practice of financial management throughout the world. Unlike Certified Public Accountants (CPAs), Certified Fraud Examiners (CFEs), and Certified Internal Auditors (CIAs), the FEI does not have a credential. They use the generic term *senior financial officers*. Nonetheless, FEI members are accountable for adhering to a Code of Ethics. The Code provides principles to which members are expected to adhere and advocate. They embody rules regarding individual and peer responsibilities, as well as responsibilities to employers, the public, and the other stakeholders. The Code reads:

All members of FEI will:

- Act with honesty and integrity, avoiding actual or apparent conflicts of interest in personal and professional relationships.
- Provide constituents with information that is accurate, complete, objective, relevant, timely, and understandable.
- Comply with applicable rules and regulations of federal, state, provincial, and local governments and other appropriate private and public regulatory agencies.
- Act in good faith, responsibly, with due care, competence and diligence, without misrepresenting material facts or allowing one's independent judgment to be subordinated.
- Respect the confidentiality of information acquired in the course of one's work except when authorized or otherwise legally obligated to disclose. Confidential information acquired in the course of one's work will not be used for personal advantage.
- Share knowledge and maintain skills important and relevant to constituents' needs.
- Proactively promote ethical behavior as a responsible partner among peers, in the work environment and the community.
- Achieve responsible use of and control over all assets and resources employed or entrusted.
- Report known or suspected violations of this Code in accordance with the FEI Rules of Procedure.
- Be accountable for adhering to this Code.

You will see these points echoed consistently in the pages ahead (lucky you, huh?!). Violations may result in censure, suspension, or expulsion under procedural rules adopted by the FEI's board of directors.

Perhaps the strongest component regarding senior executives' ethical dilemma toolbox are provisions set forth in the Sarbanes-Oxley Act of 2002 (SOX). On July 30, 2002, President Bush signed into law the Sarbanes-Oxley Act of 2002, which he characterized as "the most far-reaching reforms of American business practices since the time of Franklin Delano Roosevelt." The general objective was to enhance corporate governance, and improve overall reliability and transparency of financial reports, and to hold those responsible for their preparation and presentation accountable for their accuracy.

One of the most significant changes as it pertains to senior financial executives was the requirements set in Sections 302 and 906.

Section 302 of the Act contains three parts: (1) accuracy and fair presentation of the report's disclosure, (2) establishment and maintenance of disclosure controls and procedures, and (3) reporting of deficiencies in, and changes to, internal accounting controls. These Civil Certifications require the CEO and CFE to personally certify the following upon filing their public reports:

1. he or she has reviewed the report;
2. based on his or her knowledge, the report does not contain any untrue statement of fact or omit to state a material fact necessary in order to make the statements made, in light of the circumstances under which such statements were made, not misleading with respect to the period covered by the report; and
3. based on his or her knowledge, the financial statements, and other financial information included in the report (including, financial statements, footnotes to the financial statements, selected financial data, management's discussion and analysis of operations and financial condition and other financial information in the report), fairly present in all material respects the financial condition, results of operations and cash flows of the company as of, and for, the periods presented in the report.

A CEO and CFO must also certify that:

1. he or she and the other certifying officer:
   a. are responsible for establishing and maintaining "disclosure controls and procedures" (a newly defined term reflecting the concept of controls and other procedures of the company that are designed to ensure that information required in quarterly and annual reports is recorded, processed, summarized and reported in a timely manner) for the company;
   b. have designed such disclosure controls and procedures to ensure that material information is made known to them, particularly during the period in which the periodic report is being prepared;
   c. have evaluated the effectiveness of the company's disclosure controls and procedures within 90 days of the date of the report; and
   d. have presented in the report their conclusions about the effectiveness of the disclosure controls and procedures based on the required evaluation.
2. he or she and the other certifying officer have disclosed to the company's auditors and the audit committee (or persons fulfilling the equivalent function):
   a. all significant deficiencies in the design or operation of "internal controls" (a pre-existing term relating solely to financial reporting)

which could adversely affect the company's ability to record, process, summarize and report financial data and have identified for the company's auditors any material weaknesses in internal controls; and

b. any fraud, whether or not material, that involves management or other employees who have a significant role in the company's internal controls; and

3. he or she and the other certifying officer have indicated in the report whether or not there were significant changes in internal controls or in other factors that could significantly affect internal controls subsequent to the date of their evaluation, including any corrective actions with regard to significant deficiencies and material weaknesses.

There are a few points I would like to highlight:

1. The officer is *not* certifying that there is *no* fraud. The language clarifies that there is no fraud "based on his or her knowledge."
2. Whether the officer relies on others to oversee or address internal controls, she confirms that she, the officer, is ultimate responsible. No passing the buck!
3. Lastly, "I don't recall" is a terrible defense, as the officer confirms he has evaluated the control's effectiveness recently, i.e., within the past 90 days.

Section 906 addresses criminal penalties for certifying a misleading or fraudulent financial report. Under SOX 906, penalties can be upwards of *$5 million in fines and 20 years in prison*. Section 906 states:

1. Certification of Periodic Financial Reports. Each periodic report containing financial statements filed by an issuer with the Securities Exchange Commission pursuant to section 13(a) or 15(d) of the Securities Exchange Act of 1934 (15 U.S.C. 78m(a) or 78o(d)) shall be accompanied by a written statement by the chief executive officer and chief financial officer (or equivalent thereof) of the issuer.
2. Content. The statement required under subsection (a) shall certify that the periodic report containing the financial statements fully complies with the requirements of section 13(a) or 15(d) of the Securities Exchange Act of 1934 (15 U.S.C. 78m or 78o(d)) and that information contained in the periodic report fairly presents, in all material respects, the financial condition and results of operations of the issuer.

There are other laws and regulations that pertain to management ethical requirements. **The Securities Act of 1933**, often referred to as the "truth in securities" law, prohibits deceit, misrepresentation, and other fraud in the sale of securities. **The Security Exchange Act of 1934,** in which Congress created the Securities and Exchange Commission, established broad enforcement authority. 17 CFR § 240.10b-5 of this Act – Employment of manipulative and deceptive devices – reads:

> It shall be unlawful for any person, directly or indirectly, by the use of any means or instrumentality of interstate commerce, or of the mails or of any facility of any national securities exchange,
>
> 1. To employ any device, scheme, or artifice to defraud,
> 2. To make any untrue statement of a material fact or to omit to state a material fact necessary in order to make the statements made, in the light of the circumstances under which they were made, not misleading, or
> 3. To engage in any act, practice, or course of business which operates or would operate as a fraud or deceit upon any person.

In addition to the SEC's enforcement rights, private citizens also have the right to file lawsuits against companies and individuals for violations of Rule 10b-5. Typically, Rule 10b-5 claims are applied in lawsuits involving:

1. insider trading,
2. market manipulation,
3. fraud in connection with public offerings and takeovers, and
4. fraud in connection with the purchase or sale of securities.

Please understand. This is not an all-encompassing list by any stretch, and I know some amazing attorneys that can right volumes on even more rules. All industries, further segregated by country, state, and sometimes local municipalities, have their own laws, rules, and regulations. It is management's responsibility to familiarize themselves with these requirements. Therefore, consult your local regulators and attorneys for further compliance obligations.

Lastly, and perhaps most relevant, each publicly traded company is required to have an environment of oversight, that is, an operating environment in which the tone at the top encourages ethical behavior, and is the cultural element that drives the initiative. Corporate policies often include Codes of Conduct, Codes of Ethics, Fraud Policies, and annual training requirements for each.

The shortfall for many of these policies is the lack of practical examples within them, and the tendency to think that "one size fits all." Some countries have vastly different cultures and requirements. What is acceptable to some is offensive to others. Examples of common situations and cultural conflicts should be prevalent and highlighted.

Procedures and other controls include whistleblower hotlines – that is, employee reporting mechanisms, audit committees, and independent members on the company's board of directors. A common challenge is the lack of anonymity in the reporting process. Regardless of the policies and procedures implemented, there is no such thing as "guaranteed" anonymity or confidentiality.

EXTERNAL AUDITORS

Unlike management, as mentioned above, rules are defined and more restrictive when it comes to certifications and requirements of serving as an external auditor. Only Certified Public Accountants can complete a financial statement audit in the United States. The American Institute of Certified Public Accountants (AICPA) along with each state's Board of Accountants and the Public Company Accounting Oversight Board (PCAOB) promulgates CPAs rules. For the purpose of this text, I focus more heavily on the AICPA guidance. While the guidance of the two bodies is similar, it is important to note that the PCAOB monitors accountants that work with public entities, while the AICPA is more broad and is comprised of accountants ("members") that work across all areas. The AICPA bylaws require that *members* adhere to the rules of the code. Compliance with the rules depends primarily on *members'* understanding and voluntary actions; secondarily on reinforcement by peers and public opinion; and ultimately on disciplinary proceedings, when necessary, against *members* who fail to comply with the rules. *Members* must be prepared to justify departures from these rules. I have included (1) the AICPA Code of Professional Conduct and (2) SAS 99 procedures, as provided by the Auditing Standards Board of the AICPA in October 2002.

AICPA Code of Professional Conduct

AICPA is the leading professional organization for accountants in the United States. The AICPA's Code of Professional Conduct is among the AICPA's most important functions as well as a central piece of establishing and enforcing the profession's ethical and technical standards. The overarching purpose of the

AICPA Code is to ensure that its members serve the interests of their clients with a high degree of integrity, technical competency, and diligence. It has several component parts, including:

1. Members are obligated to act in the public interest. Members who act with honesty and in fulfillment of their obligation to the public to provide sound, ethical service also serve the best interests of their clients and their employers. The public consists of "clients, credit grantors, governments, employers, investors, the business and financial community, and others who rely on the objectivity and integrity of members to maintain the orderly functioning of commerce."
2. Standards of integrity. Acting with integrity means being honest and candid within the constraints of the accountant's professional obligations to maintain a client's confidentiality. Integrity also means that members must not subordinate service and the public trust to personal gain. The rules recognize that integrity can endure in the face of mistakes or differences of opinion, but vanishes when a professional acts with deceit or subordinates core ethical principles to selfish motives.
3. Standards of objectivity and independence. Objectivity is a distinguishing feature of the profession. It imposes an obligation to be impartial, intellectually honest, and free of conflicts of interest. Likewise, the Code requires accountants to be independent, precluding relationships that may appear to impair a professional's objectivity.
4. Standards of due care. Exercising due care is keeping the best interest of the client in mind as services are performed with diligence and competence.
5. Standards of scope of nature of services. In order to accomplish this, *members* should
   a. Practice in *firms* that have in place internal quality control procedures to ensure that services are competently delivered and adequately supervised.
   b. Determine, in their individual judgments, whether the scope and nature of other services provided to an audit *client* would create a conflict of interest in the performance of the audit function for that *client*.
   c. Assess, in their individual judgments, whether an activity is consistent with their role as professionals.

SAS 99

The generally accepted accounting principles (GAAP) also contain provisions to guide external auditors through their professional responsibilities as they relate to identifying fraud and misconduct. Those conducting financial statement audits are required to adhere to SAS 99. SAS 99 (also the source for

PCAOB Standard AU 316, and AU 2401, which becomes effective in 2020) not only requires auditors to be reasonably sure that financial statements are free of material misstatements, whether caused by error or fraud, but also gives them focused and clearer guidance on meeting their responsibilities to uncover fraud.

SAS 99 requires auditors to look for fraud throughout the entire audit process. The standard defines fraud as an intentional act resulting in a material misstatement in the financial statements. The standard aims to have the auditor's consideration of fraud seamlessly blended into the audit process and continually updated until the audit's completion.

SAS 99 describes a process in which the auditor (1) gathers information needed to identify risks of material misstatement due to fraud, (2) assesses these risks after taking into account an evaluation of the entity's programs and controls, and (3) responds to the results.

The auditor should also have an attitude that includes a questioning mind and a critical assessment of audit evidence (such as avoiding biases and over-reliance on client representations). The engagement should be conducted recognizing the possibility of material misstatement due to fraud.

There are multiple steps involved in assessing risk of fraud (see Figure 1.6):

1. *Brainstorming.* By exercising professional skepticism, generate ideas about how and where financial statements might be susceptible to fraud.
2. *Obtaining information needed to identify risk of fraud.* Obtain information from (1) management, the audit committee, internal auditors, and others within the organization; (2) analytical procedures; (3) consideration of fraud risk factors; and (4) other sources.

FIGURE 1.6 The fraud risks assessment process.

3. *Identifying and assessing the identified risks.* Analyze information about potential fraud risks; consider the type, significance, likelihood, and pervasiveness of the risk.
4. *Responding to results of the assessment.* The risks of material misstatement due to fraud have an overall effect on how the audit is conducted. As risk increases:

- ▪ The more experienced personnel and the greater amount of supervision are required on the engagement.
- ▪ SAS 99 requires the auditor to consider management's selection and application of significant accounting principles as part of the overall response to the risks of material misstatement.
- ▪ SAS 99 requires the auditor to incorporate an element of unpredictability into the procedures from year to year.

In addition, the accounts should also consult AICPA guidance in AU 240. While very similar, it provides clarity for the accountant by providing distinguishing factor between fraud and error is whether the underlying action that results in the misstatement of the financial statements is intentional or unintentional. It becomes more essential to modify the nature, timing, and extent of the audit procedures the auditor will perform to address identified risks of material misstatement due to fraud, as well as performing certain tasks to address the risk of management overriding internal control and to examine adjusting journal entries, accounting estimates, and unusual significant transactions.

1. *Evaluating audit evidence.* Reminds auditors that analytical procedures conducted as substantive procedures or as part of the overall review stage of the audit also may uncover previously unrecognized risks of material misstatement due to fraud.
2. *Communicating about fraud.* Inform the proper level of management and audit committee.
3. *Documenting consideration of fraud.* Documentation is required as follows:

- ▪ The discussion among engagement personnel in planning the audit regarding the susceptibility of the entity's financial statements to material misstatement due to fraud, including how and when the discussion occurred, the audit team members who participated, and the subjects discussed.

- ▓ The procedures performed to obtain information necessary to identify and assess the risks of material misstatement due to fraud.
- ▓ Specific risks of material misstatement due to fraud that were identified and a description of the auditor's response to those risks.
- ▓ If the auditor has not identified improper revenue recognition as a risk of material misstatement due to fraud in a particular circumstance, the reasons supporting that conclusion.
- ▓ The results of the procedures performed to further address the risk of management override of controls.
- ▓ Conditions and analytical relationships that caused the auditor to believe additional auditing procedures or other responses were required and any further responses the auditor concluded were appropriate to address such risks or other conditions.
- ▓ The nature of the communications about fraud made to management, the audit committee, and others.

The AICPA also has general standards that pertain to CPAs not conducting financial statement audits. These standards are referred to as management consulting services (MCS) standards, and accounting and review services standards. Generally, litigation services engagements are subject to the MCS standards and are exempt from the others. However, each are very similar. Consulting services that CPAs provided to their clients have evolved from advice on accounting-related matters to a wide range of services involving diverse technical disciplines, industry knowledge, and consulting skills. Most practitioners, including those who provide audit and tax services, also provide business and management-consulting services to their clients. Statements on Standards for Consulting Services are issued by the AICPA Management Consulting Services Executive Committee, the senior technical committee of the Institute designated to issue renouncements in connection with consulting services. The Council has designated the AICPA Management Consulting Services Executive Committee as a body to establish professional standards under the "Compliance with Standards Rule" of the Institute's Code of Professional Conduct (code). Members should be prepared to justify departures from this statement.

The general standards of the profession are contained in the "General Standards Rule" of the code and apply to all services performed by members. They are as follows:

a. Professional competence. Undertake only those professional services that the member or the member's firm can reasonably expect to be completed with professional competence.

b. Due professional care. Exercise due professional care in the performance of professional services.

c. Planning and supervision. Adequately plan and supervise the performance of professional services.

d. Sufficient relevant data. Obtain sufficient relevant data to afford a reasonable basis for conclusions or recommendations in relation to any professional services performed.

In "Integrity," *integrity* is described as follows: "Integrity requires a member to be, among other things, honest and candid within the constraints of client confidentiality Service and the public trust should not be subordinated to personal gain and advantage. Integrity can accommodate the inadvertent error and the honest difference of opinion; it cannot accommodate deceit or subordination of principle."

In "Objectivity and Independence," *objectivity* and *independence* are differentiated as follows: "Objectivity is a state of mind, a quality that lends value to a *member's* services. It is a distinguishing feature of the profession. The principle of objectivity imposes the obligation to be impartial, intellectually honest, and free of conflicts of interest. *Independence* precludes relationships that may appear to *impair* a *member's* objectivity in rendering attestation services."

The "Conflict of Interest Rule" states, in part, the following:

a. A conflict of interest may occur if a *member* or the *member's firm* has a relationship with another person, entity, product, or service that, in the member's professional judgment, the client or other appropriate parties may view as impairing the *member's* objectivity. . .

b. A *member* may perform the *professional service* if he or she determines that the service can be performed with objectivity because the *threats* are not significant or can be reduced to an *acceptable level* through the application of *safeguards*. . .

Additionally, an AICPA member should also consult the following, if applicable:

1. The ethical requirements of the *member's* state CPA society and authoritative regulatory bodies such as state board(s) of accountancy
2. The Securities and Exchange Commission (SEC)
3. The Public Company Accounting Oversight Board (PCAOB)
4. The Government Accountability Office (GAO)
5. The Department of Labor (DOL)
6. Federal, state, and local taxing authorities

INTERNAL AUDITORS

Internal auditing is an independent, objective assurance and consulting activity designed to add value and improve an organization's operations. It helps an organization accomplish its objectives by bringing a systematic, disciplined approach to evaluate and improve the effectiveness of risk management, control, and governance processes.

Globally, the professional is under the watchful eye of the Institute of Internal Auditors (IIA). The IIA has more than 185,000 members. The IIA in North America comprises 160 chapters serving more than 70,000 members in the United States, Canada, the Caribbean (Aruba, Bahamas, Barbados, Cayman Islands, Curacao, Jamaica, Puerto Rico, and Turks & Caicos), Bermuda, Guyana, and Trinidad & Tobago.

"Internal auditors" refers to IIA members, recipients of or candidates for IIA professional certifications, and those who perform internal audit services within the Definition of Internal Auditing.

Internal auditors serve an important function in organizations. Internal auditors can be external, meaning a company on specific assignment hires them or they can be employees to the organization. Regardless, the same standards generally apply.

The International Professional Practices Framework (IPPF) is the conceptual framework that organizes authoritative guidance promulgated by the Institute of Internal Auditors. Established in 1941, The Institute of Internal Auditors (IIA) is an international professional association with global headquarters in Lake Mary, Florida. The IIA is the internal audit profession's global voice, recognized authority, acknowledged leader, chief advocate, and principal educator. Generally, members work in internal auditing, risk management, governance, internal control, information technology audit, education, and security. The mission of The Institute of Internal Auditors is to provide dynamic leadership for the global profession of internal auditing.

The IIA Code of Ethics states the principles and expectations governing the behavior of individuals and organizations in the conduct of internal auditing. It describes the minimum requirements for conduct, and behavioral expectations rather than specific activities. The purpose of The Institute's Code of Ethics is to promote an ethical culture in the profession of internal auditing.

The IIA's Code of Ethics extends beyond the Definition of Internal Auditing to include two essential components:

1. Principles that are relevant to the profession and practice of internal auditing.

2. Rules of Conduct that describe behavior norms expected of internal auditors. These rules are an aid to interpreting the Principles into practical applications and are intended to guide the ethical conduct of internal auditors.

For IIA members and recipients of, or candidates for, IIA professional certifications, breaches of the Code of Ethics will be evaluated and administered according to The Institute's bylaws and administrative directives. The fact that a particular conduct is not mentioned in the Rules of Conduct does not prevent it from being unacceptable or discreditable, and therefore, the member, certification holder, or candidate can be liable for disciplinary action.

Code of Ethics – Principles

Internal auditors are expected to apply and uphold the following principles:

1. Integrity: The integrity of internal auditors establishes trust and thus provides the basis for reliance on their judgment.
2. Objectivity: Internal auditors exhibit the highest level of professional objectivity in gathering, evaluating, and communicating information about the activity or process being examined. Internal auditors make a balanced assessment of all the relevant circumstances and are not unduly influenced by their own interests or by others in forming judgments.
3. Confidentiality: Internal auditors respect the value and ownership of information they receive and do not disclose information without appropriate authority unless there is a legal or professional obligation to do so.
4. Competency: Internal auditors apply the knowledge, skills, and experience needed in the performance of internal audit services.[1]

Rules of Conduct

The IIA also has guidance of ethical conducts that includes the same principles above.

ETHICAL STANDARDS AROUND THE WORLD

To open our eyes to accounting ethical standards in other parts of the world, the following sections introduce the International Ethics Standards Board for

---

[1]International Standards for the Professional Practice of Internal Auditing (Standards) – IIA Standard 1210.A2.

Accountants (IESBA). The IESBA is an independent standard-setting body that serves the public interest by setting robust, internationally appropriate ethics standards, for professional accountants worldwide.[2] The IESBA is an independent standard-setting board of the International Federation of Accountants (IFAC).

IFAC is the global organization for the accountancy profession dedicated to serving the public interest by strengthening the profession and contributing to the development of strong international economies. IFAC is comprised of over 175 members and associates in more than 130 countries and jurisdictions, representing almost 3 million accountants in public practice, education, government service, industry, and commerce.[3] Members include professional organizations such as the American Institute of Public Accountants (AICPA) of the United States, the Association of Chartered Certified Accountants (ACCA) of the UK, the Chartered Accountants Australia and New Zealand, Chartered Professional Accountants Canada, Chinese Institute of Certified Public Accountants (CICPA), Institute of Chartered Accountants of India, South African Institute of Chartered Accountants, and so on. The "member bodies" of the IFAC agree to meet the standards set by IFAC-supported boards, including the IESBA.

Comparison of IESBA and AICPA Codes of Ethics

The IESBA and AICPA codes of ethics are more similar than different. Both codes address areas such as independence, due care, confidentiality, and truthful report of information. However, there are some differences between the two codes. For example, the IESBA includes three topics for professional accountants in public practice that are not specifically addressed in the AICPA Code.[4] They are:

1. Professional appointment: Ethical considerations related to the acceptance and continuance of client engagements and responsibilities of successor/predecessor accountants.
2. Second opinions: Ethical considerations related to the provision of a second opinion on the application of accounting, auditing, reporting, or other standards or principles to specific circumstances or transactions by or on behalf of a company or an entity that is not an existing client.
3. Custody of assets: Ethical considerations related to holding client assets.

---

[2]https://www.ethicsboard.org/.
[3]https://www.ifac.org/about-ifac.
[4]Catherine Allen, "Comparing the Ethics Codes: AICPA and IFAC," *Journal of Accountancy* 210, no. 4 (October 1, 2010).

Although they do not appear in the AICPA code of ethics, these topics are addressed specifically in the AICPA audit/attest literature and rules.

IESBA has more stringent requirements on the issue of independence than the AICPA Code. The IESBA splits its independence requirements into two sections: Section 290 and Section 291. Section 290 applies to audits and reviews of financial statements; Section 291 applies to all other assurance engagements. Section 290 has more restrictive independence requirements than Section 291 because Section 291 does not impose prohibitions or other requirements on public interest entities.

In many cases, applying either the IESBA or the AICPA Code of Ethics leads to similar results.

Updates and Recent Movements

The IESBA released a completely rewritten Code of Ethics for Professional Accountants in April 2018. The code incorporates key ethics advances and is clearer about how accountants should deal with ethics and independence issues. The new code, effective June 15, 2019, emphasizes three key messages to the professional accountants:

1. Comply with the fundamental principles;
2. Apply the conceptual framework to identify, evaluate, and address threats to compliance with the fundamental principles; and
3. Maintain independence, when required.

Next, let's take a closer look at each topic.

Fundamental Principles

A professional accountant shall comply with each of the fundamental principles. The five fundamental principles of ethics for professional accountants are:[5]

a. Integrity – to be straightforward and honest in all professional and business relationships.
b. Objectivity – not to compromise professional or business judgments because of bias, conflict of interest or undue influence of others. Objectivity is further mentioned in "Independence." Independence is defined as:
    i. Independence of mind – the state of mind that permits the expression of a conclusion without being affected by influences that

---

[5] *2018 Handbook of the International Code of Ethics for Professional Accountants (including International Independence Standards)*, https://www.ethicsboard.org/iesba-code.

compromise professional judgment, thereby allowing an individual to act with integrity, and exercise objectivity and professional skepticism.

  ii. Independence in appearance – the avoidance of facts and circumstances that are so significant that a reasonable and informed third party would be likely to conclude that a firm's, or an audit team member's, integrity, objectivity or professional skepticism has been compromised.

c. Professional Competence and Due Care – to:

  i. Attain and maintain professional knowledge and skill at the level required to ensure that a client or employing organization receives competent professional service, based on current technical and professional standards and relevant legislation; and

  ii. Act diligently and in accordance with applicable technical and professional standards.

d. Confidentiality – to respect the confidentiality of information acquired as a result of professional and business relationships.

e. Professional Behavior – to comply with relevant laws and regulations and avoid any conduct that the professional accountant knows or should know might discredit the profession.

Do you recognize those from before? They're very similar!

The Conceptual Framework

While the fundamental principles of ethics have not changed, major revisions have been made to the unifying conceptual framework—the approach used by all professional accountants to identify, evaluate, and address threats to compliance with the fundamental principles and, where applicable, independence.

The conceptual framework specifies an approach for a professional accountant to:[6]

a. Identify threats to compliance with the fundamental principles;

b. Evaluate the threats identified; and

c. Address the threats by eliminating or reducing them to an acceptable level.

---

[6]*2018 Handbook of the International Code of Ethics for Professional Accountants (including International Independence Standards,* https://www.ethicsboard.org/iesba-code.

New Code highlights include:[7]

   a. Revised "safeguards" provisions better aligned to threats to compliance with the fundamental principles;

   b. Stronger independence provisions regarding long association of personnel with audit clients;

   c. New and revised sections dedicated to professional accountants in business (PAIBs) relating to:

   d. Preparing and presenting information; and

   e. Pressure to breach the fundamental principles.

   f. Clear guidance for accountants in public practice that relevant PAIB provisions are applicable to them;

   g. New guidance to emphasize the importance of understanding facts and circumstances when exercising professional judgment; and

   h. New guidance to explain how compliance with the fundamental principles supports the exercise of professional skepticism in an audit or other assurance engagements.

In summary, the IESBA sets ethical principles and a conceptual framework for professional accountants to follow in more than 130 countries around the world. Many countries, such as China, put emphasis on convergence with the IESBA Code of Ethics. However, rules also vary by countries.

Ethical Standards in China

The public accounting industry is relatively new in China. The Accounting Law of 1985 was amended in 1999, and it stipulates that professional accountants must abide by ethical requirements. In June 1996, the Ministry of Finance released the Regulation of the Accounting Foundation Work, which includes ethical requirements for all accountants.

The Chinese Institute of Certified Public Accountants (CICPA) is authorized to establish professional standards and rules for CPAs. In 2009, the CICPA released the Code of Ethics for Chinese CPAs and the Code of Ethics for Non-Practicing Members of CICPA, which are aligned with the 2009 IESBA Code of Ethics for Professional Accountants. These two documents regulate the ethical conducts of CPAs and nonpracticing members.

In 2014, CICPA released Q&As related to the Code of Ethics for Chinese CPAs, consisting of over 30 specific questions in such areas as conceptual

---

[7]IFAC press release, dated April 9, 2018, http://www.ifac.org/news-events/2018-04/global-ethics-board-releases-revamped-code-ethics-professional-accountants.

framework, firm networks, requirements of audit and assurance services on independence, and Code of Ethics for nonpracticing members and so on. It provides detailed guidance and tips to help CPAs understand the Code of Ethics and solve ethical problems encountered in practice.

In 2017, CICPA utilized an extensive comparison chart to detail the differences between the CICPA Code of Ethics and the IESBA Code. CICPA provisions are more stringent than the IESBA Code in certain areas, for example:

1. The definition of immediate family, which is broader than the IESBA Code of Ethics to align with national Chinese legislation;
2. Key audit matter rotation which in the CICPA Code of Ethics is five years on, two years off as opposed to seven years on, two years off in IESBA Code; and
3. CICPA's Code states that an auditor cannot accept any gift.

Historically, unethical behaviors were not uncommon in China. Prevalent fraudulent activities include:

1. Accountants creating journal entries according to their bosses' direction to avoid taxes.
2. Companies keeping two sets of books to hide "private funds" for employees' benefits, gifts and kickbacks given to potential clients to gain business.
3. Bribes paid to government officials for business favors.

The current China government lists anticorruption as one of its top priorities. Although it will likely take generations to change the business environment completely, China is heading in the right direction in addressing corruption.

Ethical Standards in Canada

In Canada, the authority to set ethical requirements lies in the provincial accounting bodies of the Canadian Public Accountability Board (CPAB). The CPAB reported in 2018 that the ethical requirements of the Canadian CPA Code of Professional Conduct (CPA Code) have essentially converged with the IESBA Code of Ethics.

The Public Trust Committee (PTC) of Canada's CPA profession is currently considering the recent changes in the IESBA, such as noncompliance with laws and regulations (NOCLAR) in relation to the CPA profession's existing ethical standards. As a member of the IFAC, Canadian CPA professionals are required to meet or exceed the IESBA Code. The NOCLAR applies when accountants are providing a professional service to their clients or are carrying out their duties for their employer. It includes a clear pathway to disclosure of noncompliance with laws and regulations to appropriate authorities.

The laws and regulations against corruption appear to work wonders in Canada, which ranks as the ninth-least-corrupt nation out of 176 countries, and the least corrupt nation in the Americas, according to Transparency International's 2016 Corruption Perception Index.

Ethical Standards in India

Under the Chartered Accountants Act of 1949 (revised in 2013), the Institute of Chartered Accountants of India (ICAI) was established with the authority to regulate the accountancy profession and with powers to establish regulations as necessary to fulfill its duties.[8] The ICAI's membership is comprised of Chartered Accountants, a designation protected under the Act. The Act grants ICAI authority to (i) establish initial professional development and continuing professional development (CPD) requirements; (ii) maintain a register of its members; (iii) ensure members' adherence to laws and professional standards; and (iv) investigate and discipline members for professional misconduct.

In 2002, the ICAI developed the Peer Review Mechanism that covers all audit work conducted by its members. The Peer Review Mechanism's objectives are to ensure that Chartered Accountants who are authorized to conduct audits are complying with applicable standards set by the institute. In accordance with the Companies Act of 1956 (revised in 2013), all auditors must have a practicing certificate issued by ICAI in order to conduct statutory financial statement audits. In addition to being an IFAC founding member, ICAI is a member of the Confederation of Asian and Pacific Accountants (CAPA) and the South Asian Federation of Accountants (SAFA).

Recent cases of fraudulent financial reporting, accounting frauds, and the resulting outcry for transparency and honesty in reporting have given rise to disparate yet logical outcomes. The failure of the corporate communication structure has made the financial community realize that there is a great need for skilled professionals who can identify, expose, and prevent structural weaknesses in three key areas: poor corporate governance, flawed internal controls, and fraudulent financial statements. Forensic accounting skills are becoming increasingly relied upon within a corporate reporting system that emphasizes its accountability and responsibility to stakeholders.

---

[8]https://www.ifac.org/about-ifac/membership/members/institute-chartered-accountants-india.

Let's look at a recent Indian case that involves these issues. Satyam Computer Services Limited ("Satyam") was once the crown jewel of the Indian IT industry, but was brought to the ground by its founders in 2009 as a result of financial crime. Satyam's top management simply cooked the company's books by overstating its revenues, profit margins, and profits for every single quarter over a period of five years, from 2003 to 2008. Satyam's top manager stated that he overstated assets on Satyam's balance sheet by $1.47 billion, and nearly $1.04 billion in bank loans and cash that the company claimed to own was nonexistent. Satyam also under reported liabilities on its balance sheet and overstated its income nearly every quarter over the course of several years in order to meet analyst expectations.

According to the founder's own public confession, Satyam had frequently used fraudulent financial reporting practices by inflating its reported revenues by 25%, its operating margins by over 10 times, and its cash and bank balance by over $1 billion. The magnitude of this fraud makes it by far the biggest accounting scandal in India's history.[9] The Satyam reporting fraud is clearly a case of abuse of accounting, in which the accounts were adjusted upward through recording fake invoices for services not rendered, recognizing revenue on these fake receipts, falsifying bank balances and interest on fixed deposits to show these fake invoices had been converted into cash receipts and were earning interest, and so on. These types of fraudulent reporting accounting practices are both illegal and unethical.

Many experts cast partial blame for the accounting scandal on Satyam's auditor, Pricewaterhouse Coopers (PwC) India, because the fraud went undetected for so many years. In fact, the global auditing firm used Lovelock and Lewis (as their agent), who audited the Satyam's books of accounts from June 2000 until the discovery of the fraud in 2009.

The SFIO Report stated, "Statutory auditors instead of using an independent testing mechanism used Satyam's investigative tools and thereby compromised on reporting standards." PwC did not check even 1% of the invoices; neither did they pay enough attention to verification of sundry debtors, which were overstated by 23% (the SFIO report says it was overstated by almost 50%). The statutory auditors also failed in discharging their duty when it came to independently verifying cash and bank balances, both current account and fixed deposits. Hence, it was required that the PwC auditors independently check with the banks on the existence of fixed deposits, but this was not done.

---

[9]"India's Satyam Scandal: A Blessing in Disguise?" China India Institute, December 20, 2015. http://www.chinaindiainstitute.com/indias-satyam-scandal-a-blessing-in-disguise-2.

PwC audited the company for nearly nine years and did not uncover the fraud, whereas Merrill Lynch discovered the fraud as part of its due diligence in merely 10 days. Missing these red flags implied either that the auditors were grossly inept or in collusion with the company in committing the fraud. The CBI, which investigated the case, also charged the two auditors with complicity in the commission of the fraud by consciously overlooking the accounting irregularities. On April 22, 2014, The Institute of Chartered Accountants of India (ICAI) imposed a lifetime ban on four auditors involved in the Satyam CA fraud.

A point has also been raised about the unjustified increase in audit fees. The PwC received an annual fee of Rs. 37.3 million for the financial year 2007–2008, which is almost twice as much as Satyam peers (e.g., TCS, Infosys, Wipro) on average pay their auditors. This shows that the auditors were being lured by the monetary incentive to certify the cooked and manipulated financial statements. Events of such nature raised doubts about statutory auditors' discharging their duty independently. Consequently, on January 24, 2009, Andhra Pradesh CID police booked two senior partners of PwC, Mr. S. Gopalakrishna and Mr. Srinivas Talluri, on charges of fraud and criminal conspiracy. In addition, the PwC had suspended the two partners, who signed on Satyam's balance sheet and are currently in prison.

International Laws and Regulations

If I may play Captain Obvious for a minute, each country has its own laws. However, there are a few laws that transcend the borders as they relate to our fraud and misconduct responsibilities. Therefore, in addition to accounting professional Code of Ethics around the world, accountants need to understand some applicable laws and regulations that affect the profession. In this section, we compare anti-bribery laws in two counties: the Foreign Corrupt Practices Act (FCPA) of the United States and the Bribery Act of the United Kingdom, as well as touch on a few laws making the news.

US Foreign Corrupt Practices Act of 1977

The Foreign Corrupt Practices Act of 1977 ("FCPA") was enacted for the purpose of making it unlawful for certain classes of persons and entities to make payments to foreign government officials to assist in obtaining or retaining business. The FCPA has two provisions:

1. Anti-bribery: The anti-bribery provisions of the FCPA prohibit the willful use of the mails or any means of instrumentality of interstate commerce

corruptly in furtherance of any offer, payment, promise to pay, or authorization of the payment of money or anything of value to any person, while knowing that all or a portion of such money or thing of value will be offered, given or promised, directly or indirectly, to a foreign official to influence the foreign official in his or her official capacity, induce the foreign official to do or omit to do an act in violation of his or her lawful duty, or to secure any improper advantage in order to assist in obtaining or retaining business for or with, or directing business to, any person.

2. Record keeping. Companies whose securities are listed in the United States to meet their accounting provisions. These accounting provisions, which were designed to operate in tandem with the anti-bribery provisions of the FCPA, require corporations covered by the provisions to (a) make and keep books and records that accurately and fairly reflect the transactions of the corporation and (b) devise and maintain an adequate system of internal accounting controls.

Many companies that are household names become involved in FCPA investigations. Often times, the costs of investigations, fines, and penalties dwarf the bribes actually paid. For example, on December 8, 2011, Wal-Mart Stores Inc., the world's largest retailer, filed its 10-K filing and disclosed its FCPA investigation:

> During fiscal 2012, the Company began conducting a voluntary internal review of its policies, procedures and internal controls pertaining to its global anti-corruption compliance program. As a result of information obtained during that review and from other sources, the Company has begun an internal investigation into whether certain matters, including permitting, licensing and inspections, were in compliance with the U.S. Foreign Corrupt Practices Act. The Company has engaged outside counsel and other advisors to assist in the review of these matters and has implemented, and is continuing to implement, appropriate remedial measures. The Company has voluntarily disclosed its internal investigation to the U.S. Department of Justice and the Securities and Exchange Commission. We cannot reasonably estimate the potential liability, if any, related to these matters. However, based on the facts currently known, we do not believe that these matters will have a material adverse effect on our business, financial condition, results of operations or cash flows.

The Walmart allegations were sensational. Walmart was accused of paying $24 million in bribes to obtain permits to obtain permission to open stores in Mexico. It was reported that an in-house attorney in Mexico initiated the allegations. The attorney launched a preliminary investigation and reported the allegations to Walmart's general counsel. It was alleged that Walmart then interviewed outside counsel to lead an investigation, yet later decided to use their in-house investigators. Those investigators determined there was a "reasonable suspicion." However, after reviewing the findings, senior executives determined there was no clear violation of law.

In November 2017, Walmart disclosed they were in discussions to settle, in which Walmart would pay $283 million:

> As previously disclosed, the Company has been cooperating with the U.S. Department of Justice and the U.S. Securities and Exchange Commission with respect to their investigations regarding possible violations of the U.S. Foreign Corrupt Practices Act and there have been ongoing discussions regarding the possible resolution of these matters with the government agencies. These discussions have progressed to a point that the Company can now reasonably estimate a probable loss and has recorded an aggregate accrual of $283 million with respect to these matters. As the discussions are continuing, there can be no assurance that the Company's efforts to reach a final resolution with the government agencies will be successful or, if they are, what the timing or terms of such resolution will be.

Further, Walmart disclosed it had incurred $877 million in pre-enforcement professional fees and compliance enhancement expenses.

This is a surprising matter, considering the strong warnings and the enforcement trends involving FCPA actions. Enforcement continues to be a top priority for the SEC and DOJ (see Figure 1.7 for DOJ and SEC enforcement actions trending by year). In 2010, the SEC's Enforcement Division created a specialized unit to further enhance its enforcement of the FCPA. The new Office of Market Intelligence is responsible for the collection, analysis, and monitoring of the hundreds of thousands of tips, complaints, and referrals that the SEC receives each year. The new office helps provide the additional structure, resources, and expertise necessary for enforcement staff to keep pace with ever-changing markets and to more comprehensively investigate cases involving complex products, markets, regulatory regimes, practices, and transactions.

In Figures 1.7 and 1.8, we analyze the trends through 2018. While we see 2010 as still the high-water mark, please notice that 2018 nearly approached the combined action levels.

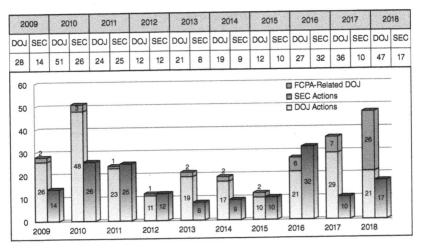

2009		2010		2011		2012		2013		2014		2015		2016		2017		2018	
DOJ	SEC	DOJ	SEC	DOJ	SEC	DOJ	SEC	DOJ	SEC	DOJ	SEC	DOJ	SEC	DOJ	SEC	DOJ	SEC	DOJ	SEC
28	14	51	26	24	25	12	12	21	8	19	9	12	10	27	32	36	10	47	17

FIGURE 1.7 FCPA + FCPA-related enforcement actions (2009–2018). *Source*: Gibson Dunn & Crutcher LLP 2018 Year-End FCPA Update, 2018.

However, the most startling trend is clearly in the monetary sanctions, where as of July, the 2019 amounts are predicted to far outpace the previous high from 2009, and to continue the historical increases that began in 2016.

UK Bribery Act

A more recent bribery law is the UK Bribery Act of 2010. This Act defines offenses as offers, promises, or providing a financial or other advantage to another person, or rewarding a person for the improper performance of a function or activity. This Act also prohibits a bribe from being paid to obtain a financial or other advantage to a relevant function or for an activity to be performed improperly. The UK's Serious Fraud Office (SFO) is a specialist prosecuting authority tackling the top level of serious or complex fraud, bribery, and corruption. It is part of the UK criminal justice system covering England, Wales, and Northern Ireland, but not Scotland, the Isle of Man, or the Channel Islands.

The largest UK Bribery Act investigation involved Rolls-Royce, another household name (although I bet there are only a few of us accountants driving them!). Following a four-year investigation, the SFO reached a settlement on January 17, 2017. The DPA enables Rolls-Royce to account to a UK court for criminal conduct spanning three decades in seven jurisdictions and involving three business sectors. The settlement involves payments of £497,252,645

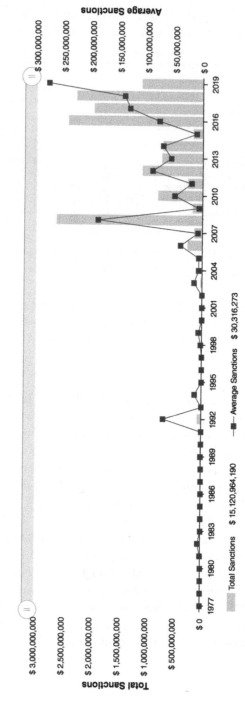

FIGURE 1.8 Total and average sanctions. *Source:* Stanford Law School in collaboration with Sullivan and Cromwell LLP.

TABLE 1.1 Differences between FCPA and the UK Bribery Act.

Element	FCPA	UK Bribery Act
Jurisdiction	Individuals affiliated with US companies, and all US companies.	Individuals who are closely connected within the UK. Companies conducting business or that are incorporated in the UK.
Enforcement	US Department of Justice (bribery provisions) and the SEC (record-keeping and internal controls).	Criminal enforcement only by the UK Serious Fraud Office (SFO).
Provisions	Record-keeping and internal control provisions.	Does not include books, records, or internal control violations.
Bribes	Prohibits bribes to foreign officials.	Prohibits bribes to foreign officials and private citizens.
Facilitation Payments	Allows payments to expedite or secure performance of a routine government action.	No facilitation payment exception.

(comprising disgorgement of profits of £258,170,000 and a financial penalty of £239,082,645) plus interest. Rolls-Royce also agreed to reimburse the SFO's costs in full (c£13m).

There are significant differences between these two Acts (see Table 1.1).

The Travel Act

While federal agencies typically use the False Claims Act (covered later), the FCPA, or the UK Bribery Act to pursue fraud, a new trend in combating health-care fraud is the use of the Travel Act. Using this law, enacted more than 60 years ago, allows for the choosing of whether to prosecute under federal law or state law due to the alleged activity, the parties involved, and the ease of proving a violation.

The Travel Act, 18 U.S.C. § 1952, forbids the use of such transmission methods as the U.S. mail, or interstate or foreign travel, to facilitate the occurrence of criminal acts. Specially, the law states that:

Whoever travels in interstate or foreign commerce or uses the mail or any facility in interstate or foreign commerce, with intent to:

1. distribute the proceeds of any unlawful activity; or
2. commit any crime of violence to further any unlawful activity;

3. or otherwise promote, manage, establish, carry on, or facilitate the promotion, management, establishment, or carrying on, of any unlawful activity, and thereafter performs or attempts to perform

   a. shall be fined under this title, imprisoned not more than 5 years, or both; or

   b. an act described in paragraph (2) shall be fined under this title, imprisoned for not more than 20 years, or both, and if death results shall be imprisoned for any term of years or for life.

The US Department of Justice recently used the Travel Act recently to obtain multiple indictments, along with numerous guilty pleas, in healthcare investigations in Texas and New Jersey.

AUDIT VERSUS FRAUD INVESTIGATION

As we proceed through this text, it is important to understand and appreciate the difference between audit and fraud investigation. I work with both auditors and auditing professionals on a daily basis, and during my career I have assisted on more audits than I can remember. I also use auditors on my engagements as a subject matter and industry experts. That combination is a perfect complement on many of my investigations. I have also hired former auditors to work directly in my group. Some have done exceptionally well while some have struggled.

While there are many white-papers and studies that highlight the difference between a financial statement audit and a fraud investigation, the standards for each are largely the same. Both professionals are responsible for detecting fraud or errors, and there are not different levels of skepticism for each. The expectations to find fraud are likely identical to the investing public.

I have also seen narratives that attempt to differentiate the personality differences of the two. I have found those comical, and even offensive to some. In my humble opinion, only significant exposure to both professions can adequately highlight differences in the professionals. I have seen plenty of good and bad on each side, but I have also seen greatness from both.I prepared Table 1.2 based on my experiences. And while there are certainly exceptions, I find this to be an accurate representation based on my exposure.The one area that I have seen that typically determines the successful transition from an auditor to a fraud investigator is operating within the world of unknowns. Not knowing the ultimate scope, the timing, the due dates. Not having last year's working papers to refer to, and in some cases, having to completely rely on nonfinancial

TABLE 1.2 Audit versus fraud investigation.

Professional	Audit	Fraud Investigation
Certification	Auditors typically are expected to take the CPA exam and obtain a CPA license. Many public accounting firms require their staff to obtain a CPA certification before being promoted to senior associate level and beyond.	White-collar fraud investigators are oftentimes CPAs. They also commonly obtain their Certified Fraud Examiner (CFE) certification. Other certifications include Certified in Financial Forensics (CFF), and the EnCE certification, which indicates that an investigator is a skilled computer examiner. Further, many states require that investigators become licensed private investigators in the states in which they work, especially when electronic data is retrieved and used.
Backgrounds	Auditors are accountants. They can have also have valuable experience in various industries.	Investigators can have numerous backgrounds, including, but not limited to accounting, law, criminal justice, law enforcement, and the military.
Training	Technical training for CPAs focuses largely on accounting, tax, and auditing updates, as well as methodology and software tools.	Fraud examiner training centers on fraud prevention, detection, and deterrence. Depending on the investigator's practice, other specialized training focuses on financial transactions, investigation techniques, laws, and interview skills. Furthermore, research, data analysis and financial modeling are all critical areas, which are driven by the licensed technology. Training courses such as mock trials and deposition preparation are necessary for those fraud examiners who serve as expert witnesses.
Client Relationships	Financial Statement Audits are required for public registrants, governmental agencies, and many others. They are also reoccurring. The learning curve for a company's audit is steep, and costly, which makes auditor retention most common. Questions and concerns can also be	Fraud investigations are a reaction to a situation where fraud is occurring, has occurred, or is expected to occur. No one likes to see a fraud investigator, which results in "throwing good money after bad." Fraud can make executives feel cheated, angry, and hostile towards the situation. This can lead to tense environment that is best avoided. Therefore, the hope is that this is

(Continued)

TABLE 1.2 (*Continued*)

Professional	Audit	Fraud Investigation
	raised when a company changes auditors, so some companies are reluctant to change. As such, there is typically a long-standing, somewhat cordial relationship with a client. The relationship is carefully scrutinized to insure independence, and for publically traded companies, the audit partner must rotate every five years.	a one-time arrangement (unless outside counsel, who represents the company, hires you). There are generally no "independence" requirements for a fraud investigator.
Engagement Letter	Audit engagement letters are signed directly with the clients, the entities being audited.	Forensic service engagement letters are signed most often with in-house attorneys or outside law firms that represent the ultimate clients. This assists in preserving the confidential nature of the investigation, and attorney-client privilege.
Scope – expected work	Based on last year's working papers and well-developed, standard methodology. The number of hours per audit is generally reasonably known, and the price is often fixed.	Entirely dependent on the allegations and the investigator's experience in similar matters. It is almost impossible to know the number of hours or cost associated with an investigation. In fact, a crafty defense attorney can use fee caps and time constraints to allege that there were scope restraints.
Skepticism	Auditors assume that the client is neither honest nor dishonest. Further, each year, an auditor has to confirm they have no reason to question the integrity of management, and that there are no outstanding disagreements between them and management.	As mentioned above, an investigator is on the scene because there is belief that fraud has occured, is occurring, or is likely to occur. Therefore, there is often a mindset that someone is or is likely to be dishonest.

TABLE 1.2 *(Continued)*

Professional	Audit	Fraud Investigation
Approach	Audit covers all accounts of the financial statements. Auditors utilize sampling, statistical sampling, or nonstatistical methods. Rarely do auditors review 100% of transactions in an account, unless the account does not have many transactions. Audit utilizes threshold and materiality in testing. Transactions below a certain threshold are not selected as testing samples. Mistakes below certain materiality pass further review.	Fraud engagements are more focused, for example, on allegations involving asset misrepresentation, corruption, or fraudulent financial statements. Scope of a fraud investigation depends on the area in which fraudulent activities occurred or are suspected. Fraud investigations typically have no materiality threshold, and most likely involve reviewing 100% of the transactions in certain accounts during a period. Sometimes it is important to wear a "disguise." To avoid disrupting operations at a client, some fraud investigations are conducted covertly, or generically referred to as an audit. They are also taught to avoid using words, such as "investigation," "interview," "fraud" when meeting at client sites.
Documentation	It is imperative for auditors to have well documented work papers on all audits. Without proper documentation of work performed, an audit cannot pass various levels of reviews performed by the seniors, managers, partners, and peer review by another firm or review by higher authorities, such as PCAOB.	Fraud investigators work with sensitive information, and there are well-defined protocols that determine what, if anything, is written. Fraud investigation documentation typically would contain qualifiers such as ATTORNEY CLIENT PRIVILEGED, FOR ATTORNEYS' EYES ONLY.
Reporting	The auditor's report contains an expression of opinion on the financial statements, taken as a whole, or an assertion that an opinion	While there are many preferred templates, fraud investigation reports vary greatly in contents and format. There is no standard format or template. They can be oral or written.

(Continued)

TABLE 1.2 (*Continued*)

Professional	Audit	Fraud Investigation
	cannot be expressed. Audit reports have four types of opinions: unqualified opinion, qualified opinion, adverse opinion, and disclaimer of opinion.	Written reports typically contain a disclaimer to limit use of the report to certain specific purpose and audience.
	Audit reports are largely standardized to express one of four opinions.	Expert witness reports that pertain to federal matters have certain requirements in order to be accepted.
Work–life balance	Auditors typically know their schedule months in advance. The hours are long, and there are certainly "surprises" along the way, but generally speaking, their whereabouts are known. Auditors have what is referred to as "busy season," which is typically from January to the end of April. Some firms require staff auditors to work 12-hour days, along with mandatory weekends during busy season. Summers are typically a slower season for auditors, allowing them to take much deserved and needed time off.	Fraud investigators rarely know what lies ahead. When one stone is overturned, whatever is hiding underneath can sprint a number of different directions (geographies, departments, current and former executives, etc.). A $5,000 assignment can explode to a $5 million project in a split second. Assignments can also go the other direction, in that what you envision as a significant undertaking can be resolved unexpectedly through settlements and employee terminations. Fraud examiners have no fixed busy season. It is feast or famine, as they jokingly put it, full of peaks and valleys. What you do in your valleys will determine how long you stay there, and also the height of your next peak. Engagements come and go at their own pace, and fraud examiners react to the demands. There are times when investigators have to work long hours for periods of time to resolve allegations. We have been known to work in 12-hour shifts, allowing coverage 24 hours per day. Further, investigations oftentimes can involve multiple countries with different time zones. Those can make for long days.

(*Continued*)

TABLE 1.2 (Continued)

Professional	Audit	Fraud Investigation
		Fraud examiners find it difficult to plan vacations, and certainly should insure their trips due to the sensitive and urgent nature of most matters that arise without notice.
Other interpersonal observations	I find auditors typically more organized and methodical. They are outstanding at ticking and tying financial data and supporting schedules. Their organization skills are also impeccable, and their working papers are strong. They can also be more accustomed to working in teams and "play well with others."	I find fraud investigators more skeptical, to the point of almost being cynical. (possibly a product of the environment in which they work). Their interview skills are generally more polished, and their written work-product can stand on its own.

information (interviews, surveillance, and absence of information). All of those can be overcome in time, if the professional becomes "comfortable" with being "uncomfortable."

I had the opportunity to spend time recently with a professional who has experienced all "branches" of the accounting and auditing profession during her 20-year career. She began her career as a forensic accounting consultant, and then moved into the internal audit department at an international Fortune 500 company. She then transitioned into a financial reporting role, where she interacts with the board of directors, company executives, and the external/internal auditors.

This has given her a unique perspective when it comes to responsibilities and being held accountable. I asked her the following questions:

Q: What differences come to mind, generally speaking, between a consultant and employee?

A: Employees have a vested interest in the company. They typically want to do what is in the best interest of the company and have genuine concern about their personal branding/reputation, which affects future roles, promotions, longevity with the company. Consultants are often influenced by the client and can be conflicted in doing the right thing. Consultants are also driven by sales, utilization rates, hours billed, and so on, which can often skew their intentions.

Q: While internal auditors are sometimes called "independent," what factors make that challenging? Can it impair objectivity?

A: Yes, because an internal auditor is an actual employee, and their vested interest in the company impairs their objectivity and independence. Internal auditors must balance controls, processes, and procedures with business operations so the controls do not impede productivity. Internal auditors frequently must mitigate competing priorities between a strong control environment and flourishing business operation.

Q: As a "member of management," do you now see fraud risks and ethical dilemmas differently? If yes, then how so? Would it make you a better consultant or auditor?

A: Yes, you're intimately involved in many aspects across the company, so you see fraud risks and ethical dilemmas through a different lens than a consultant, external auditor, or even internal auditor/investigator because of the closeness to the operations. You have a deeper understanding for why and how decisions were made and the justifications for them. However, you are also held to a much higher standard than an individual contributor or someone early in their career, which means despite the closeness, you can't hold any bias. As a leader of the company, you are expected to set the tone across your teams by encouraging healthy skepticism, challenging the status quo, and asking questions. You also must instill comfort in your teams so that they can report suspicions of fraud or misconduct without any repercussions.

One case that I remember fondly occurred in the early 2000s. It was a highly technical accounting matter involving one of the world's largest software developers. I was teamed with two of our firm's strongest auditors to explore various allegations involving the company's revenue recognition practices. There was an accusation that the company was recognizing revenue prematurely in violation of GAAP. The issue was whether the company's products were client-ready off the shelf – in which they could record revenue immediately – or whether the products required considerable customization, modification, and implementation – which would preclude revenue recognition.

The two auditors spent nearly 100% of their time in this particular industry on these very same issues. As such, I spent countless hours studying and compiling research. I felt ready (that I had obtained professional competency) once the assignment commenced.

We each obtained our sample of contracts for analysis. After the first few days, they had substantially completed their contract review, and I had only gone through three contracts and flagged each of them for anomalies, triggering a second level of review. Considering that I was the least experienced resource on the assignment, I took them home and studied them even closer. I compared the contracts to my research notes and even called an accounting college professor I knew. I could not get comfortable and provided my concerns to counsel.

The issue that I raised was that when I read the contract and traced the deliverables to the supporting documentation that triggered the immediate revenue recognition, I saw significant man-hours being charged to the jobs after "delivery." When I researched the employees who were incurring hours, they were classified as engineers, programmers, coders, developers, and other designers. If a product was ready "off the shelf," why did I continue to see such hours from those types of employees?

I wrote up my findings and presented them in draft form. It was the start of something far bigger than we imagined. The two auditors agreed, and went back through their contracts applying this insight, and they, too, found similar concerns. Much to the company's credit, they assisted us in the investigation, which helped reach a resolution. I can summarize management's position through the many discussions we had. They had "paralysis by analysis." There was so much data, so many reports. There were not sufficient resources or time in the day to chase down every anomaly or variance. (This is a fairly common statement across all industries.) The company ultimately was accused of overstating revenues by more than $1 billion, and settled for a $10 million civil penalty.

Was I smarter than the auditors were? Not by a long shot. I was simply accustomed to requesting and looking at documents that were often outside the scope of an audit, and for a completely different purpose. The supporting documentation was readily available, and every transaction reconciled to the data provided; there was simply more pieces to the puzzle that required a much deeper dive.

SUMMARY

Standards, standards, and more standards. And if that is not enough for you, laws, laws, and more laws. It is your individual responsibility to familiarize yourself with the standards and laws that govern your profession. These regulations constantly evolve and commonly vary by role, industry, and country. Despite the applicable standards and laws, fraud can happen to any company and any size. It is imperative that you consult the applicable rules to mitigate that risk, as well as address the occurrences as they arise.

 RECOMMENDATIONS

A pervasive control, if you will, over all elements contained herein is establishing strong policies that specifically include the words *fraud* and *ethics*. In addition to using those "bad" words, those policies should:

1. Define fraud and misconduct for your organization, along with the consequences for taking part in either.
2. Be specifically tailored and communicated in a way the user will comprehend. This includes special provisions in countries that have different cultures and ethical expectations. (Language/cultural barriers do not make for good defenses.)
3. Provide illustrations, "real-world" examples that employees may face. These also include financial statement fraud and examples of management override of internal controls, specifically tailored for those involved in the accounting function. Large conglomerates should also consider the different educational backgrounds of their employees, and communicate to their level and provide examples they may commonly face.
4. Guidelines and illustrations should be certified as read *and* understood by all employees (annually); this should be accompanied by tracking mechanisms to identify those employees whose certifications are incomplete. Some companies do not stop at policies; they provide annual training, in which employees are tested based on their knowledge of the applicable policies. (CPAs and CFEs know all too well about ethical training and tests. However, not everyone is so lucky!)
5. Extended beyond employees. Agents, third-party providers, consultants, and significant vendors should also adhere to your policies and inform you when they see unethical behavior from their point of view.

6. Enforced. A strong policy is nothing more than a "paper tiger" if management fails to enforce the policy and consistently administer the consequences for breaches.
7. Constantly updates based on prior experiences.

Specially speaking to the chapter at hand, to avoid becoming a victim of F – forgetting the present, I recommend the following:

1. Keep apprised of current events. It is your personal responsibility to stay apprised of new rules and regulations affecting the profession. Regulations often alter our obligations, mostly for the better. Lawsuits, news, and other events occur weekly that involve your competitors and industry. Setting aside time each week to read and network with peers can provide valuable insight to situations that may find their way to your desk.
2. Network. As you well know, not all issues are made or become public. Attending training conferences connects you with others in your field. Further, many cities have invitation-only peer groups that confidentially share insight into emerging trends and competing priorities they face in their own environments.
3. Educate others. As you will read in the chapters ahead, you will realize that nonaccountants (or those ethically challenged accountants) can apply pressure and suggest courses of actions that violate your standards and could affect your career. Take an active approach to protecting your license and inform others of your required course of action.
4. Expect the unexpected. As you gather information through continuing education and dedication to remaining curious about the profession, document potential exposures you could face. Be prepared to encounter challenges and have a contingency plan in place if the unimaginable happens.
5. Take on a new challenge. My favorite! Be dedicated to continuous learning. Write or speak on a topic that interests you, but yet is unfamiliar. Attend a training session on an emerging area that may not currently affect you, but that could eventually. Assign something similar to those that report to you. Remain curious about the profession and encourage that in others. It is a marathon, not a sprint. And the more you learn, the more you know (my own Yogi-ism!).

Case Study: The Curious Case of the Consulting Fees

Techno Inc. is a publicly traded Fortune 500 company, with international manufacturing operations. The Vice President of Internal Audit included Techno's plant in India in this year's audit plan. During the audit's fieldwork, the team identified large payments to an Indian public official. The payments were coded as "consulting fees" in the company's general ledger. The supporting documentation was limited, as invoices contained no details, just a round dollar amounts. Techno's Indian president advised internal audit that the payments were to "ensure that operations run smoothly, and that Techno could not operate without them. It's simply the cost of doing business in India." Internal audit was told there were no contracts, no agreed-upon deliverables, and no specified pay rates or dollar figures. They also could not articulate what was actually being done.

Internal audit approached the corporate accounting department to ask why such payments were coded as "consulting fees." The Accounting Manager said he was instructed to code them as consulting payments by the CFO, who is a Certified Public Accountant. The CFO was unable to make time to meet with internal audit before their report was due to the audit committee, but through email, advised internal audit that while he had not personally reviewed the transactions or underlying support, the general counsel was aware and had asked that they be recorded this way. The CFO advised that any questions be directed toward the general counsel."

The Vice President of Internal Audit determined that in her professional opinion, these payments were bribes and likely violations of the Foreign Corrupt Practices Act. She presented her draft report to Techno's audit committee. Shortly after presenting the draft report, the Vice President was called to the General Counsel's Office. The General Counsel informed the Vice President that her assessment was wrong, and that these were truly consulting payments that he directed. He had changed her report to reflect the transaction's substance and issued the final report to the audit committee.

Further, as a result of Techno's reorganization, her role was being eliminated. However, he added, that if she signed a "nondisclosure and nondisparage agreement," she would be allowed to resign and receive six-month's severance pay including benefits. Otherwise, she would receive two weeks, with pay, and would not be eligible for rehire.

1. What "red flags" suggest these payments may not be for consulting?
2. What ethical rules, laws, or regulations are relevant to management in this situation? To internal audit? To the CFO?
3. What personal exposure exists for the accounting manager? For the CFO? For VP of Internal Audit?

(Continued)

4. What legal/financial consequences might the General Counsel be attempting to avoid by altering the internal audit report and not investigating further?
5. Alternatively, what governmental incentives suggest that the best course of action is for the General Counsel to disclose the original internal audit report?
6. What ramifications, if any, does the Vice President of Internal Audit face if she accepts the severance? And if she refuses? What pressures may influence her ultimate decision? What recourse could be available to her?
7. Assuming that Techno operates in an "at-will" state, do they face any exposure in terminating the Vice President of Internal Audit? If so, what?
8. Why might this information be of interest to the company's external auditor? What action might they take if they learned of this involuntarily?
9. Provide and defend an appropriate course of actions for each professional, including:
   a. The accounting manager in recording the transaction.
   b. The CFO, prior to acceptance.
   c. The Vice President of Internal Audit's decision.
10. If you are a Certified Fraud Examiner hired to investigation this allegation, what steps would you take to provide the company's board of directors and external auditor with the determination of their financial damages, and the opinion that this incident was isolated to India?

CHAPTER TWO

R – Relying on Others

N THIS CHAPTER, WE discuss adequate supervision in the individual responsibilities placed on accountants to discharge their professional responsibilities.

INTRODUCTION

For all the parents out there, how many times have you asked your children to do something, but after an ensuing discussion uttered the words, "Forget it. I'll do it myself!" I bet more than a few of you went ahead and did it yourself, just to advance your day. Perhaps that was part of your children's plan! (And for those of you who are still children, shame on you!) I remember once, in eighth grade, my best friend and I were given after-school detention. (In fact, I don't ever remember a time from kindergarten through tenth grade when I wasn't on some sort of school probation or detention.) Part of our punishment during this stretch of hard time was painting the high school boys' restroom. The principal left us two gallons of bright blue paint, two rollers, and two brushes. When we sought further clarification on our tasks, we were cut off: *"Just paint the damn bathroom!"* So, we did. We worked well into the night. We painted EVERY-THING blue. The walls, the toilets, the sinks, urinals. All the fixtures. You name it. The only thing not blue were the two mirrors above the sinks. That's simply so we could see the big smiles on our faces. We raced to school, early that morning reveling in the handywork. We couldn't wait to show the principal. As we walked toward the latrine, my heart raced. I knew I was facing another few weeks "in the box" aka Shawshank Redemption. As the principal swung open the door, the blue glistened like a Kaye's diamond. He was furious. Trembling. However, as he looked at the two grinning eighth graders, he softened. "You boys are proud of yourselves, aren't you? Well, I must admit I admire your creativity. You'll get a couple of extra weeks of detention, but I think the students will get a kick out of this." And did they. Much as they did a number of our high school antics. Our entire school enrollment, K–12, was less than 350, so it did not take much to provide much-needed entertainment.

In our professional settings, we can sometimes assume our work "children" have completed certain tasks, rather than us doing it ourselves. Professional Standards require that CPAs, CIAs, and CFEs adequately plan and supervise their staff. Further standards (240, FAS 2, and many others) require that the practitioner assign the tasks commensurate to the associated risk.

I think we can all agree, if it weren't for people, our job would be easy. After all, many of us became accountants to avoid people! Nonetheless, we are in the people business, and we often experience challenges. Challenges in staff availability, fee constraints, and personal conflicts can cripple the best-laid plans. As such, we can sometimes place reliance on incompetence, just as my principal relied on mine, or the lack thereof, when it came to painting.

 MANAGEMENT

As we will discuss, investors place a great deal of reliance on management's trustworthiness. After all, management is the first line of defense. Since companies cannot run without people, there have been significant developments relating to a company's corporate governance and response to the risks of fraud and misconduct. The Sarbanes-Oxley language referenced earlier provides management with somewhat of a "get out of jail free" card as it relates to disclosing fraud and misconduct. The standard provides management with a limitation, stipulating such disclosure reads "to the best of your knowledge." As such, the assurances, once again, are not absolute.

However, in 2015, the Department of Justice (DOJ) put management on notice. In September 2015, Deputy Attorney General Sally Yates issued a memorandum. The subject – "Individual Accountability for Corporate Wrongdoing." The Department of Justice released the following statement:

> Fighting corporate fraud and other misconduct is a top priority of the Department of Justice. The United States' economy depends on effective enforcement of the civil and criminal laws that protect our financial system and, by extension, all our citizens. These are principles that the Department lives and breathes – as evidenced by the many attorneys, agents, and support staff who have worked tirelessly on corporate investigations.
>
> One of the most effective ways to combat corporate misconduct is by seeking accountability from the individuals who perpetrated the wrongdoing. Such accountability is important for several reasons: it deters future illegal activity; it incentivizes changes in corporate behavior; it ensures that the proper parties are held responsible for their actions; and it promotes the public's confidence in our justice system.
>
> On September 9, 2015, Deputy Attorney General Sally Q. Yates issued a memorandum entitled, "Individual Accountability for Corporate Wrongdoing" to guide department attorneys when handling corporate matters. The memo outlined six significant steps [see Figure 2.1] in Department policy in order to ensure that corporate investigations are handled consistently across the department:

1. To be eligible for any cooperation credit, corporations must provide the Department all relevant facts about individuals involved in corporate misconduct;
2. Both criminal and civil corporate investigations should focus on individuals from the inception of the investigation;
3. Criminal and civil attorneys handling corporate investigations should be in routine communication with one another;
4. Absent extraordinary circumstances, no corporate resolution should provide protection from criminal or civil liability for any individuals;
5. Corporate cases should not be resolved without a clear plan to resolve related individual cases; and

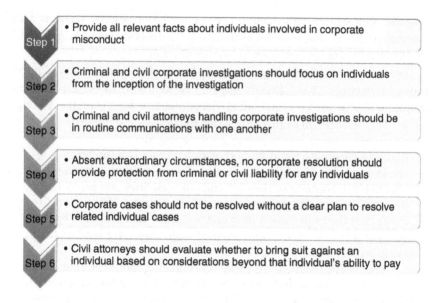

Step 1
• Provide all relevant facts about individuals involved in corporate misconduct

Step 2
• Criminal and civil corporate investigations should focus on individuals from the inception of the investigation

Step 3
• Criminal and civil attorneys handling corporate investigations should be in routine communications with one another

Step 4
• Absent extraordinary circumstances, no corporate resolution should provide protection from criminal or civil liability for any individuals

Step 5
• Corporate cases should not be resolved without a clear plan to resolve related individual cases

Step 6
• Civil attorneys should evaluate whether to bring suit against an individual based on considerations beyond that individual's ability to pay

FIGURE 2.1 Six key steps to strengthen pursuit of individual corporate wrongdoing.

6. Civil attorneys should evaluate whether to bring suit against an individual based on considerations beyond that individual's ability to pay.

As a result of this directive, the DOJ reemphasized their focus on holding individuals accountable for wrongdoing actions. When people are held responsible for their actions and receive severe consequences for wrong, it tends to deter illegal activity and correct corporate behavior. In response, the public will have more confidence in businesses and in the justice system.

In December 2018, the DOJ revised its policies to give additional clarification to the 2015 memorandum. The DOJ was very clear that they are committed to holding individuals accountable for corporate wrongdoing. These new "revised" policies did not waive the original policy, but rather enhanced discretion and focus. These revisions affect both criminal cases and civil cases. The DOJ revisions stated:

With respect to criminal cases, companies now only need to provide the DOJ with information about individuals who were "substantially" involved in the alleged misconduct to be eligible for cooperation credit, rather than all such employees, regardless of their level of involvement.

With respect to civil cases, Rosenstein announced a number of policy changes that give enforcement attorneys more discretion. Civil enforcement attorneys may now: (1) grant companies partial cooperation credit if they provide "meaningful assistance" to the DOJ, even if they do not provide information related to lower-level employees; (2) release individuals from civil liability when resolving civil corporate cases, if warranted; and (3) consider an individual's ability to pay as a determinative factor in evaluating whether to bring civil claims against him or her.[1]

There is still some room for debate in specific areas, such as the definition of "substantially" and "meaningful assistance." However, as a result of this revision, prosecution and conviction of executives have been brought to a more serious level. To keep out of negative light, companies may be more inclined to strengthen their codes of conduct and examine the tone at the top. In addition, companies could be more incentivized to cooperate due to partial cooperation credit.

Let us assume the worst. What happens when internal auditors and compliance personnel rely to their detriment on management, who, as we mentioned, should be the first line of defense? Take, for example, the 2019 news about Cognizant Technology Solutions Corp. Federal prosecutors and regulators handed down parallel criminal and civil charges for the former president and chief legal officer, accusing them of participating in a scheme to bribe an Indian official with a $2 million payment for permission to move forward on a construction project.

The charges were filed on the same day that Cognizant, an information technology and consulting services corporation with more than half its workforce in India, agreed to pay the SEC $25 million to settle its own Foreign Corrupt Practices Act charges.

The former president and former chief legal officer were accused of authorizing a contractor to pay a senior government official in Tamil Nadu $2 million to secure a planning permit needed for construction of Cognizant's 2.7-million square-foot office campus in Chennai.

---

[1]James P. Melendres, Aloke S. Chakravarty, and Carter Gee-Taylor, "Yates Memorandum: Rosenstein Announces Easier Path for Companies to Receive Cooperation Credit," Snell & Wilmer, December 11, 2018, https://www.swlaw.com/publications/legal-alerts/2574.

"The allegations in the indictment filed yesterday describe a sophisticated international bribery scheme authorized and concealed by C-suite executives of a publicly-traded multinational company," assistant US Attorney General Benczkowski said in an announcement.

According to the SEC and prosecutors, construction on the office campus hit a snag in early 2014 when Cognizant became aware that the construction company contracted for the job had not obtained a necessary planning permit due to delays with a government order.

In April of that year, the executives authorized the contractor to pay an official $2 million to get the ball rolling on needed planning and building permits and agreed to pay the contractor an additional $500,000 for carrying out the bribe, authorities claim.

The contractor was reimbursed for the $2.5 million through a series of fraudulent change orders that inflated the amount owed by Cognizant to the contractor for its construction services, all of which were approved by Coburn, according to the government.

In addition, the SEC has accused Cognizant of authorizing and concealing two additional bribes made during 2013 and 2014, totaling more than $1.6 million, to secure environmental clearance for a project in Pune, India, and construction-related permits in Siruseri, India.

While Cognizant neither admitted nor denied the SEC's allegations, they entered into a cease-and-desist order in which it agreed to disgorge approximately $19 million and pay a $6 million fine to resolve the multiple alleged federal securities law violations.

The executives now individually face federal securities law violations related to anti-bribery, books and records and internal accounting controls from the SEC, which is seeking permanent injunctions, monetary penalties, and officer-and-director bars against them.

Pause. Consider that these are exactly the level of executives – the internal auditor, an external auditor – that an expert, in addition to the investing public, generally relies on to provide relevant and reliable information.

Setting aside the risks we raise with management, accountants and management may place heavy reliance in those outside of the immediate organization. One such role that exposes companies to risks is outsourcing operations, or even management positions. A company may decide it is more efficient and effective to outsource an operational component, or may ultimately determine they do not have the proper skill set or adequate resources to perform the role. Regardless of the reason, those outsourced vendors that companies *rely* on, can, and often do, create challenges.

There are times when utilizing an interim financial executive may be necessary or advantageous, such as, for example, when:

▨ A critical financial executive wishes to transition out or has left the company suddenly
▨ The financial executive does not possess the appropriate skills the business needs for growth or to achieve goals
▨ The company needs a specific set of skills for a short period of time due to a crisis or critical initiative
▨ To provide a fresh pair of eyes or perspective or provide the company time to evaluate the longer term needs of the position before making the next hire

Unlike internal auditors (in which case it is common to co-source or out-source), C-level executives are expected to take ownership of not only the controls, but also the financial statements themselves. In the case of an interim (i.e., temporary) arrangement, there are unique risks and limitations that must be considered.

The CFO Suite, LLC focuses on filling gaps in high-level financial areas with professionals typically having 15–25 years of experience. Managing Partner Kathy Schrock is well aware of the risks associated with these arrangements and consults on risk mitigation almost daily. According to Ms. Schrock, risks of outsourcing C-suite financial executives include qualifications, expectations, and knowledge retention/transfer.

▨ *Qualifications.* Just because an individual was a great CFO for a colleague does not mean they are a great fit for your company. The demands and expectations of financial executives and titles vary more widely than you can imagine. It is not uncommon for smaller companies to give a controller a title of VP or CFO, but that does not mean they can operate as a CFO in a bigger company. Some controllers of large, complex organizations are qualified to be CFOs in a different organization/environment so the title alone does not define qualifications. Risks are greater in sourcing and finding an individual on your own, particularly in a tight market where unemployment is low, and many companies do not have the internal expertise to source and evaluate candidates quickly for this type of position or to replace the position if someone leaves. Firms that are uniquely positioned to provide these services have access to a broader pool of candidates and information to help identify a good fit or replacement.

- *Expectations.* It is very important to establish clear expectations regarding responsibilities, supervision, limitations, insurance, and disclosure when engaging an interim either directly with an individual or through a firm. Because an interim position is temporary in nature, it is appropriate to limit access to assets. Firms providing the resource do not typically have direct supervision over interim financial executives and visibility to work product; the executive is under the direction and supervision of company management (and perhaps the Board). The firm's engagement letter will typically indicate such and that the individual will not have sole decision-making authority, signatory authority, or access to assets. If the firm providing the resource has signed a nondisclosure agreement (NDA) on behalf of the firm and their employee (the interim executive), it is still recommended that an NDA be executed with the individual financial executive. Firms have basic business and liability insurance, but individuals do not. It is critical in either case that the company add the interim executive to their D&O insurance – sometimes this presents unique challenges with insurance companies, and they may request additional information. For public companies, the nature of the interim arrangement is required to be disclosed, including the payment/fee arrangement – similar to compensation disclosure for key executives. Communication is key when it comes to expectations and changes in expectations. Many good interim executives will take responsibility and ownership as if they were an "official" member of management, but companies need to be mindful that while the arrangement is interim, there are certain precautions that are imperative.
- *Knowledge retention/transfer.* As with any position, knowledge retention and transfer is important, and in the case of an interim position, that person is not as "tied" to the company as an "official" hire. It is important to establish protocol for retaining records, knowledge, and so forth and that management has appropriate communication and involvement to prevent critical knowledge, history, or information from being lost if/when this individual leaves.

Frankly, many of these risks apply even in the case of a newly appointed permanent CFO. Ensuring appropriate qualifications or engaging a firm that specializes in recruiting that type of position is important to the success of the individual and the company. Hiring "ahead" of growth or goals will provide a longer tenure than hiring an individual that the company will outgrow quickly or that doesn't possess key skills the company knows it will need in the next

12–24 months. Clear communication in establishing expectations is always important with any role, as is a method for retaining critical knowledge and information. The typical tenure of a financial executive is often shorter than you think due to many factors, including market conditions, stage of company, growth opportunity, individual goals, and so forth.

Third-party providers (such as vendors or entire companies) present unique challenges and can exhibit more risk factors than employees. There are a few reasons why:

1. They are not company employees and may have ulterior motives. Their loyalties may lie with their own company, and not yours.
2. They may not have been subjected to the same level of background investigations or training to obtain and retain their job as those within the organization they are being retained to represent.
3. They may have different cultural experiences. What is acceptable in their culture may not be in yours.
4. The retaining organization may not have adequate resources, skill sets, or experience to supervise or monitor their performance. After all, there is a reason the company is using a third party.
5. Lastly, the company that is retained may not ultimately be the company that performs the work. Subcontractors can present even more risks, as they are one step further removed from transparency.

This is especially apparent in the financial services industry, and some recent cases involving household names. In 2010, The Dodd-Frank Act gave the Consumer Financial Protection Bureau (CFPB) supervisory authority over a variety of institutions that may engage in debt collection, including:

- Certain depository institutions and their affiliates
- Nonbank entities in the residential mortgage
- Payday lending
- Private education lending markets, as well as their service providers

The Dodd-Frank Act (Section 1036 of Title X) provides guidance on the unlawful practices of financial service providers to engage in unfair, deceptive, or abusive acts or practices. Further, the CFPB affirms that the use of third-party relationships does not relinquish responsibility of the board of directors and management for compliance with federal consumer law to avoid consumer harm. Some companies learned of this too late.

For example, in 2012, the CFPB brought its first enforcement action, and reported that its examiners discovered that Capital One's third-party vendors engaged in deceptive tactics to sell ancillary products to the company's credit cards. Capital One agreed to provide between $140 million and $150 million in restitution to 2 million customers and pay an additional $60 million in penalties – $25 million to the CFPB and $35 million to the Office of the Comptroller of the Currency.

Other lenders also settled after being accused of failing to adequately monitor their vendors or subsidiaries:

- American Express – two subsidiaries were charged for discriminating against consumers in Puerto Rico, the US Virgin Islands, and other US territories by providing them with credit and charge card terms that were inferior to those available in the 50 states. American Express paid approximately $95 million in consumer redress during the course of the Bureau's review, and the order required it to pay at least another $1 million to fully compensate harmed consumers.
- Discover – its two student loan affiliates were required to refund $16 million to consumers, pay a $2.5 million penalty, and improve its billing, student loan interest reporting, and collection practices.

Further, engaging with third parties continues to be the largest risk involving the FCPA and the UK Anti-Bribery Act. There is no shortage of cases to study. For example, much like the Cognizant allegations mentioned earlier, in November 2013, the DOJ and the SEC announced a settlement with a Swiss oil services provider. A company subsidiary was accused of using a third party to funnel bribes to a foreign official in exchange for the renewal of an oil services contract. It was alleged that the company generated sham purchase orders and invoices for services that were never performed. When those invoices were paid to the third party, that party paid the foreign official with the authority to approve the contract renewal. The company paid more than $250 million in criminal fines, disgorgement, and civil penalties to the DOJ, SEC, and other government agencies.

These illustrations show the monetary exposure and litigation risks involve R – relying on others, and regardless of who provides the services, the responsible party is rarely, if ever, completely absolved. Lastly, and importantly, management can blindly on their internal controls. We have mentioned the Sarbanes-Oxley certifications that management makes regarding their ownership and effectiveness of said controls. However, many internal controls are dependent on people, or subject to management override. One analogy I have used over the years is "baby-proofing." How many of you have small children? (how many of you still behave like small children, or are married to one.) Remember when you/they baby proofed the house? I bet the belief was that everything was covered. All the risks were mitigated. Covers were over the electrical outlets. Clasps were around cabinets and doorknobs secured. The issue, is that those "controls" also make it difficult for adults to access doors and cabinets. And sometimes, in haste, the plugs or clasps may not be put back on, or not fully re-applied. That one slip is all it takes and the little one is under the sink! (don't ask me how I know). Further, that infant also probably identified gaps; dangers or risks that you or your friend hadn't considered. (again, I know this too!) Internal controls are just like this. It only takes one gap, or human error, to expose the organization to risk, despite even the best controls. It also only takes a manager (aka a parent) to override (or remove them) all together. Blindly relying on controls, that are run by others, without properly testing and constantly monitoring them, can wreak just as much havoc as junior drinking all your dishwashing liquids.

EXTERNAL AUDITORS

Dog ownership is one of the greatest things on this earth. They never talk back or argue, and they are always happy to see you and faithfully greet you at the door every time. I did not want just any dog; I wanted a very specific dog. In order to do that I went onto the rescue society's website and got to see pictures of the dogs and read their bios. Something to note is before the dogs are allowed to be posted for adoption the foster parent has to have a dog for two weeks to observe the dog so there could be a good match and place the dog in their forever home. For months I waited and waited for the perfect dog to pop up. Finally, Bailey was posted. She was over a year (so out of the young puppy stage), potty and crate trained, sweet, and cuddly and loved playing outside. In her picture she was all nice and brushed with a big pink bow around her neck and a big smile. She was perfect, I thought. I just had to have her. I put in an application for her and within a few days she was mine. It was like wrestling with a bull to get her in my car. She was absolutely terrified. She was excessively panting and had slobber everywhere. They conveniently left that off of her bio. When we got home, she was terrified of being inside. She ran in the backyard and would not come inside for the most elaborate bribes. (Oh hush! Bribes are totally appropriate for animals and toddlers.) Nothing in her bio mentioned her being terrified of the inside and only wanting to be outside. After finally convincing her to come inside, she wanted absolutely nothing to do with any sort of cuddling. Bailey was not potty trained by any stretch of the imagination and was one of the most destructive dogs I have ever seen. The couch, my books, food off the counter, shoes, you name it. The only time she ever went into her kennel is when she could not get outside and she wanted to hide from getting in trouble. Clearly Bailey did not accurately reflect her bio, which led me to have a fiasco on my hands. As silly and funny, this story may be, a valuable lesson can be learned. You can never fully rely on someone else when the stake (or in my case, the steaks!) are so high.

There are times in which auditors have to rely on other experts, or specialists. As such, external auditors (CPAs) have a thorough set of standards, that they must abide by when having to execute a financial statement audit. The Public Company Accounting Oversight Board (PCAOB) defines an external auditor's responsibility as "to plan and perform the audit to obtain reasonable assurance about whether the financial statements are free of material misstatement, whether caused by error or fraud. Because of the nature of audit evidence and the characteristics of fraud, the auditor is able to obtain reasonable, but not absolute, assurance that material misstatements are detected." When an external audit fails and there are material misstatements, the company is required to restate their financial statements. External auditors assume some level of responsibility when considering risk of material misstatement due to fraud. Some of the challenges that these companies face are class-action lawsuits from investors, and potentially other stakeholders who relied on the financial statements. In fact, a 2017 study by Caseware Analytics found that there is a 99% chance of the auditor being sued if an actual fraud is not detected as part of an audit (despite the technicality that finding fraud is not the auditor's primary responsibility). These lawsuits generally accuse the firm of violating the generally accepted auditing standards and principles.

Reliance on others is covered in elaborate detail. One standard presented in generally accepted auditing standards pertains to planning and supervision of the assignment. The first standard of fieldwork states, "The auditor must adequately plan the work and must properly supervise any assistants." Planning and supervision continue throughout the audit.

The AICPA standard AU-C Section 620 – Using the Work of an Auditor's Specialist – provides insight on how an accountant/auditor should approach such reliance.

> An auditor's specialist is an individual or organization possessing expertise in a field other than accounting or auditing, whose work in that field is used by the auditor to assist the auditor in obtaining sufficient appropriate audit evidence. The auditor should evaluate the adequacy of the work of the auditor's specialist for the auditor's purposes, including:
>
> a. The relevance and reasonableness of the findings and conclusions of the auditor's specialist and their consistency with other audit evidence.
> b. If the work of the auditor's specialist involves the use of significant assumptions and methods,
>   i. Obtaining an understanding of those assumptions and methods and
>   ii. Evaluating the relevance and reasonableness of those assumptions and methods in the circumstances, giving consideration

to the rationale and support provided by the specialist, and in relation to the auditor's other findings and conclusions.

The auditor has sole responsibility for the audit opinion expressed, and that responsibility is not reduced by the auditor's use of the work of an auditor's specialist. Nonetheless, if the auditor using the work of an auditor's specialist, having followed this section, concludes that the work of that specialist is adequate for the auditor's purposes, the auditor may accept that specialist's findings or conclusions in the specialist's field as appropriate audit evidence.

The American Institute of Certified Public Accounts (AICPA) also released standards that address adequate supervision as well as professional competence. Audit Standards AU 311.28–311.32 specifically address supervision.

.28 Supervision involves directing the efforts of assistants who are involved in accomplishing the objectives of the audit and determining whether those objectives were accomplished. Elements of supervision include instructing assistants, keeping informed of significant issues encountered, reviewing the work performed, and dealing with differences of opinion among firm personnel. The extent of supervision appropriate in a given instance depends on many factors, including the complexity of the subject matter and the qualifications of persons performing the work, including knowledge of the client's business and industry.

.29 The auditor with final responsibility for the audit should communicate with members of the audit team regarding the susceptibility of the entity's financial statements to material misstatement due to error or fraud, with special emphasis on fraud. Such discussion helps all audit team members understand the entity and its environment, including its internal control, and how risks that the entity faces may affect the audit. The discussion should emphasize the need to maintain a questioning mind and to exercise professional skepticism in gathering and evaluating evidence throughout the audit.

.30 In addition, assistants should be informed of their responsibilities and the objectives of the audit procedures they are to perform. They should be informed of matters that may affect the nature, timing, and extent of audit procedures they are to perform, such as the nature of the entity's business as it relates to their assignments and possible accounting and auditing issues. The auditor with final responsibility for the audit should direct assistants to bring to his or her attention accounting and auditing issues raised during the audit that the assistant believes are of significance to the financial statements or auditor's report so the auditor with final responsibility may assess their significance. Assistants also should be directed to bring to the attention of appropriate individuals in the firm difficulties encountered in performing the audit, such as missing documents or resistance from client personnel in providing access to information or in responding to inquiries.

.31 The work performed by each assistant, including the audit documentation, should be reviewed to determine whether it was adequately performed and documented and to evaluate the results, relative to the conclusions to be presented in the auditor's report. The person with final responsibility for the audit may delegate parts of the review responsibility to other assistants, in accordance with the firm's quality control system. See section 339, Audit Documentation, for guidance on documenting the review of audit documentation.

.32 Each assistant has a professional responsibility to bring to the attention of appropriate individuals in the firm disagreements or concerns with respect to accounting and auditing issues that the assistant believes are of significance to the financial statements or auditor's report, however those disagreements or concerns may have arisen. The auditor with final responsibility for the audit and assistants should be aware of the procedures to be followed when differences of opinion concerning accounting and auditing issues exist among firm personnel involved in the audit. Such procedures should enable an assistant to document his or her disagreement with the conclusions reached if, after appropriate consultation, he or she believes it necessary to disassociate himself or herself from the resolution of the matter. In this situation, the basis for the final resolution should also be documented.

Auditor partners, those professionals ultimately responsible for the audit, also rely on their staff. Audits are generally staffed on a pyramid basis (see Figure 2.2). That means each assignment has one partner, yet various levels of staff are assigned tasks in order to complete the audit. A partner leads the assignment and is responsible for its completion in accordance with GAAP/ GAAS. However, partner time per engagement varies, and it is not unusual to see partner time represent less than 10% of total audit engagement hours. Nonetheless, companies routinely ask for rate concessions and discounts, and expect audit fees to decrease over time, as the audit team becomes more familiar with the company's operations. Since partner rates are the highest on the assignment, one way of reducing costs is to reduce partner time. Another way to reduce costs is for the auditor to rely on the organization's internal auditor's work, instead of the audit firm's own . . . hence, partners can rely heavily on others to help execute their assignments.

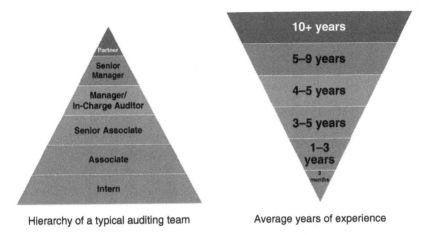

Hierarchy of a typical auditing team   Average years of experience

FIGURE 2.2 Inverse relationship between audit team hierarchy level and average years of experience.

I sat down and interviewed recent college graduates that had joined professional accounting firms as staff, working for different partners. Following is the summary of those discussions:

1. **What were some of the obstacles you faced as an entry-level staff?**
   a. Low level of knowledge and experience
   b. Expectations to perform and beat benchmarks
   c. Feeling overwhelmed by the firm's expectations and the expectations for myself
2. **How often did you feel pressured to perform a task in which you lack the qualifications and experience?**
   a. I would not necessarily say "pressured" but I found myself being assigned harder tasks when working with a new manager. Almost as if it's a test.
3. **How receptive was your direct supervisor when you asked for guidance?**
   a. They were very receptive and friendly. Once they know that you have an issue, they will connect with you more often.
   b. However, if I ask too many questions or they notice I am really struggling, they'll just do it or won't assign you anything else.
4. **Was there a situation where you were scared to ask for help?**
   a. No, one of the things I appreciate about the firm is that everyone is willing to help.

5. How do your supervisors help guide you through tough projects?
   a. They assign me sections that they did last year and wait for me to ask questions.
6. What is the biggest mistake you made as a staff?
   a. Not asking enough questions when it comes to new tasks.
   b. Saying yes to everything, which often led me to working until past midnight.

   In fact, each staff ranked "being overworked" and "feeling unqualified" as their top two professional concerns (see Figure 2.3).

   Let us pause. Supervisors – in relying on others, what comforts and concerns do you have when reading the summaries? Staff – what would you add to the notes above?

   One critical and interlinked concept to adequate staffing, and ultimate reliance, is professional competency. Auditing Standard AS 1010 provides a blue-print for the training and level of proficiency each independent

FIGURE 2.3 Concerns facing entry-level accounting firm staff. *Source:* Interviews with various entry-level staff.

auditor should have. There are six key factors in order to be "qualified" as an independent auditor:

1. Performed by a person having adequate technical training and proficiency as an auditor.
2. Recognizes however capable a person may be, the person cannot meet the requirements of the auditing standards without proper education and experience in the field of auditing.
3. The independent auditor holds himself out as one who is proficient in accounting and auditing.
   a. The attainment of that proficiency begins with the auditor's formal education and extends into his subsequent experience.
   b. The independent auditor must undergo training adequate to meet the requirements of a professional.
   c. The junior assistant, just entering upon an auditing career, must obtain his professional experience with the proper supervision and review of his work by a more experienced superior.
   d. The engagement partner must exercise seasoned judgment in the varying degrees of his supervision and review of the work done and judgments exercised by his subordinates.
4. The independent auditor's formal education and professional experience complement one another.
5. He must study, understand, and apply new pronouncements on accounting principles and auditing procedures as they are developed by authoritative bodies within the accounting profession.
6. Acquired the ability to consider objectively and to exercise independent judgment with respect to the information recorded in books of account or otherwise disclosed by his audit.

Regardless of whether you are an audit partner or staff, you still have to comply with professional standards. In the General Standards of Code of Professional Conduct professional competence is defined as "Undertaking only those professional services that the member or the member's firm can reasonably expect to be completed with professional competence." The professional standard goes on to provide interpretations of competence under rule 201:

.02 201-1—Competence. A member's agreement to perform professional services implies that the member has the necessary competence to complete those professional services according to professional standards, applying his or her knowledge and skill with reasonable care and diligence, but the member does not assume a responsibility for infallibility of knowledge or judgment.

Competence to perform professional services involves both the technical qualifications of the member and the member's staff and the ability to supervise and evaluate the quality of the work performed. Competence relates both to knowledge of the profession's standards, techniques and the technical subject matter involved, and to the capability to exercise sound judgment in applying such knowledge in the performance of professional services.

The member may have the knowledge required to complete the services in accordance with professional standards prior to performance. In some cases, however, additional research or consultation with others may be necessary during the performance of the professional services. This does not ordinarily represent a lack of competence, but rather is a normal part of the performance of professional services.

However, if a member is unable to gain sufficient competence through these means, the member should suggest, in fairness to the client and the public, the engagement of someone competent to perform the needed professional service, either independently or as an associate.

In order to maintain and/or develop competency for new and/or current staff, a company will invest time and money toward the proper training to develop their staff.

Training magazine's Training Industry report was recognized in 2017 as the training industry's most trusted source on data budgets, staffing, and programs. The magazine would send an annual e-mail containing invitations to participate in online surveys representing a cross-section of industries and companies. In 2017 companies started investing more time and putting aside money toward training their employees and other training expenditures. These companies would spend on travel, facilities, and equipment. More than 28% of organizations had increased staff. Companies not only spent more on training and recruiting staff, but also invested in their staff by carving out more hours to train their staff when compared against other years. Employees received 47.6 hours of training. When put against the figures from the prior year, they've added 4 more hours. Although training expenditure and hours steadily increased in 2017, 36% of participants of the study have reported an increase in training budgets. Most of the budget increases were modest (less than 18%) and most who reported an increase in their training budgets attributed it to (see Figure 2.4):

1. Increase in scope of training
2. Added training staff
3. Increased number of learners served
4. Purchased new technologies/equipment

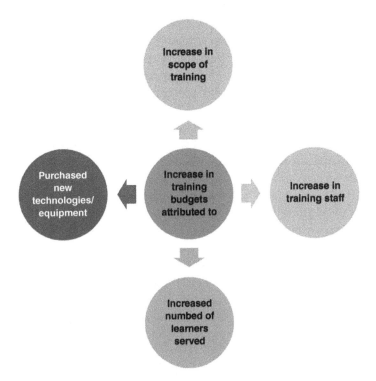

FIGURE 2.4 Drivers of increased training budgets.

Budget cuts vary across industries, and the greatest risk for budget cuts comes from the education industry while government and military was the most stable.

The most common training delivery came in the form of instructors in classrooms seating up to 41% of the respondents' answers, although technology classes are starting to catch up due to new online or computer-based technologies at 28.6%.

Corporate spending is on the rise and steadily increasing. US spending on corporate training grew by 15% when compared to the prior year, which is the highest growth rate experienced in the past seven years.[2] Studies suggest that this increase in corporate training is a great indicator of economic activity. When companies slow down, one of the first areas to receive less attention is training, and one of the first cuts in budget would be employee training. As the business's financial performance climbs its way back is when you'll see companies bring

---

[2]Josh Bersin, "Spending on Corporate Training Soars: Employee Capabilities Now a Priority," *Forbes*, February 4, 2014.

their attention to training current and incoming staff. Companies have more to spend on their employees. The *Forbes* study suggests that rapid growth in corporate spending on training is due to the "skills supply chain."[3]

The theory presents itself as such, that many companies believe it takes three to five years to arrive at a fully seasoned professional in their company and have them fully productive. The learning curve is incredibly high, and doesn't reach a point where it tops off. Companies can finally harvest the returns of investing in their employees at the three- to five-year mark. With this, it's still difficult to keep up with the demand of qualified staff. Take for example the petrochemical engineer demand in 2016; the oil and gas industry needed 60,000 petrochemical engineers, yet only 1,300 actually graduated from school each year. What was often found was that companies that were performing well financially offered more training to employees (see Figure 2.5). This is also attributed to technology revolutionizing the market and allowing training to be more accessible, easier, and cheaper to put the employees through training. This is exciting news. While skills gaps (we call it the "supply chain of skills") continue to challenge companies, an increased investment in training is good for everyone: employees, businesses, and job seekers. This level of increase shows that businesses are aggressively expanding and companies need skilled workers to grow.

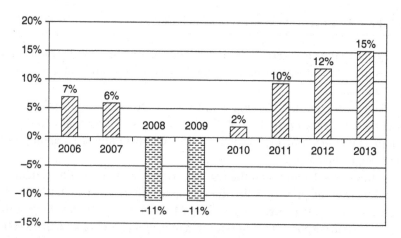

FIGURE 2.5 Year-over-year change in training spending in the United States, 2006 to 2013. *Source:* Based on data from Bersin by Deloitte, 2013.

---

[3]Ibid.

Training is not only achieved through attending seminars and conferences. "Real-time" and "on-the-Job" training through performance reviews and timely feedback is equally and perhaps even more effective.

I was baptized by fire at the start of my career. I relied far more on instincts than I did on education. However, I studied a lot. I passed both my CPA and CFE exams within the first couple of years of my career, and actively pursued speaking engagements almost weekly. Then, as now, I chose speaking opportunities that required research. I wanted it to be current, and relevant to my specific audience. It was a lot of work, but I knew I would not study and learn new things on my own. Most of the training offered through the profession was very basic. I was curious about our profession, and I still seek out learning opportunities.

When I left government and moved to Dallas to work for accounting firms there, the training focused solely on "soft skills." And trust me; I needed a lot of that! I often-times felt insecure working around such brilliant minds. Those professionals, who graduated from much more prestigious universities, had PhDs and multiple business degrees. I then forced myself to study even harder.

My first performance review did not go as well as I had hoped. Looking back, this was understandable because I was doing work in which I had no experience or training. But I did not think that way at the time. That lackluster review "nudged" me into overdrive on my learning. And within a couple of months, I had received a spot bonus and merit increase for outstanding work.

The experience I had with my less-than-stellar, first-ever performance review left a lasting mark. Never again did I not want to "have the answer." The fear became entrenched, and I found myself rushing to find answers to my interpretation of issues we faced, rather than simply asking questions. If I did not understand something, I obsessed until I thought I did. I viewed not knowing answers and not understanding something as signs of weakness. As such, I was reluctant to speak up.

That changed in a dramatic way. I began working for a partner who had recently retired, but agreed to extend his arrangement with the firm for a few more years. He was "retiring" from audit engagements, but had found new energy in working on fraud and litigation assignments with me. To my guess, he had well over 40 years' experience and was simply brilliant. He had forgotten more than I likely will ever know. I loved taking him to client meetings because he had "all the answers." Until he did not. Words I thought I would never hear from him, rolled so easily off his tongue. In perhaps one of the largest client pitches of my career, the client asked us a difficult question. His response: "I don't know the answer to that. Would you give me a day or two? I know just who to ask." I was stunned. I thought for sure we had lost the assignment. But you know what? We won it, and it was not even close.

I learned so much through that simple exchange. If this man, who had more experience that my entire team combined, could admit he did not know the answer to something, how egotistical must I be to not be comfortable admitting the same. From that moment on, I felt comfortable not knowing an answer. And rather than rambling, I give the client assurance that I will find the answer.

Reflect on the lesson learned on a work situation. A partner receives a big project and has to have the perfect team for it. Let's say the project requires very specific skills and a particular knowledge base. If the partner picks the team members based only on their performance reviews and those performance reviews are 100% accurate, then that project could turn into a catastrophe if the members do not have the necessary knowledge. This could lead to losing a client and revenues, and hurt an organization's reputation.

Performance reviews and timely feedback are critical to both employees and employers. This process is key to learning and growth. It allows employers to give constructive criticism and critique an employee's work. In response, this allows employees to correct bad habits, enhance their knowledge and skills, and become more efficient. If possible, it is always important to get a performance review when working under different managers. This allows the employee to get different perspectives on their work. Performance reviews often reflect employees' weaknesses and strengths. They are often relied upon whenever a boss is trying to effectively put together a team for a project. If a project requires very specific skills and a boss picks the team members based on performance review and those performance reviews are 100% accurate, then that project could turn into a catastrophe.

In the performance review process it is very important that the feedback be given timely. It is not all that beneficial if reviews are received long after a project is complete. Much of the context is lost, and the content is not fresh in your mind. In addition to timeliness, feedback needs to be objective, clear, and specific. Vague feedback can be quite confusing. It does not validate whether the person is doing a good job, nor does it correct someone if there are issues or concerns. During a performance review the communication process needs to be respectful and not degrading. Even positive reviews, delivered poorly, can strip a person of all their confidence, and it can destroy office morale. It may even cause employees to be fearful to ask questions in the future because they are scared of getting graded harshly, or "looked at like they're stupid." When employees are afraid to ask questions, it causes a slew of other issues. I am an avid sports fan and often use this analogy. Let's say a college football player receives a multitude of awards while representing his university on the football field. He receives praise upon praise, so he decides to enter the pro football draft. However, leading up to the draft, he is criticized every way imaginable. Everything from his body-fat percentage to the height of his jump. His draft value plummets and he loses millions of dollars. If this is the first time the athlete has heard of these criticisms, was it fair that he was not given the opportunity to address them before it cost him dearly? This can also happen to staff, who are holding out hope for a promotion or incentive compensation. Overall, performance reviews are meant to help improve business performance and strengthen the company as a whole, not to create fear, stress and anxiety.

The auditors (and their staff) are relied upon by the public. The public does not differentiate between the trust they place on the partners and the staff we mentioned earlier. The public trusts the firm. The firm's process. The signature and assurances provided within the report. "Auditors are entrusted with significant responsibility when auditing public companies," said Shamoil Shipchandler, former director of the SEC's Fort Worth Regional Office. "Public accountants who manipulate their files to conceal audit deficiencies represent a serious breach of those professional obligations, and the commission will impose suspensions to protect investors."[4]

With that burden in mind, note that these same auditors can be at the mercy of their clients. External auditors rely heavily on their client's management during the audit process. To help provide a level of assurance to the management's role, nduer GAAS, auditors are required to obtain written representations from management and those charged with governance in an audit of financial statements. In addition to management's representation that the financial statements are presented fairly, auditors also require that management provide written representations that it:

    a. acknowledges its responsibility for the design, implementation, and maintenance of internal controls to prevent and detect fraud;

    b. has disclosed to the auditor the results of its assessment of the risk that the financial statements may be materially misstated as a result of fraud;

    c. has disclosed to the auditor its knowledge of fraud or suspected fraud affecting the entity involving

      i. management,

      ii. employees who have significant roles in internal control,

      iii. others when the fraud could have a material effect on the financial statements; and

    d. has disclosed to the auditor its knowledge of any allegations of fraud or suspected fraud affecting the entity's financial statements communicated by employees, former employees, regulators, or others.

---

[4]Interview with author.

This highlights that an individual audit partner can demonstrate the reliance they place on others is reasonable by obtaining written representations of management.

Another level of "insulation" is the fact that in the United States, a firm signs the financial statement audit, not the individual partner. However, this has been a heavily debated subject in years past.

Effective December 15, 2016, the International Auditing and Assurance Standards Board that sets auditing standards on a global capacity required that engagement partners physically sign the audit reports with their names and not the name of the firm, as in the United States. According to PCAOB chairman James Doty: "All the major markets, except the US, have such a signature requirement. Auditors are living with it in most countries around the world except here," Doty said. "By knowing who the engagement partner is, investors would be able to track certain aspects of the individual engagement partner's history, including his or her industry expertise, restatement history, and involvement in disciplinary proceedings or other litigation. All of these factors provide valuable information for an investor to fully understand the riskiness of an audit. And it sharpens the mind."[5]

This debate is ongoing in the United States. In India there isn't even a debate. Let's bring our attention to Satyam. This is a great example that will highlight the importance of professional responsibilities.

There was a time that Satyam was one of India's leading software providers. They were armed with 53,000 employees, and had nearly 700 clients. B. Ramalinga Raju, the chairman of one of India's largest information technology companies, brought to light a confession to padding the company's balance sheet by $1 billion, cash. He acknowledged his involvement in inflating Satyam's profits with fabricated assets, cash that didn't exist, and misreporting the debts the company owed. He was sentenced to seven years in jail along with nine co-conspirators in 2015.

PricewaterhouseCoopers (PwC) audited Satyam. The Securities and Exchange Board of India (SEBI) pursued charges against PwC and stated PwC overlooked "several red flags. . . . which were all too obvious for any reasonable professional auditor to miss."

SEBI also arrested two of PwC's senior partners for fraud and criminal conspiracy. The partners were found guilty for their role and in 2015 were given seven-year sentences for their assistance to cover up the scandal. The court claimed they "knowingly failed to point out the fraud and actively connived" with top senior executives. They were also required to pay a monetary fine, and the Institute of Chartered Accountants India (ICAI) barred them from practicing as chartered accountants. The ICAI also barred a third member

---

[5]https://www.workplaceethicsadvice.com/archives.html.

Prabhakar Gupta, Satyam's internal auditor, sentenced on the same grounds as the two ex-PwC partners.

In January 2018, SEBI banned PwC from auditing listed companies in India for two years. SEBI punished PwC, and the individual PwC partners for failing to spot fraud of over $1 billion at the defunct tech firm Satyam Computer Services. SEBI also ordered the accounting firm to relinquish "wrongful gains" of around 130 million rupees ($2 million), plus 12% interest per year for the past eight years.

As a result of the Satyam scandal, Indian corporate laws introduced bold measures to engage auditors in the early detection of fraud. Under the recently enacted Companies Act, auditors who suspect that fraud has been committed against the audited company have to report it immediately to the central government.

ICAI issued guidance in 2019 to comply with the regulatory changes, which according to the institute placed an unprecedented level of responsibility on auditors, envisaging them in the role of whistle blowers.

According to these rules, auditors who have sufficient reason to believe an offense involving fraud is being, or has been, committed by its officers or employees are required to forward a report to the company's board or audit committee immediately and seek their reply or observations on the report within 45 days.

Once auditors receive the feedback from the board or audit committee, they must forward it alongside the initial report to the central government within 15 days, which will be no later than 60 days from when the alleged fraud came to the auditor's knowledge.

So as you can see, the environment for external auditors is changing, and while audit partners in the United States may not "technically" be on the hook for personal liability, they do have clear responsibilities to plan, supervise, and staff assignments accordingly, despite relying on staff to execute and management to affirm. In other countries, as evidenced in the Satyam example, this is not the case.

 ## INTERNAL AUDITORS

Internal auditors report to the audit committee, board of directors, and executive management. Occasionally, internal auditors report to the general counsel. Management relies on internal audit to verify the adequacy and efficiency of internal controls. Internal auditors provide assurance and almost act as consultants. The internal auditors are responsible for maintaining lines of communication between the external auditor and the board of directors. The Institute of Internal Auditors (IIA) states that the internal auditors should meet separately with the audit committee without management at least once a year. The purpose of this is to help prevent management from covering up any fraud that could be occurring.

Enron and WorldCom are two classic examples of internal audit failure. Enron's external auditors did both the external and internal audit, which eliminated any checks and balances and created a conflict of interest. WorldCom's internal auditor, Cynthia Cooper, is the one who originally caught the fraudulent activity. When Cooper reported to the CFO, who was a part of the scandal, no action was taken. If Cooper had reported to the audit committee rather than management, corrective action could have been taken immediately.

External auditors' reliance on internal auditors is addressed in AU-C Section 610, "Using the Work of Internal Auditors." Although external auditors are solely responsible for the audit, they can use internal auditors' work or direct assistance in obtaining audit evidence. More specifically, internal auditors can be used to help obtain an understanding of internal controls, help assess risk of material misstatements, and help obtain direct evidence for substantive procedures. Internal auditors cannot be in any way a part of audit decisions, judgments, or assessments. Because the internal auditors are employees of the entity, they are not independent. External auditors can use internal auditors to help in obtaining and understanding internal controls and assessing risks. The external auditor should supervise and review the work performed by the internal auditors.

Everyone knows when a commercial starts playing "in the arms of an Angel" what is coming next. It is some awful, heart-wrenching pictures and videos of abandoned and abused animals. Other similar commercials show poor, sick, and starving children. These commercials stab at people's emotions and even can guilt-trip them into donating to the charity. The pathos effect at its finest. The big question is how much money actually goes toward the cause and how much do people personally profit from it? One big platform that has emerged for raising money is Internet sites. What are these websites' internal auditors doing to evaluate and validate that the campaigns posted are legitimate? The GoFundMe internal audit failed at thoroughly vetting campaigns, which led to a huge fraud scandal in October 2017. The story that led to the campaign went viral. It was all over the news and flooded social media. Katelyn McClure, a 27-year-old woman, was on her way to Philadelphia one evening when she ran out of gas on Interstate 95. Johnny Bobbitt Jr., a homeless veteran, saw Katelyn on the side on the road. He approached her and told her to stay in the car and lock the door because it was not a good area. He had $20 and would go get her some gas. Katelyn didn't have any cash on her to repay him that night. To repay him for his kindness, she later paid him back and in addition frequently stopped by his spot with clothes, food, and water. Katelyn and her boyfriend, Mark D'Amico, set up a GoFundMe campaign to help raise money for Johnny to get back on his feet and give him a second chance at life. Shortly after the account was set up, $400,000 was raised by about 14,000 donors. Katelyn and Mark were in complete control of the money. They were fearful that Johnny would spend the money on drugs. Within a few months, the money was blown on lavish vacations, extravagant cars, shopping sprees, and gambling. They had purchased a pickup truck and RV for Johnny in their same campaign, but sold it when they needed more cash. Out of the $400,000 raised, Johnny claims he only received a small part of it. This led Johnny to file a civil complaint against Katelyn and Mark. From here on out, the real story unraveled through a series of text messages and audio recordings. The whole story was a hoax. Katelyn and Johnny already knew each other from a casino and the whole scheme was fabricated. GoFundMe refunded every donor who contributed to the campaign. GoFundMe spokesman Bobby Whithorne stated cases of misuse "make up less than one-tenth of 1 percent" of GoFundMe campaigns. Shouldn't have GoFundMe's internal auditors caught the fraud from the beginning if they had done their due diligence? What started as a feel-good story led to all three being charged with theft by deception and conspiracy to commit theft by deception.

Those donors relied on the TV stations to vet these charities, not objectively assessing the risk. It can happen to accountants, when they rely on others to do their vetting. That could leave auditors soliciting for their own gofundme campaign. Don't be that accountant!

 ## EXPERT WITNESSES

In civil and criminal proceedings, there might be accounting principles too technical or advanced for the juror or judge to understand. This will usually prompt the attorneys to call upon an expert witness to give their opinion on a matter. Especially in the case of high-profile or high-risk cases, it's common practice that both the defendants and plaintiffs are willing to spend millions and millions of dollars defending and/or prosecuting alleged fraud. This makes the cost of fighting fraud very high. The process to become an expert witness is known as voir dire. The judge rules whether an expert witness qualifies to provide their own opinion as evidence on a matter before court. Aside from the report during the discovery phase, an expert witness deposition is considered the scariest time. The expert witness is cross-examined by the opposing attorneys in an attempt to ruin the expert witness's credibility. This is why it's important to stay grounded in these circumstances. Given their unique experience, education, and training, expert witnesses can offer opinions in court. Although there are many types of expert witnesses, there is only room for one in the world of accounting.

The Federal Rule of Evidence 702 defines that expert witness as follows:

A witness who is qualified as an expert by knowledge, skill, experience, training, or education may testify in the form of an opinion or otherwise if:

a. the expert's scientific, technical, or other specialized knowledge will help the trier of fact to understand the evidence or to determine a fact in issue;
b. the testimony is based on sufficient facts or data;
c. the testimony is the product of reliable principles and methods; and
d. the expert has reliably applied the principles and methods to the facts of the case.

In addition to the legal requirements, an expert witness will likely be cross-examined before trial. The judge will have the ultimate decision on determining if the expert witness is credible. There are no standards that specify the minimal amount of time one must spend on an engagement to be considered an expert.

Particularly in mass tort litigation, attorneys often face choices about how many experts to disclose, what specialty (or specialties) are necessary for the litigation, and – as part and parcel of those considerations – whether one expert witness can address topics that ideally might be handled by another expert or even by other nondesignated witnesses. Minimizing the total number of expert witnesses may be strategically appropriate for a variety of reasons: It can make a case more palatable for the jury, and it can be an effective way to reduce costs to the client. Courts also may limit the number of experts under case management orders.

Against these competing interests, counsel must balance the need for efficiency with the limitations imposed by civil rules and case law. The following material explores, under federal law, instances where experts may offer opinions based on other experts' opinions, as well as situations where an expert may rely on an undisclosed witness's findings to support his or her opinion.

Engaging in this balancing act is not without risks, perhaps akin to a game of Jenga: If the court strikes the underlying expert's (or witness's) testimony, then other, surviving experts may be left on precariously thin ice. This section examines those scenarios, contrasts situations where the court found an expert's reliance on another expert or witness or materials to be permissible and appropriate, and concludes by offering a few suggestions to strengthen an expert's foundation.

In providing expert witness testimony, experts rely on management and attorneys to provide evidence through a process called discovery. We have covered the risks associated with that reliance, and how the roles of an expert differ from management and attorneys. However, experts may also find themselves relying on other experts, or specialists, as mentioned in the regulations for auditors. Federal Rule 703 provides additional guidance in covering the bases of opinion testimony of an expert.

Federal Rule of Evidence 703 provides the foundation for permitting an expert to rely on another witness or underlying materials. Titled "Bases of Opinion Testimony by Experts," Rule 703 states in full as follows:

> An expert may base an opinion on facts or data in the case that the expert has been made aware of or personally observed. If experts in the particular field would reasonably rely on those kinds of facts or data in forming an opinion on the subject, they need not be admissible for the opinion to be admitted. But if the facts or data would otherwise be inadmissible, the proponents of the opinion may disclose them to the jury only if their probative value in helping the jury evaluate the opinion substantially outweighs their prejudicial effect.

Put differently, an expert is entitled to rely on inadmissible facts or data where the "magic phrase" in Rule 703 has been satisfied: that is, that the items are the "kinds of facts or data" that "experts in the particular field would reasonably rely on." There is, accordingly, support in the plain text of the rule to permit one expert to rely on another expert, another witness, or other facts or data. The phrase that is repeated often through case law is the determination that the information, or specialist's report, is "that of a type that reasonably may be relied upon by an expert in forming an opinion upon the subject to which his testimony relates."

Case law supports this basic proposition. For instance, a physician expert's reference to an underlying pathology report may be considered "routine procedure in medical treatment" and thus appropriate and permissible under Rule 703 (physician's reliance on a pathology report to confirm his diagnosis did not reflect negatively on his qualifications or ability to diagnose his patient; to the contrary, it reflected routine procedure in medical treatment).

Having begun with the basic premise that experts may appropriately rely on other people or information in forming their conclusions, it is worthwhile to evaluate possible weak points in the strategy of one expert relying on another.

As explained below, federal courts have excluded certain experts deemed to be "merely a mouthpiece for," "merely parroting," or "merely regurgitating" another expert's or witness's findings and conclusions.

The expert's obligations remain the same: to gain comfort that the other expert is qualified and objective, and has used sound, generally accepted methodology, as well as adhered to the same standards.

Dura was a case involving the cleanup of an Environmental Protection Agency Superfund site. Dura designated only one expert, a hydrogeologist, who admitted at his deposition that he was not an expert in mathematical models of groundwater flow. Instead, he relied on mathematical modeling prepared by other employees of his firm. CTS moved to exclude that expert, and Dura responded by submitting affidavits from four employees who worked on the underlying mathematical models.

CTS moved to strike those affidavits as untimely under Rule 37. The district court granted the motion to strike. Without those affidavits, there was insufficient evidence of the reliability of the models that the expert relied on – so the court excluded Dura's expert. In a one–two punch, because Dura had no expert, summary judgement was granted in CTS's favor.

Judge Posner began from a threshold premise: There is nothing wrong with an expert using "assistants" (as in this case, the employees at the expert's firm) to formulate an expert opinion, because the opposing party may depose them and the expert to determine if Rule 703 has been satisfied. The court continued, however, that "analysis becomes more complicated if the assistants aren't merely gofers or data gatherers but exercise professional judgment that is beyond the expert's ken." The court cited Rule 703's advisory committee notes, which provide the example of a "physician who, though not an expert in radiology, relied for a diagnosis on an x-ray. We too do not believe that the leader of a clinical medical team must be qualified as an expert in every individual discipline encompassed by the team in order to testify as to the team's conclusions."

 ## ADDITIONAL CONSIDERATIONS

In September 2018, *The Economist* cited a Gallup survey that determined Americans were leaving their jobs at a 17-year high. Further, *The Economist* cited a Deloitte study that suggested the combination of hiring costs and lost productivity totaled $121,000 for each departing employee. Consider our profession, and the value of experience and training. Think of the importance of a particular firm's methodology and engagement continuity. Think of an internal audit practice, where seasoned employees have years of rapport established with other departments. With each employee departure and new hire, the risk of relying on inadequate resources increases.

 ## SUMMARY

It is impossible to completely eliminate the reliance on others. Accountants rely on staff, management, and other professionals. The investing public relies on us all. It is imperative that accountants assess the trustworthiness and competence of those in whom they place material reliance. Further, staff, management, and professionals need to understand the importance of adhering to professional standards and maintaining their professional competency. Creating a culture that fosters continuous learning and accurate and timely feedback, and encouraging open dialogue can prevent accountants from relying on inadequate resources.

 ## RECOMMENDATIONS

To avoid overrelying on others, accountants should consider the following:

1. *Know your role.* Are you the supervisor relying on others? Or are you the one being relied on? Both? It helps to know this prior to accepting the role. Having that open dialogue at the beginning of an assignment can avoid dire straits at the end. Further, when performing fraud risk assessments, include those responsible for enforcing the internal controls, as well as those that are part of the controls. If gaps are identified, which is likely, list those responsible for remediation. This will add a layer of accountability in the process.
2. *Expand your diligence.* Obtain a full appreciation of those third parties that are working under your supervision, at your direction, or on your behalf. They create just as much, if not more, risk. Confirm that their background investigations are as thorough as the ones for your own employees (including reference checks). Ensure they have acknowledged your policies and procedures, and be sure to subject them to continuous oversight and monitoring.
3. *Risk-rank tasks.* For those large assignments with multiple work-streams and deliverables, rank them by complexity and risk. Make sure the staff

assigned to each task is commensurate with the complexity and risk. This also includes third parties and the associated risks of foreign lands.

4. *Analyze hours by professional.* Ensure the hours incurred on an assignment support adequate supervision and monitoring, and are consistent with other projects with similar risk characteristics.

5. *Training.* Formalized training at all levels of an organization is imperative. It is very difficult to rely entirely on "on the job training" at any level, considering the pace of our profession and the associated demands. Keeping records of such training affords an opportunity for supervisors, employers, and clients to decide which professionals have the best skills to accomplish a given task.

6. *Give feedback.* Performance reviews can be a pain and a source of stress to the preparer and recipient, but they are extremely valuable. Meaningful feedback will not only protect you, but also protect the employee. Performance reviews can help determine which employees are most appropriate for an assignment, and which they should avoid. It will also give a heads-up to supervisors on areas to monitor more closely while supervising them. If an employee is a constantly poor performer, counsel them out of your organization. Retaining poor performers hinders your ability to execute assignments, and also prevents the employee from finding a better long-term fit. It can also drive your best performers away, or spread apathy among the organization, sending a signal that quality isn't a priority.

7. *Maintain an open door policy, and encourage its use.* Encourage supervisors to ask if staff feel qualified, and to re-connect often. Encourage staff to speak up when they do not understand. Perhaps take it a step further by including staff's willingness to learn in their performance review. Encourage staff to evaluate their supervisor's willingness to teach.

8. *Establish a review protocol.* I hate using the word "checklist," as it often stifles creativity. However, checklists can be helpful in situations that require multiple levels of review. It is easy for one person to overlook an item, but having a qualified second set of eyes reduces the likelihood. Establish a requirement that includes a peer review prior to delivering the final product.

DISCUSSION QUESTIONS

1. For seasoned accountants, think back to a time when you were a staff. Were you ever "afraid" to ask questions, for fear of "looking stupid"? Discuss.

2. At those times, what did some supervisors do to help overcome those fears? Made them worse?
3. What risks exist in situations where an organization's staff are afraid to speak up when they do not fully grasp a concept?
4. Investors rely on management's trustworthiness in making decisions. Describe some ways management can be transparent to help enhance trustworthiness throughout an organization.
5. If you are working under the direction of top management and you believe they are involved with fraudulent activity, what would you do:
   a. If you were an internal auditor?
   b. If you were retained by management as their external auditor?
6. Discuss the risks of an expert spending too little time on an engagement. And how about an expert that spends too much time?
7. What are pros and cons of detailed performance reviews, as well as the risks of relying on them?

Case Study: The Time the New Hire Was Thrown to the Fire

Accounting Firm LLP (AF) is one of the world's largest and most prestigious accounting firms. In fact, for every 100 applicants, only five are hired. You are at the top of your accounting class, and are thrilled when you hear that you have been hired as a staff auditor. It is a dream come true.

You are immediately put on one of the firm's large audit clients, Global Shipping Inc. (GSI). However, you have received very little training. In fact, the only training you have received is on AF's auditing software and time-keeping system. You approach your direct supervisor, an AF manager, and express concerns. Your manager, who is a Certified Public Accountant and Certified Fraud Examiner, assures you that "you're a quick learner and a go-getter. You will pick this up in no time," then asks you not mention your lack of experience to GSI, as "we do not want them to think we are using them as a staff training tool. If asked, tell them you have four years' experience. After all, college counts. I will give you the AR confirmation. I did it last year, so just follow what I did and you will be fine."

You are assigned the task of confirming and reconciling GSI's Accounts Receivable. Your job is essentially to email GSI's clients to confirm their outstanding account balances, and AF has a pre-set form for you to send. You review last year's audit working papers and see where 20 client confirmations were completed with no exceptions. You know from your accounting classes

(Continued)

(Continued)

that changing sample sizes and criteria from year-to-year is important, so you select 50 clients based on sales volume and frequency. Upon sending 50 confirmations, several respondents claim they have never heard of GSI while several others claim the amounts listed are overstated because "we returned the merchandise shortly after the quarter's end, just as we agreed upon." In researching these discrepancies, you are unable to locate many of the contracts. For those you can locate, only a few are actually signed, and some have handwritten changes to the prices and terms.

From your days in college, you remember the revenue recognition standards and criteria for recording accounts receivable. These commends do not support "evidence of an agreement" or the "reasonable certainty of the amount of payment, if any." Your findings suggest a likelihood of fraud, and are indicative of schemes involving channel stuffing and fictitious clients. You document in AF's audit software that the client has failed the AR Confirmation process, and that you have reason to suspect fraud.

Word somehow gets back to the CEO of GSI, who immediately calls AF's Audit Partner. The CEO reminds the audit partner of their long-time relationships, the trips their families have taken together, and challenges the fees GSI has paid AF. The CEO provides the Audit Partner with a list of 20 clients to confirm.

Shortly after the call, the Audit Partner scolds you for not having the proper training or authority within the firm to make these types of decisions and issues. You agree, and acknowledge know you have not had the proper training and that you could actually be mistaken. The Audit Partner gives you the list of the 20 clients to confirm, which you do without exception. You rewrite your submission in AF's audit software, and GSI is given a clean, unqualified audit opinion.

1. Who in the above scenario has possibly violated professional standards, rules, and regulations? Explain.
2. What professional legislation has a provision that directly addresses the tenure of a company's audit partner?
3. If the fraud is ultimately exposed, what are the likely consequences to the firm? To the Audit Partner? To the Manager? To you as the staff?
4. How did the Audit Partner take advantage of you, the young, inexperienced staff, in "managing" the findings?
5. What possible incentives could exist for assigning an inexperienced staff to such a material role on an audit such as this?
6. In what ways does GSI benefit from having a close relationship with AF's Audit Partner? How about AF? In what ways could this relationship be a violation of professional standards?

(Continued)

7. What concerns might you have, in that the CEO learned of your findings before the Audit Partner?
8. How might this impact you and your decision to bring findings such as this to your superiors in the future?
9. What would the impact be to GSI, had the Audit Partner supported the staff's findings? Impact to AF?
10. Would you be concerned if the CEO called and asked you to investigate, so that he could "give the auditors some comfort these allegations are meritless"? Why? If you are hired by GSI's audit committee to investigate this allegation, what steps might you take?

CHAPTER THREE

A – Accepting, Not Verifying

N THIS CHAPTER, WE discuss the significance of obtaining sufficient relevant data, and ensuring that accountants and auditors do not simply accept, but verify.

 INTRODUCTION

Did your parents take your word when you told them your room was clean, or did they check? For those of you who have children, do you look under their bed when they claim they are finished? Of course you do, just as your parents did! My first boss, the Legislative Auditor for the State of Louisiana, Dr. Dan Kyle, had a plaque on his desk that read, IN GOD WE TRUST. IN ALL OTHERS, WE AUDIT. And boy, did he mean it. I remember having an expense report returned, as I submitted a receipt and sought reimbursement for a two-pack of AAA batters, totaling $2.88. Ms. Mary

Smith, who was in charge of the expense report verification in the accounting department, asked: *"Where is the other battery? Your pager only takes one."* I am fairly certain it was rolling around the floor of the car I had lived in for the last six weeks. Nonetheless, I was only paid $1.44 for the purchase. Such was the life of a state auditor for the State of Louisiana.

It takes a lot of courage to challenge someone's assertions. One of my favorite cases involved another Louisiana sheriff. Through various analytics, we noticed that the sheriff's office had spent millions in renovations to their parish office and the jail. However, upon our inspection of the premises, the dilapidated condition of both clearly indicated the funds had gone elsewhere. We commenced the investigation and asked for supporting documentation for the expenditures. The sheriff complied. Almost every item was supported by a receipt, but there was one problem. Where were the materials? What construction had been done? One could sling a cat through the paper-thin walls of the building. Accept, *then* verify.

We began conducting interviews and things began to make more sense. We were told that the sheriff had built a number of houses for friends and family members. He had also condemned various schools and gymnasiums, and allegedly installed a basketball floor but actually in his own home. Lastly, he had used inmate labor to do so, in an apparent violation of state law.

The majority of the materials had been purchased at the locally owned hardware store. When we approached the owner of the hardware store, he challenged our "fortitude" and whether we had sufficient experience to interview him. I say that literally, as some of the first words I recorded out of his mouth were "Boy, you don't have enough hair on your balls to be asking me those kinds of questions." To which I replied, "Sir, the hair on my bathroom parts has nothing to do with what these materials were used for." Not my best reply, and I was humiliated when the tapes were replayed in court.

He then gave me his opinion of accountants. "The Big Four accounting firms take the best and the brightest. Those who have decent grades go to work for companies. The fuckups go to government. So you must be a fuckup."

So within the first 10 minutes of meeting this owner of the hardware store, my anatomy and my intelligence were both assaulted. A double whammy!

We asked about the allegations involving the use of inmate labor. He had another colorful response. "At least someone's getting something out of them. If it were up to me, I'd grind up their bones to pave highways and use their teeth for driveways."

He concluded the interview with a salute to Hitler.

A lovely gentleman he was not!

Our big break in the case came when a former inmate became an informant. He rode with us all throughout the county and showed us the homes that he allegedly helped the sheriff build, and where the schools had been. The only location the inmate would not show us was that of the deputy sheriff, who was also the sitting mayor. His nickname was "Gun," so it was probably for the best.

The informant also gave us names of the inmates that helped him. He suggested that we approach the prison's warden, who had recently had a disagreement with the sheriff. The informant rode with me and my partner to the warden's house.

We drove forever, so it seemed, down a long, lonely single-lane gravel road. I secretly wondered if there had been any dead bodies dumped in the shallow ditches, and prayed that this rural route road would not be my final resting place. When we arrived at the warden's house, the inmate shrieked and hit the floor in the back seat. We counted a dozen inmates in the warden's front yard, burying a septic tank. We hit reverse and sped back down the red dirt road in hopes of reaching the sheriff's office, or our home base, whichever we could get to first. As we approached the end of the gravel road, we saw a sheriff's blockade with guns in their hands or on their hip. We slammed on our brakes and asked the inmate, "You know these people! What do we do now?" The inmate returned my look of terror, slung the door open, exited with his hands raised high, screaming, "Don't shoot! Don't shoot!" And you know what? My partner and I did the exact same thing! We immediately identified ourselves with our state badges. They lowered their weapons and we approached. Of course, that was after we changed our shorts.

The next day, when we returned to the sheriff's office to retrieve the rest of our records, Gun approached me, and stood inches from my face to inform me that he intended to shoot me if I set foot on his property. (That recorded conversation that came in handy during sentencing. More on that later.)

We eventually were able to speak to the warden, who was forthcoming and transparent. The Sheriff ultimately pled guilty to having his office buy building materials for him, pay his utility bills, and provide inmate labor for his personal use. He received 16 months of jail time, and was ordered to repay $27,000. He was the second parish sheriff, in a string of three sheriffs in a row, who served prison time. The latter, well, to no surprise, was indeed our old friend Gun. The hardware store owner got a little more than four years. Certain tapes were replayed at each of their sentencing hearings, and it was of great benefit to the Department of Justice in their determination of the appropriate sentences.

Think back on how this began. We had supporting documentation on the receipts. That is where some auditors might have ended. However, the explanation made no sense. The actual materials were not there. We owed it to the taxpayers of Louisiana to pursue further. Imagine the difficulty we would have faced had the money been spent on nontangible items, like services.

In lectures across the world, I've often referred to this phenomenon as "Hey Fever"; that is, failing to exclaim "Hey, this explanation and documentation make no sense" when an explanation or documentation doesn't support a transaction. I've also referred to it as "Yellow Fever," afraid to go with your instinct that something doesn't quite feel right.

I recently rescued two six-week-old kittens, Mittens and Patches, from the shelter. I am intrigued by their instincts. They hide while stalking their prey (aka each other). They pounce to attack one another at opportune times. They know exactly when to head to the litter box (most of the time). They play, and play, and play. It's amazing how they know these basic things, despite being infants and never receiving "training" from their parents. I truly do believe we possess even more powerful instincts, and should learn to trust them more often. In our profession, we often-times have hunches, ideas that spring from years of experience. However, sometimes, whether due to time and budget restraints, or even intimidation, we let it pass. I am a big fan of Marc and Angela; uber-bloggers of the site "Marc and Angela Hack Life." One nugget they recently offered was regarding the doubts we have in ourselves. *Doubt your doubts more than you doubt your faith."* Rather than pushing forward when something is amiss, we retreat. Think of Enron, which employed "the Smartest Men in the Room. Imagine how easy it must have been for them to convince a young staffer to come around to their way of thinking. You, my friends, are smart men and women. If you cannot understand a concept or explanation, trust your instincts. If you cannot seem to get comfortable, or find the courage to pursue further support for a transaction based solely on a feeling, blame your responsibility to push forward on professional standards. Professional standards require that you obtain sufficient evidential matter to support your conclusions and opinions.

 ## SUFFICIENT EVIDENTIAL MATTER

The PCAOB (AS 3) and the AICPA (AU 200 and AU 230) both have similar provisions pertaining to sufficient evidential matter, or supporting documentation. The basic premise is for auditors to obtain sufficient, appropriate audit evidence to reduce audit risk to an acceptable level, thereby enabling them to reach a reasonable conclusion. Support can take many forms. Paper documents, electronic data, and interviews. Paper documents can be voluminous, and can disguise forgeries and alterations. While accountants are not expecting to be handwriting or forgery experts, there are things that can be done to help test the validity of documents. Ask questions, such as:

1. Was there an unusual delay in the document's production? (Think executed contracts – which should be readily available on significant transactions.)
2. Was it provided to you by someone who should not have it, or perhaps obtained it illegally? (Think of a divorce situation in which a spouse provides cell phone records of their significant other.)
3. Can it be easily replicated by online templates or tools? (Think employee expense receipts.)

Further, do any of the documents contradict others. Were the contract terms actually enforced? Were they subject to oral agreements or subsequent, "unsigned" amendments or change orders? Were you told procedures were completed or tasks were performed, but yet there is not a single ounce of supporting documentation? All of this is critical to consider. Lastly, if documents are provided electronically, an accountant can easily analyze file properties to see when it was created, and by whom. Along with the last printed and last modified dates.

Data and the Technology Element

There certainly is no shortage of data to obtain, test, and verify (as opposed to merely accepting). It's overwhelming. In the past 30 years, there has been a push to rely on technology to make our jobs more efficient, and thorough. The world of accounting has never been more automated, and that is expected to continue. Computer-aided audit tools (CAAT) have been around since at least 1985, with the creation of Excel for Macintosh. A Windows version followed in November 1987. Another common CAAT program also became available about this time. Almost 35 years later, we are seeing artificial intelligence (AI) take automated programs incredible steps further. Whereas CAAT tools run based on criteria, formulas, and tests with the parameters generally set by humans, AI is a technology whereby the machines can actually think and process independently – like humans. We are seeing this used extensively within the financial services industry, as companies address money laundering and grapple with the enormous, and growing volume of international transactions. Some suggest that by 2050, the processing power of AI will exceed the entire universe's combined brainpower.

Regardless of how exciting this transformation has been, as we saw with our use of CAATs, errors can be made, and results misconstrued or ignored. Further, we can be lulled into a false sense of security.

1. *Errors in the data.* Input data can be inaccurate, incomplete, or otherwise biased. Garbage in and garbage out is very easy to remember. Without the trained eye to interpret the results to identify anomalies, red flags, or a reasonableness test, the technology can be wasted.
2. *Data ignored.* The data must be analyzed to make strategic decisions and gather risks. It must be tested, even if it is on a sample or exception basis. I often hear professionals complain: "It is not about the lack of the data. It is about having the time to review it. About the time I begin reviewing the information, I receive updated data that supersedes what I have. I can never keep up."
3. *Overstated capabilities.* The capabilities of technology can be overstated and give a false sense of security. As AI becomes more common in our profession and software developers perfect their clever marketing concepts, it must not be seen as a substitute for our individual skepticism, diligence, and dedication. Marketing companies can sometimes make unsubstantiated claims, or disclose limitations in ways the user cannot understand.

The increase in artificial intelligence brings both excitement and trepidation. Auditors rely extensively on information generated by technology, and companies lean heavily on automated internal controls. Auditors, experts, CEOs, and other C-suite executives often turn to Peter Vogel, a partner with Foley Gardere, on the confluence of technology issues. His practice focuses on technology involved in all business operations, including complex enterprise systems and IT platforms. Peter is also routinely appointed as a Special Master representing the court in IT disputes. Mr. Vogel cautions on the overreliance of technology. According to him, auditors, CEOs, and other executives should remember that technology is fallible, and that nothing can replace the analytical capability and well-honed skepticism of a skillful and diligent user. The professional should be aware of the technology's limitations and educate other users early, and remind them often. Failures can result in significant financial exposure and catastrophic damage to the company's reputation. Additionally, Mr. Vogel advises:

1. Understand the potential risk factors associated with AI.
2. Discuss the ethical and legal questions that have surfaced regarding AI.
3. Identify best practices for AI and other machine learning enterprise strategies.

4. Consult with experts, if and when you identify knowledge gaps as you advance through the knowledge gaps.

Acknowledging what you know and what you don't know is critical to adequately addressing technology risks, and can help prevent overreliance.

Data and the Human Element

Further, some areas are simply best attacked by people power. You cannot replace our ability to think in abstract terms or our creativity. Do you think a fraudster's creativity is ever at rest? Further, some controls around critical areas simply cannot be effectively automated. No automated controls or AI can prevent a person from intentionally lying, or carelessly speaking or tweeting. Few automated controls can identify patterns many companies and many individuals removed from the registrant. The strongest control continues to be people, enforcing the existing policies and procedures, and administering the consequences when they are breached.

The biggest fraud of our generation, and of many generations before that, was Bernie Madoff and his $50 billion Ponzi scheme. While AI and data analytics certainly raised red flags, think about the peripheral information. Two big ones rank near the top.

1. The majority of his victims were Jewish. This is known as "affinity fraud," which refers to investment scams that prey upon members of identifiable groups, such as religious or ethnic communities, the elderly, or professional groups. These swindles build trust on being "part of the club" and exploit the alleged common bond.
   - ▦ Do you recall having to list your religious affiliation on any investment or loan document? Likely not. Therefore, it would be very challenging to run a query to identify this particular risk.
2. Madoff was audited by a firm that was not capable of adequately auditing such a large company. The firm consisted of two principals and an administrative assistant, and ultimately pled guilty in the scandal. Look at the allegations levied by the SEC:
   - ▦ The firm did not perform a meaningful audit, and did not perform procedures to confirm that the securities purportedly held on behalf of its customers even existed.
   - ▦ The firm merely pretended to conduct minimal audit procedures of certain accounts to make it seem as though it were conducting an audit, and then failed to document its purported findings and conclusions as required under GAAS.

▪ Similarly, the firm did not conduct any audit procedures with respect to internal controls, and had no basis to represent that the company had no material inadequacies.

Highlight areas above that were accepted without verification. The auditor pled guilty and was sentenced to 12 months of in-home confinement after cooperating with US authorities. "His crime came down to his failure to do his job," said Randall W. Jackson, an assistant federal prosecutor under Preet Bharara, the United States attorney for Manhattan.

Those two elements are qualitative and are not easily discovered through analytics or technology. The latter goes directly to what we are addressing in this chapter – accepting without verifying.

That is also largely the case with insider trading. Illegal insider trading generally refers to buying or selling a security, in breach of a fiduciary duty or other relationship of trust and confidence, on the basis of material, nonpublic information about the security. One of the many difficulties in investigating insider trading is identifying the "insider" who makes the trades. Think of all the many aliases, friends, or relatives' names a corporate executive could use to trade under that would prove difficult to trace, without a tip. What about when the unthinkable happens – and it is the external auditor or consultant who trades on the information? This has happened twice in the recent past when partners of a Big Four accounting firm were found guilty in separate matters.

In 2013, the SEC alleged that a Big Four partner and his friend made more than $1.2 million in illicit profits trading ahead of earnings releases and merger announcements of the firm's clients. It was said that the partner provided the information to his friend, who made the trades and took profits. In exchange, the friend paid the partner at least $50,000 in cash – delivered in bags outside of a jewelry store – along with a Rolex watch, other jewelry, meals, and entertainment.

After losing his job and his reputation, the partner pled guilty in 2014. He agreed to serve 14 months in federal prison. He was also fined $100,000. The Big Four firm also withdrew several audits of two of the large companies in which the partner and his friend had traded.

Almost simultaneously, and within the same Big Four firm, Switzerland's top criminal court announced suspicions that an auditor had used direct knowledge of confidential information pertaining to a takeover bid to trade and net profits of 29,000 francs. He was found guilty in 2018 and fined 5,000 Swiss francs and placed on two years' probation.

Imagine how difficult it is for a company to police and monitor the actions of its external consultants and auditors. And think of the investing public, which relies on the ethics of them both, and often accepts them on their word without verification, or assumes others have already done the vetting.

 MANAGEMENT

One area for management that is susceptible to "accepting without verifying" is the Management's Discussion and Analysis. I will not burden you with all of the rules and regulations pertaining to Management's Discussion and Analysis. The SEC states simply that MD&A is a narrative explanation of the financial statements and other statistical data that the registrant believes will enhance a readers' understanding of its financial condition, changes in financial condition, and results of operation.

The objectives of MD&A are:

1. To provide a narrative explanation of a company's financial statements that enables investors to see the company through the eyes of management;
2. To enhance the overall financial disclosure and provide the context within which financial information should be analyzed; and
3. To provide information about the quality of, and potential variability of, a company's earnings and cash flow so that investors can ascertain the likelihood that past performance is indicative of future performance.

They further provide that MD&A should not consist of generic or boilerplate disclosure. Rather, it should reflect the facts and circumstances specific to each individual organization. However simply stated this may be, the substance can take many forms. Investors may not limit their reliance on MD&A to 10-Ks, 10-Qs, press releases, or appearances. They can also obsess over and rely on social media. Take Tesla, for example.

Tesla is an American automotive and energy company. Tesla's mission is to accelerate the world's transition to sustainable energy. Since their founding in 2003, Tesla has broken new barriers in developing high-performance automobiles that are not only the world's best and highest-selling pure electric vehicles – with long range and absolutely no tailpipe emissions – but also the safest, highest-rated cars on the road in the world. Its co-founder and chief executive officer is Elon Musk.

On April 1, 2018, Mr. Musk tweeted, "Despite intense efforts to raise money, including a last-ditch mass sale of Easter eggs, we are sad to report that Tesla has gone completely and totally bankrupt. So bankrupt, you can't believe it."

How was this information verified? Well, it wasn't. It was an April Fool's joke. The investors failed to see the humor. The next day, Tesla's stock fell 7%. Was it simply a coincidence, or reaction to the tweet?

On August 7, 2018, Musk tweeted that he could take Tesla private at $420 per share, which was significantly higher than it was trading at the time. He tweeted that the funding had been secured and that only a shareholder vote remained. However, the SEC alleged that Musk knew the potential transaction was uncertain and fraught with contingencies. Musk had not discussed the terms with his partners, and his statements lacked an adequate basis in fact. Further, the SEC noted that Tesla had notified them in 2013 that it intended to use the tweets as a means of announcing material information. This is despite the fact, according to the SEC, that Tesla had no disclosure controls or procedures in place to determine whether the tweets should have been disclosed in filings, nor sufficient controls to confirm whether the tweets were accurate or complete.

Nonetheless, the stock shot up over 6%, and the SEC filed suit. The suit was settled a few months later. Musk and Tesla agreed to settle the charges against them without admitting or denying the SEC's allegations. Among other relief, the settlements require that:

1. Musk steps down as Tesla's chairman and is replaced by an independent chairman. Musk will be ineligible to be reelected Chairman for three years;
2. Tesla appoints a total of two new independent directors to its board;
3. Tesla will establish a new committee of independent directors and put in place additional controls and procedures to oversee Musk's communications;
4. Musk and Tesla pay a separate $20 million penalty. The $40 million in penalties will be distributed to harmed investors under a court-approved process.

Jay A. Dubow is the former branch chief in the Division of Enforcement of the US Securities and Exchange Commission in Washington, DC. He is a partner with Pepper Hamilton, a member of the firm's White Collar Litigation and Investigations Practice Group and a co-chair of the Securities and Financial Services Enforcement Group. Mr. Dubow was quoted in several articles after the Securities and Exchange Commission (SEC) announced they had reached a settlement with Tesla CEO Elon Musk. The SEC alleged in a lawsuit that Musk made "false and misleading statements" in August 2018 about the possibility of taking Tesla private. Under the terms of the settlement, Musk doesn't admit or deny the allegations in the agency's lawsuit against him, but he will step down as the chairman of Tesla's board of directors for three years and pay a $20 million fine.

Mr. Dubow says, "It's unusual that Musk will step down as chairman but remain CEO, since executives usually have to resign from both positions when they settle with the SEC in similar situations. The SEC may have determined that removing Musk as CEO would have been bad for shareholders. The settlement is good for Musk and Tesla since it eliminates the uncertainty the company would have faced if it had to find a new CEO. The settlement is good for the SEC since it received a lot of attention and sent a message to other executives."

Shockingly, this was not the end of the tweet controversy. Shortly before this book was published, the SEC accused Musk of violating the settlement agreement by tweeting production forecasts that were contrary to previous forecasts provided by Tesla. Part of the settlement agreement had been a requirement that Musk obtain approval before tweeting messages about the company.

This story continues to develop. Think of all the stakeholders that rely on management, and that relied on the settlement agreement and the requirement that controls be implemented, and accepted this information without verification.

What other areas can you think of that are manual, and overly dependent on people? Did you happen to think of the risk of an executive lying on a resume? Well, it happened to Radio Shack, when its chief executive admitted to lying on his resume by claiming he had two college degrees when he really had none. The kicker: One of the degrees was said to have been from a Baptist Bible college. How could this be? Don't we all assume the information on our resumes will be verified?

While many may consider that a small, innocent exaggeration, just consider the risk of relying on the CEO for much larger, material financial matters. How would the external auditors answer their question: "Do you have any reason to question the integrity of management?"

It is funny what you learn in this business. I once found myself working with quite a spin doctor. He was accused of orchestrating a $20 million Ponzi scheme. The solicitation materials he used to recruit investors explained how he intended on using the funds to make commercial loans to the "underbanked" community. However, the loans were ultimately made to companies he either owned or controlled. It was questioned as to whether those facts had been adequately disclosed to the investors. Some investors claimed they knew while others did not.

The day I met him, he told me that he was a "Big Four partner by marriage." Insert big eye emoji right here!

"Partner by marriage?" I asked. "As in, your spouse is a partner?"

He said no. "I was a partner in a small firm, and that firm was acquired by a Big Four. Therefore, I'm really a partner at the Big Four."

Are you as confused now as I was then? I clearly wasn't following what he was saying.

I shook my head. (It is *never* a good sign when *your* expert shakes his head!) I asked him to explain further. "So why 'through marriage'? Didn't you become a partner when they acquired you?"

He said, "No. I had left the firm eight years before. However, had I stayed, I would have been a partner. That's what I mean by 'in marriage.'"

Can you imagine? The nerve! He claimed he was a partner, yet he had resigned almost 10 years before the acquisition. Claiming to be a partner at a Big Four was meant to give him credibility. Imagine the impact that statement would have on an investor. Making such a statement would obviously be a material misrepresentation and provide false confidence. At that point, I asked him to excuse himself while I discussed this outlandish claim with the attorneys. You can imagine how that conversation went. Ha! Nonetheless, that career title was retired shortly thereafter, and thankfully, I have never seen it listed on anyone's resume.

Another area subject to the risk of acceptance without verification is when organizations partner with one another. Management occasionally enters into joint venture arrangements with other organizations. This is prevalent in oil and gas projects, international pursuits, and large construction projects. Keeping in mind the risk of accepting without verifying, management often operates in the dark when it comes to project execution. While there are laws and industry standards that govern such operations, contracts can oftentimes override best practices. There are risks that accompany such arrangements, and many times, handshake agreements can be upended by ambiguous contract terms. Perhaps the largest risk is the use of related parties and terms inconsistent with the market.

Take, for example, the following provisions in a contract:

All services shall be provided on a competitive contract basis at the usual rates prevailing in the area. If it so desires, the General Partner may employ its own resources and/or affiliates, as long as the rates and terms used for any such goods or services are not greater than the amount paid for similar goods or services in arm's length transactions between unrelated parties, and such transactions are disclosed, and the majority of the investors have consented to such transaction.

On its face, this provision appears to offer a sound internal control. Specifically, the General Partner responsible for the project is allowed use-related parties, only and as long as the transactions are disclosed and approved by the majority of the partners. However, if you continue reading, the contract later provides the following:

> Notwithstanding the prior section or any other section in the agreement, the following transactions will not require consent of the Partners:
>
> ▪ Management services provided by or through the General Partner;
> ▪ Payment of Expense Advances;
> ▪ Any business established by the General Partner, which is established for the primary purpose of operating the business.

Reading those two provisions in concert, you can easily ascertain the first paragraph isn't a control at all. In fact, the second paragraph gives the General Partner an open checkbook and sweeping authority. In such situations, management could be powerless to dispute charges they deem inappropriate without engaging in expensive litigation.

Another area in which management can face the risk of acceptance without verification is when acquiring another company. When management enters into a buy/sell transaction, each side exchanges certain representations and warranties. There are practice aids, textbooks, and college courses that share masses of information on transactions of this nature. As such, I will share the most common representation and warranty that I encounter:

> The accompanying Financial Statements fairly present the financial position and combined results of operations of the Sellers and present the combined financial position and results of operations of the Sellers at the respective dates thereof in accordance with Generally Accepted Accounting Principles, and are consistent with the Seller's historical practices.

What due diligence did management undertake before accepting this representation and warranty? Has the company making such a statement undertaken an external audit by an independent certified or chartered accountant? How many prior years are consistent and reliable? Think of the risks of a US public company acquiring a small, independent company. Is the small company capable of complying with rules and regulations required? What other concerns might you raise?

Much like the examples given in the financial services industry, any organization may face similar risks when acquiring or partnering with a third party. Each of these risks can be mitigated by verifying the terms and provisions of a buy/sell representation and warranty or contract terms prior to acceptance.

One of the best tools to address these contract terms, as well as verifying the representations and warranties, is through a Right-to-Audit Clause. These contract provisions give management, or agents on their behalf, an avenue to access and analyze books, records, and information necessary to confirm performance and accuracy. They also provide remedies, such as payment of the legal and audit expenses of the offended party and a process to resolve disputes to avoid unnecessary litigation that may harm the future of the agreement between the parties.

One challenge I have seen for accountants is that they are not always consulted on the terms and conditions necessary to adequately complete the audit. Many times, attorneys draft audit language without considering auditing or accounting needs. Further, companies may be pressed for time and rush through the contract process assuming, as we mentioned in Chapter 1, that bad things can never happen to them.

Nonetheless, here are a few problematic areas accountants can help address in an effort to ensure proper measures are taken to avoid ambiguity and allow for a productive audit:

1. *Performance.* Management should know whether the audit should be discharged through their in-house accountants, or whether an external party is required. Keep in mind, if management is responsible for completing the audit, the accountant will still have to determine whether or not they possess the professional competency, have the resources, and are able to demonstrate their objectivity. If an external accountant or accounting firm is required, it must be determined who selects them. Further, the party responsible for the payment should also be confirmed.

2. *Notice.* Management should also know how much, if any, notice of an audit is required. If so, how much time is appropriate?

3. *Information provided.* "Information" should include both people and data. There may be time limitations placed on the audit's completion; as such it is critical that people most familiar with the data changed be available to help interpret such, and shorten any perceived learning curve. Relating to data, identify early on what data will be available, electronically or in hardcopy. The exchange of information always results in concerns over privacy, so be prepared to address security. It is not uncommon for one country to prohibit data from leaving their country, so plan accordingly.

a. A subcomponent of this section relates to document retention. The length of time the "auditee" is required to maintain books and records should coincide with dates of the contract performance.

Each of those elements is important *prior* to taking on the assignment. You can imagine all the challenges faced on the execution – the part where you verify! I remember one occasion where I was executing a royalty audit on behalf of a large manufacturer. The "auditee" was based in New Mexico, and it was in the dead of the summer with temperatures in the 110 range. When we arrived at the location, our "office" was an abandoned tractor-trailer rig, turned storage unit. This was an awful time to have worn a suit. After reviewing the first of about 100 boxes, and nearly having a heat stroke, my partner and I left and went to a second-hand clothing store. We bought shorts and tee-shirts, and I bought a pair of used flip-flops. We looked like tourists! When we returned, the business owners had dropped off about 10 barking bloodhound hunting dogs in a pin right outside our "cell." The barking was nonstop. When the client called for an update that afternoon, all she could hear was dogs howling. Jokingly, she asked if we were really working. Imagine what she would have thought if she could have seen what we were wearing! The business owner was simply playing games. He was trying to make our lives as miserable as possible, hoping we would miss something or leave prematurely. This is a common tactic. However, also beware of an "auditee" that is too nice. Don't be fooled; rarely is ANYONE happy to see auditors.

As the economy becomes more global, management also faces the inherent risk of accepting information from certain countries. Similar to the buy/sell and contract examples above, the further away management is from those responsible for designing, executing, or monitoring the internal controls, the less transparency and therefore, greater risk, exists.

In 1993, a few individuals decided to take a stance against global corruption and created Transparency International. With more than 100 national chapters worldwide and an international secretariat in Berlin, Transparency International works with partners in government, business, and civil society to put effective measures in place to tackle corruption.

The movement works relentlessly to stir the world's collective conscience and bring about change. Much remains to be done to stop corruption, but much has also been achieved, including:

- ▦ The creation of international anti-corruption conventions
- ▦ The prosecution of corrupt leaders and seizures of their illicitly gained riches
- ▦ National elections won and lost on tackling corruption
- ▦ Companies held accountable for their behavior both at home and abroad

FIGURE 3.1 Corruption risks by country.

Each year, Transparency International performs research to score countries on how corrupt their public sectors are seen to be. The Corruption Perceptions Index sends a powerful message and governments have been forced to take notice and act.

Figure 3.1 and the accompanying table show corruption risks by country. As such, exercise caution and heightened diligence when receiving information from those countries with high risks. Further, companies doing business in those countries should maintain oversight and continuous monitoring. Above all else, verify before acceptance.

 EXTERNAL AUDITORS

External auditors face a relatively straightforward standard in *sufficient relevant data*, as we mentioned earlier. An auditor is required to obtain sufficient relevant data to afford a reasonable basis for conclusions or recommendations in relation to any professional services performed. The PCAOB also emphasises this concept in Auditing Standard 15, Audit Evidence (and to a degree in AS 3). This standard explains what constitutes audit evidence and establishes requirements regarding designing and performing audit procedures to obtain sufficient appropriate audit evidence. Audit evidence is all the information, whether obtained from audit procedures or other sources, that is used by the auditor in arriving at the conclusions on which the auditor's opinion is based. Audit evidence consists of both information that supports and corroborates management's assertions regarding the financial statements or internal control over financial reporting and information that contradicts such assertions. The auditor must plan and perform audit procedures to obtain sufficient appropriate audit evidence to provide a reasonable basis for his or her opinion. Further, the AICPA issues similar guidance in AU 230.

This is a serious challenge to external auditors.

The largest accounting malpractice matter concluded in July 2018. The FDIC, as receiver for Colonial Bank brought, suit against PwC. Colonial was one of the United States' largest banks, managing over $26 billion in assets and more than 340 branches.

Colonial's failure was precipitated by a massive fraud perpetrated by Colonial's largest customer, Taylor, Bean & Whitaker Mortgage (TWB). PwC served as Colonial's parent company's audit in years that Taylor Bean victimized Colonial.

The case was complex, but the failures were explained clearly in the court's findings. Colonial provided short-term funding for mortgages TBW originated. To oversimplify, Colonial advanced TBW funds in exchange for participation and was repaid when the underlying loans were sold to third-party investors. However, in the spring of 2002, TBW began to overdraw on its Colonial accounts. At first, it was stated that money began to move between accounts to disguise the overdrafts. Later, more sophisticated methods were unveiled. TWB began selling Colonial interest in mortgages that had already been sold to other investors, and interest in mortgages that did not yet exist. By the time the fraud was discovered in 2009, $1.473 billion in mortgage trades were fake or otherwise impaired. On April 14, 2009, the Alabama State Department closed Colonial.

PwC issued clean, that is, "unqualified" opinions for Colonial. As required by professional standards, and explicitly stated in the independent auditor's report, PwC affirmed:

1. They had performed the audit in accordance with GAAP/GAAS.
2. Colonial's year-end financial statements fairly and accurately presented in all material respects Colonial's financial position.
3. Colonial maintained, in all material respects, effective internal controls.

However, the court ruled that PwC violated its professional duties to Colonial in various years' audits. The court determined that it was reasonably foreseeable that PwC's failure to uncover the fraud allowed it to continue. The Order on the Damages Phase of the PwC Bench Trial filed on July 2, 2018, cited two determinations:

1. PwC did not design its audits so as to enable it to detect fraud, and
2. PwC did not obtain sufficient competent evidence.

The court noted errors, such as failure to inspect loans, follow up on illogical dates in financial reports, and failing to physically inspect collateral. As a result of these findings, the court found that the FDIC, as Colonial's Receiver, was entitled to $625,309,085 in damages from PwC.

The FDIC also brought claims against Crowe Horwath, who served as Colonial's internal auditor during relevant years. The FDIC claimed that Crowe "consistently overlooked serious internal control issues." However, Crowe claimed their agreement with Colonial's parent expressly prohibits other parties from relying on Crowe's work, and it was only meant for management and not the FDIC.

Notwithstanding Crowe's claim, PwC's working papers mentioned how they relied on Crowe's work.

While the FDIC alleged gross negligence against Crowe, they alleged that PwC failed to perform procedures sufficient to compensate for any failings or verify the assertions about internal controls Crowe made on behalf of Colonial management.

Crow settled before their matter was brought to trial. It was reported they paid approximately $60 million in restitution.

Look at how many layers of "acceptance" are in this recent case. These are not situations in which rules have since provided guidance that could have helped the firms navigate to safe passage. Crowe undoubtedly relied on management, who were shown to have colluded and conspired to avoid detection. PwC relied on Crowe and management. What verification could Crowe have done? Would the outcome have been the same? Why or why not? How about PwC? What emphasis, both good and bad, would you have placed on PwC's comments on Crowe's work? Despite Crowe's representation that their work was not intended for third parties, is it fair to say they should have known others sought to rely on them?

Some cases are so outlandish they become movies. A recent movie is *All the Queen's Horses*.

It highlights a matter involving the treasurer for the City of Dixon. Dixon was a city with an annual budget of $6 to $8 million and a treasurer who found a way to steal almost $54 million over more than 20 years. How, you might ask? It started with a lot of trust and acceptance, yet few questions and verifications.

In 2013, the treasurer for the City of Dixon was sentenced to almost 20 years in prison, and ordered to repay nearly $54 million, after pleading guilty to bank fraud and money laundering. While her scheme was simple, the failures of the entities surrounding the fraud was puzzling. The scheme was elementary. The treasurer created almost 180 fictitious invoices for bogus capital projects. The city paid them, and the money went to the secret account. The treasurer then used it to fund a lavish lifestyle, including a successful horse-breeding business. The treasurer had vacation properties, other acreage, and used funds for jewelry, spas, and trips. Let's visit the parties and elements involved.

Bank

The treasurer opened a bank account at the city's long-time bank, unbeknownst to any other city official. Considering the long-standing relationship between the bank and the city (trust), the bank did not require any authorizations or any signatures from other officials. They did not ask questions about the money moving between the accounts.

The Auditors

The city used the same accounting firm for more than 20 years. The city also prepared the personal tax returns for the treasurer. The auditors failed to notice that the bogus invoices contained misspellings and was not on any sort of letterhead. The auditors did not follow up (verify) with others regarding the projects reflected in the invoices. They also did not verify the source of the hundreds of thousands of dollars of undocumented income on her tax returns, "assuming" it pertained to her horse business (verify).

City Officials

Despite having an annual budget of between $6 and $8 million, there were years in which the treasurer stole $5.6 and $5.8 million. However, the officials relied on the "independent" auditor, and the annual reviews by the State. When they questioned the treasurer about shortfalls, they were told the state was late in remitting funds they owed to the city. This was plausible, as the state was sometimes late in providing funds, and as such, there was no confirmation or, you got it, no verification.

Lack of Controls

The only internal control appeared to be trust. The AICPA published an article in which Dr. Kelly Richmond Pope reported that people characterized the treasurer as "sweet as pie" and "the nicest person in the world."

The city reached a settlement with the bank and the auditor for $40 million. Your guess is as good as mine as to whether they will recover the remaining $14 million in losses (which may seem small in comparison to the loss, but is two full years of an operating budget).

What could have been done differently? By the bank? By the auditor? By the executives? How would you have found it?

 OTHERS: EXPERT WITNESSES

Verification is also a significant objective for those accountants serving as expert witnesses in commercial disputes. Rule 702 of the Federal Rules of Evidence provides guidance on Testimony by Expert Witnesses. A witness who is qualified as an expert by knowledge, skill, experience, training, or education may testify in the form of an opinion or otherwise if:

  (a) the expert's scientific, technical, or other specialized knowledge will help the trier of fact to understand the evidence or to determine a fact in issue;
  (b) the testimony is based on sufficient facts or data;
  (c) the testimony is the product of reliable principles and methods; and
  (d) the expert has reliably applied the principles and methods to the facts of the case.

Notice anything familiar in point (b)? Indeed, in litigation, the process of exchanging documents is called discovery. In essence, the Plaintiff, the party bringing the suit, and the Defendant each produce information, called production, that they deem relevant to the dispute. Each side often hires an expert to formulate an opinion, that is, damages or violations of GAAP or GAAS, based on the information provided. The expert must disclose the documents he or she relied upon in formulating their opinion. The extent to which an expert tests, or validates, the information they relied upon is almost always a contentious subject. While the expert is clearly not performing an audit or a review, how far should they go in providing assurance that the data is both sufficient and reliable?

Further guidance can be obtained through an analysis of situations in which the expert is ultimately excluded, or not allowed to offer testimony, under what is known as a *Daubert* challenge. This standard comes from the

Supreme Court case, *Daubert v. Merrell Dow Pharmaceuticals Inc.*, 509 U.S. 579 (1993). Under the *Daubert* standard, the overarching objective is to ensure that the expert's testimony (A) is "relevant to the task at hand" and (B) it rests "on a reliable foundation," and is based on scientific knowledge and a generally accepted, valid methodology.

In determining the foundation and methodology, the factors that may be considered in determining whether the methodology is valid are (1) whether the theory or technique in question can be and has been tested; (2) whether it has been subjected to peer review and publication; (3) its known or potential error rate; (4) the existence and maintenance of standards controlling its operation; and (5) whether it has attracted widespread acceptance within a relevant scientific community.

As you can see, if sufficient relevant data is not present or obtained, it is impossible to determine two of the three overarching objectives: whether the opinion is reliable and/or accepted. Without those two, it is highly doubtful an expert would meet the third objective of relevance.

In 2015, the American Institute of Certified Public Accountants (AICPA) issued AICPA Forensic and Valuation Services Practice Aid, "Attaining Reasonable Certainty in Economic Damages Calculations" (AICPA Reasonable Certainty Practice Aid). Many relevant topics are discussed in this practice aid, including Chapter 1 on Client Supplied Information, which addresses issues confronted by damages experts when information integral to the damages analysis was provided by the client or retaining counsel. Before we get too far into this topic, it is important to note that as forensic accountants, we sometimes get involved in cases that have been going on for a long time, and the attorneys have gathered a ton of information in discovery and have prepared schedules and analyses. Similar to not blindly accepting information from clients, we cannot merely accept these schedules and analyses from the attorneys. It is our responsibility to verify/confirm that the schedules and analyses prepared by the attorneys are accurate and that they utilize the data needed to properly support our conclusions and opinions. For those of you who work in a large full-service accounting firm and/or have access to subject-matter experts, the same verification applies. For example, if there is a certain tax issue and you consult a tax professional, do you take their word for it? The expert should definitely research the information provided by other professionals/subject-matter experts to ensure that the information is accurate.

Forensic accounting experts have different training and experience from other accounting professionals. Other professionals, such as tax preparers and auditors, do not often operate in the economic damages world. Therefore, if the expert does not supply them with specific information and ask questions correctly, they may not be able to provide an answer necessary to meet the assignment's objective.

Now, back to the AICPA Practice Aid on Client Supplied Information. When performing economic damages calculations, accounting experts receive various data from clients, including:

■ Projections of financial performance – including lost revenues, associated costs, loss of value, out-of-pocket costs, and so on;

■ Assumptions regarding growth rates, pricing, financing opportunities, and cost structure;

■ Business information – such as markets served, competitors, market share, and industry trends; or

■ Technical information – such as product features and specifications, and how those features and specifications contribute to the operation of a product.

There are a number of different things forensic accountants can do to test information provided by the client. Let us consider the income statement that is provided by the client. One of the easiest verifications for the income statement is to compare it to the client's filed income tax return. In some situations, depending on the size and sophistication of the client, there may have been an audit performed. If an accounting expert has access to audited financial statements, it is still a good idea to compare the audited financial statements to the filed tax return. Further, if the economic damages model includes future lost profits and projections are necessary, the expert needs to determine if they can rely on the projections provided by the client. This is a bit easier if the business is mature as there is a history of growth. In situations where the business is not mature, the expert should analyze prior-year projections and determine if management projections were in line with actual prior performance.

Experts can and do rely on management's representations, but should make certain considerations when doing so. As mentioned in the AICPA Reasonable Certainty Practice Aid, "Numerous court opinions address the issue within the context of the evaluation of the admissibility of expert testimony, and within the context of the evaluation of the weight that should be accorded to the expert opinions regarding damages." Experts who are CPAs should adhere to the AICPAs CS Section 100, Consulting Services: Definitions and Standards. For CPAs acting as experts, it is important to know the Standards of Consulting Services provided by the AICPA. These standards are the same as the general standards that apply to all services performed by members of the AICPA. These general standards are as follows:

- **Professional competence.** Undertake only those professional services that the member or the member's firm can reasonably expect to be completed with professional competence.
- **Due professional care.** Exercise due professional care in the performance of professional services.
- **Planning and supervision.** Adequately plan and supervise the performance of professional services.
- **Sufficient relevant data.** Obtain sufficient relevant data to afford a reasonable basis for conclusions or recommendations in relation to any professional services performed.

All of the above general standards are important to know, as you can never tell when you could be tested. A few years ago, an expert friend of mine was helping her client examine the opposing expert. The opposing expert was a CPA and was required to adhere to the general standards listed above. My expert friend told her attorney to ask the opposing expert, "As a CPA, are your required to adhere to standards provided by the AICPA?" The opposing expert answered with a "Yes." Then the attorney asked, "Which standards?" The opposing expert responded, "The standards that the AICPA require." The attorney then asked, "Can you list the standards that you adhered to as required by the AICPA?" The opposing expert, who was a very seasoned expert who had been around for a long time, could not name any of the general standards.

Then the attorney asked again, "Did you adhere to the standards as a consulting expert provided by the AICPA?" The opposing expert again responded, "Yes." Then, of course, the next question the attorney asked is, "If you cannot tell me what the standards are as we sit here today, how do you know that you adhered to those standards?" The opposing expert's response was, "I have been doing this so long that [I] know what the standards are, and I do not need to memorize them."

In this particular situation, the opposing expert was so experienced and confident that this line of questioning did not shake him. However, if you still have that new testifying smell, this line of questioning could shake your confidence and make for a bad performance. Further, it could impact the judge and/or jury's opinion as to whether you are qualified, and whether your testimony is relevant and reliable.

When dealing with professional standards, as the previous chapter mentioned, the key element is that experts have to be careful to investigate the materials they rely upon.

Two particular cases come to mind in which the expert was excluded due to relying on materials that were not fully vetted. A third case was related to an expert ignoring various factors that should have been looked at before relying on materials that were produced in the case. As discussed by Mr. Jeffrey Klenk in an article dated August 29, 2017, in the District of New Jersey the court excluded an expert's testimony for its reliance on an internal corporate document that, while produced as part of the discovery process, had not been independently investigated by the expert. In constructing his model, a key input used by the expert was data contained in that document purporting to show that certain products tainted by the alleged misconduct carried a sizable price premium relative to similar products not tainted by that conduct. According to the court, though, "to extract a [. . .] price premium for the [product] based on this document, without any independent investigation into the data depicted in the document, is just too much." The court went on to conclude that "[t]here are simply too many unknown variables that would affect the data" and that "[w]ithout more serious investigation of the basis for the figures, they cannot furnish a reasonable basis" for the price premium.

A case in the Middle District of Pennsylvania likewise excluded expert testimony for failing to independently "verify" the "accuracy or reliability" of the data upon which the experts were relying. As explained by the court, "blind adherence to data absent any sort of investigation stops short of the type of reliability contemplated by *Daubert*."[1]

Notable in this case is that the court specifically addressed whether the failure to independently investigate the data contained in a document should go to the "weight" or the "admissibility" of the experts' testimony. Given that the "flaws" in the data pointed out by defendants went to the "core body of the proffered evidence," the court excluded the experts' testimony rather than risking that the jury would be "unduly prejudice[d] and confus[ed]."

Weaving this all together brings us to the curious case of Christopher Faulkner, the self-proclaimed "Frack Master" in reference to his purported hydraulic fracturing expertise. This matter involves acceptance without verification of investors, media, auditors, and an attack on an expert in an attempt to gain acceptance of the court. In 2016, the SEC brought charges against Mr. Faulkner, alleging that he engaged in a wide-ranging securities fraud scheme that raised more than $80 million. As we go through this example, think of all the "acceptances" that occurred along the way and allowed this fraud to flourish.

---

[1]*Giterman v. Pocono Med. Ctr.*, United States District Court Middle District of Pennsylvania, April 2, 2019 (Civil Action No. 3:16-0402 (M.D. Pa. April 2, 2019)).

Mr. Faulkner ran this swindle through the privately held Breitling Oil and Gas Corporation. The SEC claimed that he deceived investors by soliciting their funds through false and misleading offering documents. The list of misrepresentations in the offering document was extensive, and included baseless projections and estimated drilling costs, the intended use of the funds, and his experience. It seems Mr. Faulkner had very little experience, yet, in addition to achieving the trust (acceptance) of the investors, he was able to persuade CNBC, CNN International, Fox Business News, and the BBC to feature (acceptance) him in oil and gas discussions.

Mr. Faulkner was also accused of misappropriating millions of dollars by using investor funds on extravagant meals and entertainment, travel, cars, jewelry, gentlemen's clubs, and personal escorts.

His scheme included victims beyond the investors. As the case proceeded, Breitling management was accused of lying to the auditors and violating certain provisions of the Sarbanes-Oxley Act and other securities laws. (Think of the auditor's role, and the risk they face when accepting information from management.)

While the SEC was conducting this investigation in Texas, Mr. Faulkner resurfaced in California. In September 2017, a lawsuit was unsealed and claimed that Mr. Faulkner and two of his associates "repackaged" the Texas scheme and applied it to the real estate market. The allegations were almost identical, in that he claimed an extensive track record and promised excessive returns. (Think of these investors. Had they done their research, they certainly would have had reason to verify his claims, rather than accepting them.)

The SEC settled with Mr. Faulkner in October 2018. Mr. Faulkner agreed to repay $25 million fine, and serve 12 years in federal prison for securities fraud, money laundering, and tax evasion.

To add more intrigue to an intriguing tale, Mr. Faulkner's mom was also involved in the matter. Carole Faulkner, a Texas attorney, was sanctioned for misrepresenting the status of a state lawsuit. Following a contempt order, Ms. Faulkner claimed the receiver (the accounting, financial, or legal expert) appointed to oversee Breitling incurred significant, unnecessary legal fees responding to a suit that she asserted she had already agreed to end. However, the judge stated that Ms. Faulkner produced no evidence of such an agreement while the receiver produced evidenced contracting her claim (an example of verifying, and not simply accepting).

Think of all the roles accountants played, or should have played in the Breitling example above. Accountants would be, or should be, the likely source of the revenue, expense, and anticipated rate of return projections in the offering memorandums provided to the investing public. Accountants should have been advising investors on their due diligence prior to investing. The external auditor (accountants) would be working with management (also probably accountants) on obtaining supporting documentation in support of the figures, the notes, and the assertions in the financial statements. Accountants would also likely be part of the team conducting the investigation once the allegations surfaced, to help identify the misappropriated funds, calculate any damages, and help lead the recovery efforts on behalf of the court and investors. As for the media, do we think they need any more reasons to be distrusted?

 ## SUMMARY

Whether you serve as an external auditor, an expert, or a member of management or the investing public, you must verify any material information before reliance or "acceptance." Our tendency to blindly accept results from artificial intelligence or other technological testing can also provide false confidence and lead to errors and omissions. Technology alone is not a sound proxy to mitigate fraud or rise to meet the professional standards. That is especially true for some schemes that possess more qualitative red flags. Further, accountants should be aware that some transactions and countries present pervasive risks by their very nature. Lastly, litigation experts should be cognizant of the fact that their objective of being an advocate for their opinion, can conflict with their client's objective of advocating their position. In those situations, it is imperative to test the underlying support to any material transaction to insure the expert's work is relevant and reliable.

 ## RECOMMENDATIONS

In an effort to avoid A – Accepting, not Verifying, I recommend the following:

1. *Communicate.* Adhering to a "trust but verify" mindset pays big dividends. Informing others of missing, incomplete, unreliable, or irrelevant documentation, early and often, can help the document owners understand and share your sense of importance.
2. *Prioritize document requests.* Categorize documents by importance or relevance: must-have, nice-to-have. Providers could be overwhelmed by the volume of documents requested. Informing them of those most critical to

the assignment allows them to deliver documents as they get them. However, be able to defend reaching a conclusion or an opinion when certain documents are not received.

3. *Obtain confirmations.* Have clients or those providing documents provide a confirmation, representations, and/or warranties that the documents they have provided you are accurate, and that they have provided all documentation pertinent to your request.

4. *Test assumptions and support.* Test the analysis provided, even if it is only on a well-defined sample basis. Obtain native formats and live databases to identify any hard-coded or inconsistent data points. Ensure the file properties for "paper" documents support contemporaneous dates or those that were represented.

5. *Perform independent research.* Even when documentation is provided and tested, corroborate information by obtaining objective third-party data in areas that can become highly contested or possess a heightened risk. If your research turns up conflicting information, be prepared to analyze and disclose the impact of using one over the other.

6. *Disclose deficiencies.* There are times when sufficient documentation simply does not exist. Say so! Do not fabricate or force the issue. Limit the reliance in those areas you find weak. Honesty is the best policy.

7. *Know when to say when.* If the deficiencies cannot be overcome, know when to walk away and to call it a day. It is better to walk away at this point. It is far better to withdraw, resign, or recuse yourself than to live with an adverse ruling, or worse, for the rest of your career.

Case Study – Technology on Trial

You are hired by an attorney in their representation of Plaintiffs in a breach-of-contract matter. The Plaintiffs allege that they had a contract in place with defendants to manufacture and sell 10,000 laptops at $1,000 apiece. And that upon delivering the laptops for inspection, the Defendants rejected them and refused to pay. The Plaintiffs allege the rejection was actually due to the Defendant's deteriorating cash flows, and their desire to simply avoid their obligations after the Plaintiff had incurred extensive costs and expended significant resources to meet the contract requirements.

(Continued)

(Continued)

The Defendants claim the laptops did not meet industry standards, and as such, they had the contractual right to terminate the agreement and did so. Further, the Defendants claim the laptops were delivered after the due date, and they lost sales as a result of the delay. They filed a countersuit for damages. They hired an accounting expert. The expert, a CPA, wrote a report and opined, "While I have not been asked to audit or review the underlying facts associated with lost clients or contracts, I was told the Defendant lost the following clients as a result of the delay. The revenues associated with those lost clients total $750,000, and approximates damages in this matter."

Word of the termination spread, and had a negative impact on the Plaintiff's business. Your job as the Plaintiff's expert is to determine the lost profits associated with the Defendant's breach of contract, and to calculate the financial impact to the Plaintiff's business as a result of the Defendant's slander and/or wrongful termination.

1. As the Plaintiff's expert, what type of information would you need to determine the lost profits? Loss of other revenue?
2. If the Plaintiff was unable to provide you with supporting documentation for their calculation of the dollar amount associated with actual clients lost as a result of the slander, how would you go about determining a number, assuming you could?
3. How would you respond if the Defendant produced information you had not seen at the time you completed the report, which includes Plaintiff's email and correspondence, showing that other actions caused the Plaintiff to lose clients, and that it was not due to the termination?
4. If the Plaintiff asked you, a Certified Public Accountant, to opine on whether the machines complied with industry standards, what would you do?
5. In assessing the Defendant's damages, what types of questions would you propose to their expert?
6. What professional standards exist for both experts, and what negative actions might they face if they are found to have violated them?

CHAPTER FOUR

U – Underestimating the Effort

Accounting Humor

Q – What do accountants suffer from that other people don't?
A – Depreciation.

THIS CHAPTER ADDRESSES PROFESSIONAL competency, sufficient relevant data, and scope restrictions. We also discuss accounting expert witnesses and challenges faced during litigation matters.

INTRODUCTION

In this chapter, I focus on what I refer to as underestimating the effort and discuss how it can affect different categories of professionals:

1. Management of the company
2. Internal auditors
3. External auditors
4. Others, such as outside experts and consultants

This profession is demanding, and is accompanied by a stress that few appreciate. We walk around with large targets on our backs. Whether you serve as an accountant, an auditor, an investigator, or even a whistleblower, each of these comes with a personal risk. I have actually served in all these capacities, and have faced multiple ethical dilemmas in each role.

I have always trusted my abilities in my professional career, even though I have faced insecurities coming from such a small town. I am the first to admit that I did not graduate at the top of my class from a GPA perspective. While my GPA was very respectable, no one worked harder than me, nor were they as involved in the level of professional (and social) activities as I was. However, in this stressful line of work, every adversary you face has the primary objective of capitalizing on your particular insecurities or weaknesses. Whether it is an opposing expert challenging your assertions, or the fraudster you're interrogating challenging you to a spitting contest, you will often be called to defend your abilities and position.

Remember the investigation I mentioned in the previous chapter – the assignment where we had to follow up on allegations that a parish sheriff had used inmate labor and public funds to build homes for his friends and family? We had analyzed millions of dollars in lumber and building supplies, yet not one of the parish facilities had been renovated or remodeled. We also interviewed the crusty 70-year-old owner of the hardware store.

Shortly after we met him, and he refused to shake our hands, he launched into his belief that only the dumbest accountants worked for the government and that I lacked certain "manly" attributes. Think of what he was actually challenging. He attacked our education and our expertise. In the crudest of fashions, he was questioning our expertise. That example is a poignant, overexaggeration of a challenge, but you will face similar challenges countless times in this profession.

Let's hope you never have to defend your anatomy or hairstyle. Thankfully, the standards for accountants, auditors, and investigators are more evolved and well-defined. There are decades of analyses and court cases that provide guidance and best practices in supporting your conclusions and defending your qualifications. However, we can sometimes bite off more than we can chew. I have been known to promise the moon, causing my staff relentless stress to meet our lofty expectations. I am aware of my tendencies, as well as those of many of my peers in the industry. I keep wise counsel and before committing, ultimately reach a consensus, and we deliver. To quote Ben Franklin, "We must, indeed, all hang together or, most assuredly, we will all hang separately."

In our business, it is not unusual to face situations that may result in becoming overextended. Allowing yourself to be overextended, without proper care or measured caution, can lead to violations. Common offenses include accepting an assignment:

1. Without fully understanding the objectives
2. When there is not sufficient time or resources to complete the task
3. In which sufficient data do not exist
4. That does not fit within your area of expertise

Going back to the four categories of professionals discussed in the opening, mistakes and their consequences can vary, and their impact can be felt at all levels. The four categories of professionals are bound by certain professional standards that were created to help prevent these kinds of situations. For example, AICPA members are bound by the AICPA Code of Professional Conduct with two principles that directly relate to this chapter: due care and the scope and nature of services. The principle of due care indicates that members should abide by the profession's technical and ethical standards. The scope and nature of services should determine the level of competence necessary for the engagement. First, we will discuss external auditors.

EXTERNAL AUDITORS

Some of the most common mistakes that can derail an audit include not spending enough time planning the engagement, not having a specific scope defined prior to the audit starting, and not having enough functional expertise on the team. These dilemmas can be very detrimental to the audit and have lasting repercussions to those responsible. Further, reporting deadlines can become excruciating, and fraught with risks beyond an auditor's control. Client delays, unexpected disruptions to the engagement team, and even natural catastrophes can derail the best-laid plans. Further, unanticipated findings or lack of supporting documentation can also alter engagement planning and scope.

Take for example a recent matter in which the SEC filed an administrative order against leaders at BDO,[1] the world's fifth-largest accounting firm. On October 12, 2018, the SEC instituted administrative proceedings involving BDO's financial statement audit of AmTrust Financial Services, Inc. AmTrust

---

[1]Order Instituting Administrative Proceedings Pursuant to Section 4C of the Securities Exchange Act of 1934 and Rule 102(e) of the Commission's Rules of Practice, Making Findings and Imposing Remedial Sanctions in the SEC Matter against Richard J. Bertuglia, CPA, John W. Green, CPA, and Lev Nagdimov, CPA.

had engaged BDO to conduct an audit of their 2013 consolidated annual financial statements. The SEC's opening summary explained that the matter concerned improper professional conduct by the individuals during the audit. The leaders served in three roles: the engagement partner, the engagement quality review partner, and a senior manager. Yes, that's right. The senior manager, or in other words, the boots on the ground, was charged. In fact, the SEC goes on to state that it was the senior manager who instructed the audit team to sign off on all of their work papers and audit programs – regardless of whether their work was finished. This was so the audit procedures would appear complete before the release date for the report. This "order" included loading blank documents or placeholder documents into the electronic work paper files. This created a "predating" situation, in that the audit documentation did not accurately reflect the dates when audit procedures were actually completed or audit documentation was actually obtained.

As we dive deeper into this matter, we notice that it touches on many of the points we pondered in prior chapters. It was reported that at the time of the report, the partners did not know the team had failed to complete the necessary procedures. The partners stated that they did not discover these deficiencies until a week after the report was issued. Now, the SEC responded that had the partners exercised "due professional care," they could have identified these deficiencies before they released the report. The SEC stated that the senior manager not only failed to exercise due professional care but also failed to "properly supervise staff."

Let us pause; that is a lot to unpack. Perhaps we can revisit some concepts.

1. R – relying on others. Can you see the liability the partners created in relying on the senior manager, and the team? How about the senior manager, who failed to properly supervise? Whom did he rely on? It all rolls downhill.
2. A – accepting without verifying. Was the SEC right in determining that the auditors had not adhered to "due professional care"? How could this have been avoided?

The circumstances become clearer, as the SEC provided the root cause of the issue.

The audit team fell behind schedule during the fourth quarter of 2013. On December 18, 2013, the manager emailed a status report to the partners. The report estimated the audit team was 870 total hours behind schedule as a group, and roughly 14 weeks behind, based on current staffing and 60-hour work weeks. To cure this deficit, the partner staffed four more auditors to the engagement, including two managers.

3. That brings us right back to you – U – underestimating the effort. We continue.

The "due date" of February 28 was met, and over the course of the next month, the team completed the required procedures. However, ultimately, it was determined that BDO did not have sufficient audit evidence to support their report. The following summaries describes the significant audit deficiencies and documentation failures existing on that date:

1. Incomplete journal entry testing
2. Incomplete internal controls testing
3. Incomplete substantive testing for material accounts
4. Other incomplete audit procedures

The SEC concluded that violations of PCAOB professional standards occurred, and listed the following failures:

1. Failure to supervise and exercise due professional care
2. Failure to properly examine journal entries for evidence of possible misstatements due to fraud
3. Failure to perform sufficient tests of internal controls and substantive audit procedures to obtain sufficient evidence to support the audit opinions
4. Failure to prepare and retain required audit documentation
5. Failure to perform appropriate engagement quality review

The SEC concluded that, based on their findings, the engagement partner would be denied the privilege of appearing or practicing before the SEC as an accountant for three years. The quality control partner was denied for one year; the senior manager, five years.

This single, recent, significant matter reminds us that regardless of which of these chapters are your most and least favorite, they are all important and interlocking. It is unfortunate that these types of matters must arise to provide us teaching moments.

The Public Company Accounting Oversight Board (PCAOB) provides standards intended to prevent some of the issues that can arise when auditing financial statements of public companies. It makes a distinction between auditor's and management's responsibilities.

The independent auditor is to present the financial position, results of operations, and cash flow of a company by opining they are in conformity with generally accepted accounting principles (GAAP). Auditors have a "responsibility to plan and perform the audit to obtain reasonable assurance about whether the financial statements are free of material misstatement, whether caused by error or fraud . . . and assurance that material misstatements are detected."[2] On the other hand, the accuracy and truthfulness of the financial statements are management's responsibility. That is achieved by "adopting sound accounting policies and for establishing and maintaining internal control that will, among other things, initiate, record, process, and report transactions (as well as events and conditions) consistent with management's assertions embodied in the financial statements."[3] Again, PCAOB recommends using due professional care in the planning and performance of the audit as well as the preparation of the report.

Imagine for a second that the auditors in the BDO example mentioned earlier were not "allowed" to perform those tasks necessary to complete their work, or that relevant or reliable documents were not available, or that management was unavailable to the extent the auditors needed to obtain the reasonable assurances they required. What if the auditors were not allowed to investigate certain areas?

The AICPA and the PCAOB are both very clear in situations such as these. In fact, external auditors are required to modify their report if there is a restriction on the scope of an assignment. The guidance provides that auditors can only express an opinion if they have been afforded the opportunity to apply the procedures they deem necessary to reach a conclusion. If the approach is restricted, the auditor is required to withdraw from the assignment and disclaim their opinion.

An agreed-upon procedure assignment is different, in that the parties agree to the procedures prior to commencement, and the reports are limited accordingly. The conditions necessary for undertaking such an exam require that the party engaging the accountant be responsible for the subject matter at issue, or if they are not, provide the accountant with evidence of a third party's responsibility for the subject matter.

The relationship between the PCAOB and accounting firms is currently a hot topic, as is audit quality. The Sarbanes-Oxley Act granted the PCAOB the oversight responsibility for accounting firms providing attest services. The

---

[2]PCAOB, AU 110, "Responsibilities and Functions of the Independent Auditor," paragraph .02.
[3]PCAOB, AU 110, "Responsibilities and Functions of the Independent Auditor," paragraph .03.

PCAOB has standards with regards to audit quality control for audits of public companies. PCAOB Auditing Standard No. 7, Engagement Quality Review requires an auditor, the engagement partner, to obtain a concurring partner review. The concurring partner must be competent, and comply with the same professional standards as the engagement partner. Further, the concurring partner should also have equivalent experience. Additionally, accounting firms are subject to PCAOB inspections. The PCAOB inspects registered public accounting firms to assess compliance with Sarbanes Oxley, the rules of the Securities and Exchange Commission, and professional standards, in connection with the firm's performance of audits, issuance of audit reports, and related matters involving U.S. public companies, other issuers, brokers and dealers. The AICPA also requires member firms to enroll in a Peer Review Program if they perform services that fall within the scope of the AICPA professional standards, and they have similar guidance that requires a concurring partner (AU 230).

Ralph Q. Summerford is the president of Forensic Strategic Solutions, LLC. Mr. Summerford was recognized by the ACFE with the 2010 Cressey Award. The Cressey Award is the ACFE's highest honor, which recognizes a lifetime of achievement in the detection and deterrence of fraud. Mr. Summerford also served as the vice chairman for the ACFE Board of Regents, past chairman of its Professional Standards and Practices Committee, and past chairman of its Board of Review. He is a guest lecturer at seminars, colleges, and universities where he strives to enhance the understanding of fraud and forensic accounting. He has published articles that have appeared in *Accounting Today*, *Preventing Business Fraud*, *Financial Fraud*, *Bank Fraud & IT Security Report*, *Dunn on Damages*, and *Fraud Magazine*. In a recent blog post Mr. Summerford took note of a serious violation of trust by an accounting firm.

A matter in which he recently blogged involved a Big Four accounting firm and the government watchdog, the PCAOB. The accounting firm had been under scrutiny for years for failing to find problems at audit clients. The PCAOB had recently released reports disclosing that almost half of the firm's audits had serious deficiencies. What happened next was unconscionable. The accounting firm obtained advanced notice of which client audits would be subject to review. This was perpetrated in part by the hiring of PCAOB personnel.

When the PCAOB replaced the compromised reviews with new ones, the new audits had a much higher rate of problems. Thus, the accounting firm had obviously been helped by the advanced warning.

The *Wall Street Journal* reported on March 11, 2019, that the auditor and the former employee of the PCAOB had been convicted in a Manhattan federal court. The federal prosecutors termed their actions a "steal the exam" conspiracy.

Mr. Summerford commented that it was "the case of the auditor and the regulator who oversees the auditor both being convicted of fraud." In his remarks, he mentions that auditors have received a lot of publicity about their failures to detect fraud. Just a year ago in March 2018, federal judge Barbara Rothstein ruled that an accounting firm failed to design their audit to detect fraud at one of their clients who later failed. She entered a judgment of $625 million against the firm.

In the more recent case where auditors "stole the exam" and knew which audits would be reviewed by the regulator, they took actions to cover their failures. The audit firm wanted to improve their performance on inspections because they had performed poorly in past reviews. For example, they were under close scrutiny by the SEC for their failure to detect problems at two other clients.

Rather than focus efforts on improvements such as performing their work at an acceptable level of care and committing to higher-quality work, the defendant took an easier approach – he illegally obtained knowledge of which audits the inspectors would review, and made poor work appear better than it actually was.

We now see a fraud scheme where we didn't expect to ever see one – among the group whose duty it is to detect it. And this is a question of ethics – both personal ethics and business ethics. I don't see how you separate the two. How does this happen? As a fraud examiner, I was taught the Fraud Triangle. One of the three legs of the triangle is rationalization – the mindset of a person who rationalizes their fraudulent action. However, I will never understand how fraudsters rationalize these actions!

Auditors must be taught how to recognize fraud – and we have a mandate to teach them. Unlike a cat that attempts to cover its tracks, cover-ups and stealing the exam are unacceptable. It is simply fraud.

Mr. Summerford also added that he assumes the role of "Guardian of Trust" in discharging his responsibilities. "I recently read a post by CEO of the Institute of Internal Auditors Richard Chambers. He reminded internal auditors that 'I am respected and admired, because I am a guardian of trust.' I could not agree more."

If we conduct additional rearch, in anticipation of being challenged in courts, a legal treatise – *Cooley on Torts* – describes the obligation for due care as follows:

> Every man who offers his services to another and is employed assumes the duty to exercise in the employment such skill as he possesses with reasonable care and diligence. In all these employments where peculiar skill is requisite, if one offers his services, he is understood as holding himself out to the public as possessing the degree of skill commonly possessed by others in the same employment, and if his pretentions are unfounded, he commits a species of fraud upon every man who employs him in reliance on his public profession. But no man, whether skilled or unskilled,

undertakes that the task he assumes shall be performed successfully, and without fault or error; he undertakes for good faith and
integrity, but not for infallibility, and he is liable to his employer for
negligence, bad faith, or dishonesty, but not for losses consequent
upon pure errors of judgment.

The matter of due professional care concerns what the independent
auditor does and how well he or she does it. The quotation from *Cooley on Torts*
provides yet another source from which an auditor's responsibility for conducting an audit with due professional care can be derived. The remainder of the
section discusses the auditor's responsibility in the context of an audit.

An auditor should possess "the degree of skill commonly possessed" by
other auditors and should exercise it with "reasonable care and diligence"
(that is, with due professional care).

Auditors should be assigned to tasks and supervised commensurate
with their level of knowledge, skill, and ability so that they can evaluate the
audit evidence they are examining. The engagement partner should know, at
a minimum, the relevant professional accounting and auditing standards and
should be knowledgeable about the client. The engagement partner is responsible for the assignment of tasks to, and supervision of, the members of the
engagement team.

Due professional care requires the auditor to exercise professional skepticism. Professional skepticism is an attitude that includes a questioning mind and
a critical assessment of audit evidence. The auditor uses the knowledge, skill, and
ability called for by the profession of public accounting to diligently perform, in
good faith and with integrity, the gathering and objective evaluation of evidence.

Gathering and objectively evaluating audit evidence requires the auditor
to consider the competency and sufficiency of the evidence. Since evidence is
gathered and evaluated throughout the audit, professional skepticism should
be exercised throughout the audit process. The auditor neither assumes that
management is dishonest nor assumes unquestioned honesty. In exercising
professional skepticism, the auditor should not be satisfied with less than persuasive evidence because of a belief that management is honest.

The exercise of due professional care does not speak in "absolute" terms.
It allows the auditor to obtain *reasonable* assurance about whether the financial statements are free of material misstatement, whether caused by error
or fraud, or whether any material weaknesses exist as of the date of management's assessment. Absolute assurance is not attainable because of the
nature of audit evidence and the characteristics of fraud. Although not absolute assurance, reasonable assurance is a high level of assurance. Therefore,

an audit conducted in accordance with the standards of the Public Company Accounting Oversight Board (United States) may not detect a material weakness in internal control over financial reporting or a material misstatement to the financial statements.

EXPERT WITNESSES, FRAUD EXAMINERS, AND CONSULTING EXPERTS

In this chapter, we expand on the discussions we had in the previous chapter, with regard to expert witness and consulting services that accountants provide. One big distinguishing difference in ethical standards between those providing expert witness, as well as consulting services, and those providing external audits are the independence requirements. As mentioned, the AICPA is responsible for establishing standards for CPAs. While these standards are mandatory for CPAs providing attestation services, these standards often find their way into nonattestation services, specifically the area of litigation, due to the fact that CPA's who provide expert testimony have to follow the rules governing them.

The AICPA's Professional Ethics Executive Committee's (PEEC's) standard specifically addresses forensic accounting services, among other types of nonattest services. The PEEC revision to Interpretation No. 101-3, Performance of Nonattest Services, influences how CPAs interact with attorneys regarding expert testimony, investigatory services, and dispute resolution.

The standard is intended to preserve CPA independence when performing auditing services – or other "attest" services – for a client. One of the biggest obstacles is that oftentimes the performance of certain nonattest services would impair a CPA's independence (and the independence of the firm) when conducting attest services.[4]

When the CPA is providing expert witness testimony for a large group of plaintiffs or defendants that includes one or more of the CPA's attest clients, independence is not impaired if:

1. The CPA's attest clients represent less than 20 percent of a) the group, b) the group's voting interests, and c) the claim;
2. No attest client within the group is designated as the lead plaintiff or defendant; and

---

[4]http://www.mondaq.com/unitedstates/x/48664/Taking+a+Stand+Or+Not+New+Ethics+Rule+Could+Compromise+Your+Experts+Testimony.

3. No attest client holds sole decision-making power to select or approve the expert witness.
4. Independence also is not impaired if, while testifying as a fact witness, a CPA is solicited for opinions pertaining to matters within his or her expertise. Therefore, where a CPA who audited a client is subpoenaed as a fact witness, the CPA could testify without compromising independence.

A CPA can provide advice about the facts, issues, and strategy of a matter, as long as he or she complies with the general requirements discussed below.

1. *Neutral services.* The standard states that these services create the appearance the CPA is not independent. Independence would not be impaired, though, if the CPA does not make any decisions on behalf of the parties but instead acts as a facilitator for the parties to reach their own agreement.
2. *Investigative services.* The standard defines investigative services as including all forensic services not involving actual or threatened litigation. CPAs can deliver such services for attest clients without impairing their independence, again assuming compliance with the general requirements below and they are not expected to testify as an expert.

Let's go back to 2002, the year of Sarbanes-Oxley. One of the many catalysts that ushered in a new professional landscape was the Enron scandal and the demise of Arthur Andersen. At the time of the Enron fraud, Arthur Andersen was their external auditor. However, the fees from the external audit paled in comparison to the other services Arthur Andersen provided Enron.

In Enron's case, consulting work accounted for more than half of the $52 million that Andersen received in fees in 2000. According to John C. Coffee Jr., a law professor at Columbia, "Enron was a potential market for $50 million or $100 million in consulting fees."[5] This amount was enough to make Enron Andersen's second-largest account in 2000.

Auditors, according to GAAS, are to remain independent in both fact and appearance. This means that if an auditor appears to have a connection with their client, even though they may not have, they should drop the audit immediately. Andersen, on the other hand, took a very active role in Enron's business operations through both auditing and consulting.[6]

---

[5]Reed Abelson and Jonathan D. Glater, "Enron's Collapse: The Auditors; Who's Keeping the Accountants Accountable?" *New York Times*, January 15, 2002, https://www.nytimes.com/2002/01/15/business/enron-s-collapse-the-auditors-who-s-keeping-the-accountants-accountable.html.
[6]Ibid.

It is difficult to remain independent when Andersen was collecting fees in the area of consulting and auditing services. The rules established by GAAS challenges the rules for the audit cycle of companies. What GAAS has provided is that if an auditor has a preexisting relationship with the client, they should drop the audit immediately, which should have been enough to raise a red flag in the case of Andersen's independence, since Andersen was performing another service on top of already performing an audit.[7]

In fact, it was generally known in the industry that Arthur Andersen actually incentivized partners to cross-sell far more consulting services than their own service lines. Other firms, and Andersen were known to incentivize cross-selling nonattest services on top of the auditing services already provided. Andersen had a reputation for isolating accountants who didn't want to take on the direction that Andersen was going in. Repeatedly, Andersen rewarded those involved with the firm's most troubled clients, while others were shown the door. The goal was to take a preexisting audit, and use it as a segue into the area of consulting, a lucrative service.

There were partners and others who had business relationships with Andersen who highlighted the fact that there was a strong incentive to sell clients additional consulting services. In the past, there were firms who introduced formulas that reward cross-selling services. Some firms even docked the pay of their auditors.

Accounting firms have in the past routinely determined annual partner pay raises using formulas that reward cross-selling – selling nonaudit services to audit clients, according to sources. Concern about how much the companies – much less the individual auditors – profit from that has already inspired substantial investor concern about the quality of audits and the reliability of corporate financial results.

"It used to be that the audit partners hung garlic outside their doors to keep the consulting guys away. Then firms started to incent partners to cross-sell in the 1980s," said John Rothschild, a former public accounting partner at a large firm, though not one of today's Big Five, whose pay was also based in part on his winning business.

There have been some who experienced these selling pressures who noted that "audit partners were those who never put their career in jeopardy." But, at the end of the day, cross-selling was rewarded and highly encouraged.[8]

---

[7] https://www.mckendree.edu/academics/scholars/issue4/stinson.htm.
[8] http://www.chicagotribune.com/news/chi-0209010315sep01-story.html.

When Sarbanes-Oxley was ultimately passed, it restricted the ancillary services that external auditors provided their clients. More specifically, Sarbanes-Oxley stated:

The auditor is prohibited from providing the following nonaudit services to an audit client, including its affiliates:

1. Bookkeeping
2. Financial information systems design and implementation
3. Appraisal or valuation services, fairness opinions, or contribution-in-kind reports
4. Actuarial services
5. Internal audit outsourcing services
6. Management functions or human resources
7. Broker-dealer, investment adviser, or investment banking services
8. Legal services and expert services unrelated to the audit

In addition to the specific prohibited services, audit committees should consider whether any service provided by the audit firm may impair the firm's independence in fact or appearance.[9]

That had a significant impact on the remaining Big Four accounting firms.

In 2018, three of the Big Four accounting firms (PWC, EY, and KPMG) announced their efforts to stop offering consulting services to audit customers in an effort to restore public trust in a sector shaken by corporate scandals.

KPMG released a statement in November 2017 that the firm will phase out advisory work for its British accounting clients. Meanwhile PwC UK CEO, Kevin Ellis, announced their involvement with providing unrelated audit services for their audit clients.[10]

Death begets life. The mandatory prohibition of providing a wide range of nonattestation and consulting services and pressure to be and appear independent have bred new life for the consulting departments once engrained in public accounting firms. From Arthur Andersen's closure, firms

---

[9]https://www.sec.gov/info/accountants/audit042707.htm.

[10]https://www.reuters.com/article/us-britain-accounts/pwc-ey-join-kpmg-in-banning-consulting-for-audit-customers-idUSKCN1PO1RC.

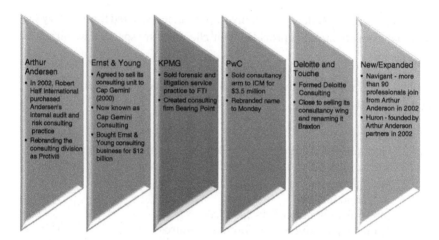

FIGURE 4.1 Notable firm acquisitions and divestitures.

like Accenture, Huron, Protiviti, and Navigant were born. See Figure 4.1 for a firm's efforts and impacts, in regard to continuing auditing services while maintaining the strict level of independence.[11]

In 2019, the AICPA Independence rules stated that AICPA professional standards require firms, including the firm's partners and professional employees, to be independent in accordance with the "Independence Rule" whenever the firm performs an attest engagement for an attest client.

A firm and its staffs are not required to be independent to perform services that are not attest services (for example, financial statement preparation, tax preparation, or advice or consulting services, such as personal financial planning) if they are the only services the firm provides to a client.[12]

That is consistent with the PCAOB rules, which state that a member or his or her firm performing an attest engagement for a client may also perform other nonattest services for that client. Before a member performs other services for an attest client, he or she must evaluate the effect of such services on his or her independence. In particular, care should be taken not to perform management functions or make management decisions for the attest client.

[11]https://www.consultancy.eu/news/1131/the-history-of-management-and-technology-consultancy-bearingpoint.

[12]https://www.aicpa.org/interestareas/professionalethics/resources/tools/downloadabledocu-ments/plain%20english%20guide.pdf.

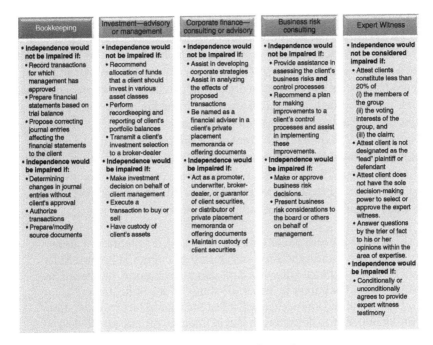

Bookkeeping	Investment—advisory or management	Corporate finance—consulting or advisory	Business risk consulting	Expert Witness
• Independence would not be impaired if: • Record transactions for which management has approved • Prepare financial statements based on trial balance • Propose correcting journal entries affecting the financial statements to the client • Independence would be impaired if: • Determining changes in journal entries without client's approval • Authorize transactions • Prepare/modify source documents	• Independence would not be impaired if: • Recommend allocation of funds that a client should invest in various asset classes • Perform recordkeeping and reporting of client's portfolio balances • Transmit a client's investment selection to a broker-dealer • Independence would be impaired if: • Make investment decision on behalf of client management • Execute a transaction to buy or sell • Have custody of client's assets	• Independence would not be impaired if: • Assist in developing corporate strategies • Assist in analyzing the effects of proposed transactions • Be named as a financial adviser in a client's private placement memoranda or offering documents • Independence would be impaired if: • Act as a promoter, underwriter, broker-dealer, or guarantor of client securities, or distributor of private placement memoranda or offering documents • Maintain custody of client securities	• Independence would not be impaired if: • Provide assistance in assessing the client's business risks and control processes • Recommend a plan for making improvements to a client's control processes and assist in implementing these improvements. • Independence would be impaired if: • Make or approve business risk decisions. • Present business risk considerations to the board or others on behalf of management.	• Independence would not be considered impaired if: • Attest clients constitute less than 20% of (i) the members of the group (ii) the voting interests of the group, and (iii) the claim; • Attest client is not designated as the "lead" plaintiff or defendant • Attest client does not have the sole decision-making power to select or approve the expert witness. • Answer questions by the trier of fact to his or her opinions within the area of expertise. • Independence would be impaired if: • Conditionally or unconditionally agrees to provide expert witness testimony

FIGURE 4.2 Services and their impact on independence.

Before performing other services, the member should establish an understanding with the client regarding the objectives of the engagement, the services to be performed, management's responsibilities, the member's responsibilities, and the limitations of the engagement. It is preferable that this understanding be documented in an engagement letter.

The examples in Figure 4.2 identify the effect that performance of other services for an attest client can have on a member's independence. These examples are not intended to be all-inclusive of the types of other services performed by members.[13]

In addition to independence, the general standards listed under the AICPA Code of Professional Conduct apply to litigation services such as competence, due professional care, planning and supervision, and sufficient relevant data. Gathering sufficient data is a key aspect of the supporting work performed by an expert, one that can have crucial consequences on whether the work product can be relied upon in a court of law and whether the expert will be allowed to testify.

---

[13]https://pcaobus.org//Standards/EI/Pages/ET101.aspx.

Additionally, the AICPA also publishes the Litigation Services and Applicable Professional Standards Special Report, which states that a practitioner has to obtain sufficient data to "provide a reasonable basis for his conclusions or recommendations for any professional services performed. In litigation, data are usually obtained through discovery, including depositions, interrogatories, and document production motions. In addition, the data-gathering process may include a review of relevant documents, research and analysis, and interviews. The nature and extent of the data will vary with each engagement and may include the practitioner's computations and analysis and other information-supporting conclusions." The expert can rely on the attorney to comply with the applicable rules of evidence. However, the expert's conclusions and judgments can only be based on sufficient relevant data.

The courts have also established rules for the determination of admissible evidence and expert testimony. In particular, the Federal Rules of Evidence address opinions and expert testimony. For example, Rule 702, "Testimony by Experts," states: If scientific, technical, or other specialized knowledge will assist the trier of fact to understand the evidence or to determine a fact in issue, a witness qualified as an expert by knowledge, skill, experience, training, or education, may testify thereto in the form of an opinion or otherwise, if:

1. the testimony is based upon sufficient facts or data,
2. the testimony is the product of reliable principles and methods, and
3. the witness has applied the principles and methods reliably to the facts of the case.

In addition, Rule 703, "Bases of Opinion Testimony by Experts," also states:

The facts or data in the particular case upon which an expert bases an opinion or inference may be those perceived by or made known to the expert at or before the hearing. If of a type reasonably relied upon by experts in the particular field in forming opinions or inferences upon the subject, the facts or data need not be admissible in evidence in order for the opinion or inference to be admitted. The proponent of the opinion or inference shall not disclose facts or data that are otherwise inadmissible to the jury unless the court determines that their probative value in assisting the jury to evaluate the expert's opinion substantially outweighs their prejudicial effect.

Interestingly, Canadian expert witnesses must certify with the court their acknowledgement of expert's duty (Form 53), a form that has to be signed by the expert. The mandatory requirements for expert reports are set out in sub-rule 53.03(2.1) of the Rules of Civil Procedure that state that expert reports must contain the following information:

1. The expert's name, address, and area of expertise.
2. The expert's qualifications and employment and educational experiences in his or her area of expertise.
3. The instructions provided to the expert in relation to the proceeding.
4. The nature of the opinion being sought and each issue in the proceeding to which the opinion relates.
5. The expert's opinion respecting each issue and, where there is a range of opinions given, a summary of the range and the reasons for the expert's own opinion within that range.
6. The expert's reasons for his or her opinion, including a description of the factual assumptions on which the opinion is based, a description of any research conducted by the expert that led him or her to form the opinion, and a list of every document, if any, relied on by the expert in forming the opinion.
7. An acknowledgment of expert's duty (Form 53) signed by the expert.

One item in this checklist that may be of particular concern for lawyers is the express requirement for the expert to disclose in their report the instructions provided to them in relation to the proceeding. While this is not something new, lawyers must be aware that they may not be able to withdraw instructions given to an expert, especially when you consider this requirement in conjunction with the newly codified Expert's Duty section.

U.S. accounting and financial experts can be subject to *Daubert* challenges resulting in their exclusion and inability to testify on the issues they have been hired to opine on. According to Rule 702 of the Federal Rules of Evidence,

A witness who is qualified as an expert by knowledge, skill, experience, training, or education may testify in the form of an opinion or otherwise if:

(a) the expert's scientific, technical, or other specialized knowledge will help the trier of fact to understand the evidence or to determine a fact in issue;

(b) the testimony is based on sufficient facts or data;

(c) the testimony is the product of reliable principles and methods; and

(d) the expert has reliably applied the principles and methods to the facts of the case.[14]

Big Four accounting firm PricewaterhouseCoopers (PwC) publishes an annual study on *Daubert* challenges to financial and accounting experts. The study explores recurring themes they see in *Daubert* challenges and presents recent, illustrative cases. PwC partner Doug Branch leads the study, which has been published annually for the past 18 years. According to Mr. Branch, nearly half (48%) of financial experts are excluded. "That number of exclusions presented in our study is artificially low, as it does not include 'motions in limine' that are granted, thereby limiting the expert's testimony. If one was to incorporate those rulings, rates could be much higher." A *motion in limine* is a *motion* filed by a party to a lawsuit that asks the court for an order or ruling limiting or preventing certain evidence from being presented by the other side at the trial of the case. This can restrict the expert's opinions, findings and analysis, and negatively impact their position.

Mr. Branch anticipates this trend will continue. "As more case law becomes available, it provides attorneys with a playbook on how to address financial experts. Financial experts face a challenging task. Unlike other experts, such as those that address highly scientific areas such as medical and engineers, accountants rely heavily on financial data. Many times that data is imperfect and/or incomplete. That can open an accounting or financial expert to weaknesses that are exploited during their testimony."

Mr. Branch advises experts to remain diligent by focusing on avoiding data-related exclusions. As stated by Mr. Branch, the "use and misuse of data is a common stumbling block for financial experts." Errors include "not including enough data, using data selectively, or failing to verify the reasonableness of data provided by third parties."

According to the annual survey, testimony not being based on sufficient facts or data has been the most frequent reason for reliability exclusions. PwC has been studying this issue since 2000, collecting data and statistics from actual cases. In its latest 2018 publication and in the 18 years since the U.S. Supreme Court's 1999 ruling in *Kumho Tire Co. v. Carmichael*, PwC has analyzed 2,410 financial expert challenges, including 206 financial expert challenges decided during calendar year 2017.

---

[14]Rule 702 of Federal Rules of Evidence.

One of the recurring themes identified in the past 18 years that resulted in exclusion of experts includes the use and misuse of data: Which data are relevant and applicable, how much data are enough, are the data reliable and applicable to your case?

PwC notes that this year the exclusion rate of financial expert testimony, 48%, is in line with the 18-year average. Of these excluded financial experts, 29% were partially excluded, and only 19% were fully excluded, indicating that the majority of financial experts challenged were ultimately permitted to testify in some form.

The Supreme Court's decision in the *Daubert* case entrusted to judges a "gatekeeping" role in evaluating the qualifications of expert witnesses and the relevance and reliability of their testimony. In performing this gatekeeping role, courts generally prefer not to keep "a heavy hand on the gate" and tend to work under the presumption of admissibility.[15] This approach is demonstrated by a 55% average acceptance rate of financial expert testimony after a challenge is filed over the last five years.

Rule No. 702 of the Federal Rules of Evidence (FRE) permits a qualified expert to testify if, among other factors, the testimony is based on "sufficient facts or data." This factor has been a common stumbling block for financial experts, and is the most frequent reason for reliability exclusions. Common errors by experts include not collecting sufficient data, using data selectively, or failing to verify the accuracy of data provided by third parties.

FRE No. 702 indicates that an expert can be qualified to testify based on his or her "knowledge, skill, experience, training, or education." Depending on the situation, each of these factors may be ascribed a different weight. For example, deep industry experience may not be necessary in a lost profits case if the expert has significant experience in lost profits calculations across a range of industries. Similarly, experience working in an accounting department may not be a sufficient demonstration of qualifications if such experience is not accompanied by accounting education and training.

Daubert challenges have become more prominent in the last few years. Michael Wagner is a senior adviser at a damages consulting firm who has testified as a financial expert in more than 140 trials. He says, "It's no surprise to have his testimony challenged or even occasionally ruled inadmissible, but that in recent years I have seen *Daubert* motions take over. Every case I'm in, there's extensive *Daubert* motions, probably every single one," he said. "That didn't used to be the case, but now it is standard practice."[16]

---

[15]PwC, "Daubert Challenges to Financial Experts," yearly study of trends and outcomes, 2000–2016.
[16]Interview with author.

Mr. Wagner has had his entire testimony excluded before, based on lack of methodology. Recently, a district judge excluded a significant portion of his testimony for an upcoming trial over damages, holding that he failed to explain a key assumption in his survey-based opinions about what portions of profits were attributable to the other party's designs.

According to Mr. Wagner, "Rather than try to attack an expert's opinion on the stand during trial, patent attorneys are going hard and heavy to try to get expert testimony ruled out ahead of time via *Daubert* motions. It's become so common and that's where all the argument goes, there's more resolution going on there," he said. "Whether that's right or wrong I'm not in a position to say, that's a public policy issue, but I do think it's just gotten totally out of control."

Mr. Wagner now made the decision to retire and stopped taking on new cases when he turned 70 years old after a 41-year career as a financial expert. He says that "the inability to predict which opinions will be excluded under *Daubert* and the impact such an exclusion has on an expert's business is a punishing combination . . . because if this trend keeps going, everyone who takes any position is eventually going to be *Daubert*-ed a number of times."

As described in the PwC survey, "Federal Rule of Evidence 702 is the gate an expert witness must pass through on his way to court – one both inviting and imposing at the same time. Courts open it, often welcoming expert testimony into cases . . . . But when an expert witness's passage is challenged, the party sponsoring him must produce the three keys the gate requires: proving that the witness is qualified, his testimony relevant, and his opinions reliably formed. Produce all three, and the witness may pass on through. But forget even one and the gate will block his way."

Legal issues, such as contract interpretation or a conclusion of fraud, are the domain of the trier of fact. When financial experts veer into this territory, they typically find themselves being prevented from testifying on these issues. Financial experts can stay in the safe zone by testifying to issues within the domain of their expertise – for example, how a case demonstrates indicia of fraud, without making the ultimate legal conclusion of whether fraud occurred.

Federal Rule of Evidence No. 702, "Testimony by Experts," governs the admissibility of expert witness testimony and incorporates the precedents set by *Daubert*, *Kumho Tire*, and other rulings. Rule 702 provides that a qualified expert's testimony is admissible if it is both relevant and reliable, and identifies criteria for evaluating relevance and reliability. We used the criteria from Rule 702 to evaluate the reasons for financial expert witness exclusions.

- In 2017, **economists** faced the highest number of *Daubert* challenges. Over the last 18 years, of the three most common financial expert types, accountants and economists have been the most frequently challenged experts.

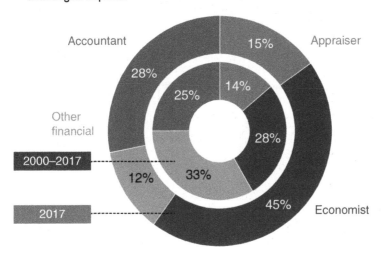

FIGURE 4.3 Expert challenges by area of expertise.

Lack of reliability, either on its own or in combination with other factors, has consistently been the main reason for financial expert witness exclusions over the course of our study. This pattern held true for 2017. When excluding testimony due to a lack of reliability, courts most frequently cited a lack of sufficient data or the use of methods that are not generally accepted as reasons for exclusion.

The second most common reason for exclusion in 2017 was that the testimony was not considered relevant to the case. This, again, is consistent with historical trends. When a financial expert is excluded for lack of relevance, it is often caused by testimony that was beyond the scope of the financial expert's role (e.g., testimony related to legal matters) or testimony that will not help the trier of fact (e.g., the opinion is not tied to the specific facts of the case).

The most common types of experts engaged to provide financial expert witness testimony are accountants, appraisers, and economists (see Figure 4.3). We also see other financial experts such as statisticians, financial analysts, finance professors, and so on.

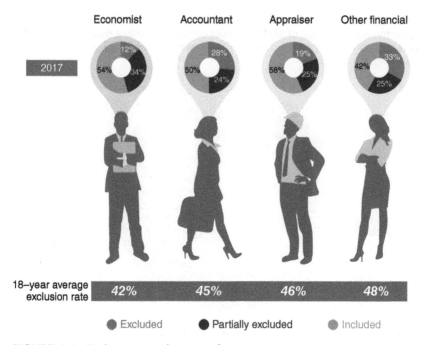

FIGURE 4.4 Exclusion rates by area of expertise.

In 2017, accountants had the highest exclusion rate of the three most common financial expert types (see Figure 4.4): 50% of *Daubert* challenges to accountants resulted in full or partial exclusion during 2017 – a rate that is 5% higher than the 18-year average exclusion rate for accountants.

There are times in which experts make a "fatal error" by "overestimating" the amount of data that are available, and the work they will be allowed to do to gain confirmation. They underestimate the obstacles standing in their way of completing the necessary tasks. It is common for experts to provide clients with a document request and work plans and an accompanying budget. If the expert provides an extensive request or work plan, yet only receives a small portion in response or is unable to complete certain steps, he or she can be challenged on the ground of not reviewing sufficient relevant data. In those circumstances, experts must seek alternatives and be able to explain how they were otherwise able to gain comfort.

The same goes for costs and budgets. If clients have an unreasonably restrictive budget, an expert can be accused of taking shortcuts, when a more thorough exam may have yielded different results.

In the UK, Civil Procedure Rule (CPR) 35 establishes rules on expert evidence, and stipulates that the parties may only rely on expert evidence with the court's permission, and where such evidence is reasonably required to resolve the proceedings. The purpose of CPR is to ensure that courts deal with cases efficiently and in a cost-effective matter. Oftentimes, judges determine they can assess the evidence without the assistance of an expert. Therefore, it is imperative that those involved in the dispute adequately assess the need for an expert early on, in the case management conference, and not underestimate the complexity of the financial matters. Making the complexity known can be a significant factor in whether an expert is accepted.

Further, Section 3 of the Civil Evidence Act 1972 provides that evidence is admissible in any case where the court accepts:

1. There exists a recognized expertise governed by recognized standards and rules of conduct
2. Capable of influencing the court's decision on any issue it has to decide
3. The witness to be called satisfies the court and has sufficient familiarity with and knowledge of the expertise in question

Further, opinion evidence, as offered by experts, must not only be relevant, which is similar to U.S. standards discussed earlier, it must also be necessary and reasonably required to resolve the issue.

Unreasonable conduct can also lead to penalties. The case often cited is *Arroyo and others v. Equion Energia Ltd.* In that matter, the unsuccessful claimant was penalized for the unreasonable behavior of its experts. A large portion of the ruling pertained to litigation costs. The 2016 decision reads:

> The costs incurred in the litigation are huge by any standard. They run to tens of millions of pounds on each side and dwarf any sums that Claimant might have hoped to recover at trial even on the most optimistic projections.

In describing the work of various experts, the decision contained the following remarks, in that the experts:

> lost those qualities of objectivity and independence of mind which are essential for an expert in contested litigation and that he had become caught up in the siege-mentality which was painfully obvious on a number of occasions (on both sides) during the trial.

lacked the objectivity and scientific rigour that was required both by the task and the standards he would set himself and by the Court

showed (unknowing) bias, and that he was prepared to include information in support of his conclusions without verifying it

the fourth report constituted a deliberate and serious breach of the Court's order limiting the scope of additional reports, was a serious error in judgement and placed unfair burdens on others.

That one case mentioned so many of the concepts included in this text. I bet you can underline them. It underscores the need to estimate the direction the matter can take at any turn.

Toby Galloway is co-chair of Winstead's Securities Litigation & Enforcement Practice Group. He also practices in the areas of white-collar defense, governmental & internal investigations, and business litigation. Before developing his private practice, he served as an attorney with the United States Securities and Exchange Commission, in roles of increasing responsibility, for more than 11 years. During his last four years at the SEC, Toby was the chief trial counsel for the Commission's Fort Worth Regional Office. In this capacity, he supervised all litigation for a four-station region. In addition, he handled his own caseload, prosecuting civil enforcement actions involving alleged violations of the federal securities laws. He also served as a Special Assistant United States Attorney for the Northern District of Texas, prosecuting white-collar crime. Mr. Galloway routinely works with experts, including myself. I remember Mr. Galloway sharing some great advice. "Say what you mean, and mean what you say. If accountants and other professionals would follow this rule, it would drastically reduce the number of regulatory actions and prosecutions involving financial reporting and accounting. Accountants should also stick to their guns. After all, it is their licenses that are on the line. This can be difficult when the pressure is on, but it pays off in the end."

I co-chair the TAG Alliances Litigation and Alternative Disputes Resolutions Committee with some fascinating professionals from around the globe. One such gentleman is John Sullivan, co-chair of Commercial Litigation Group Harper Grey LLP, in Vancouver. He has written and lectured on a variety of commercial litigation topics. He has been published in both Canada and the United States in such journals as the *Canadian Bar Review*, the *Washington Bar News*, and the *Oregon Creditor-Debtor Newsletter*. He has been a guest lecturer for the Canadian Institute as well as the BC Continuing Legal Education Society. He routinely works on litigation matters involving accountants. Mr. Sullivan mentioned that while he has not encountered "evil, ill-willed accountants," he has seen those who ventured into areas they were best to have avoided. According to Mr. Sullivan, "Accountants should stick to what they know best. Accepting a matter, while knowing they lack the requisite skillset is a recipe for disaster. It can not only lead to decisions that are detrimental to the client, it can also lead to damages to unintended third parties that rely on the information." He added that sometimes, the accountants do not realize the magnitude of their offerings. "As the markets become more globalized, the reliance on accountants and the financial information they produce is even more paramount. If confidence in the accountants wavers, it's felt through the entire system."

A particular case I worked on a few years ago is particularly representative of the issues addressed in this chapter. The case involved a False Claims Act (FCA) allegation first filed in the first half of 2012 with a final conclusion after appeal in favor of our client rendered toward the end of 2017.

The False Claim Act, otherwise known as the Lincoln Law, is another law that tasks organizations to prevent fraud and misconduct when working with governmental agencies. According to the False Claim Act, §3729, liability arises for any person who

(A) knowingly presents, or causes to be presented, a false or fraudulent claim for payment or approval; (B) knowingly makes, uses, or causes to be made or used, a false record or statement material to a false or fraudulent claim; (C) conspires to commit a violation of subparagraph (A), (B), (D), (E), (F), or (G); (D) has possession, custody, or control of property or money used, or to be used, by the Government and knowingly delivers, or causes to be delivered, less than all of that money or property; (E) is authorized to make or deliver a document certifying receipt of property used, or to be used, by the Government and, intending to defraud the Government, makes or delivers the receipt without completely knowing that the information on the receipt is true; (F) knowingly buys, or receives as a pledge of an obligation or debt, public property from an officer or employee of the Government, or a member of the Armed Forces, who lawfully may not sell or pledge property; or (G) knowingly makes, uses, or causes to be made or used, a false record or statement material to an obligation to pay or transmit money or property to the Government, or knowingly conceals or knowingly and improperly avoids or decreases an obligation to pay or transmit money or property to the Government . . . .[17]

---

[17]FCA §3729.

Simply submitting a false claim does not make one liable. To be liable, a person must have knowledge of the falsity of the information provided. According to the FCA, it means that a person "(i) has actual knowledge of the information; (ii) acts in deliberate ignorance of the truth or falsity of the information; or (iii) acts in reckless disregard of the truth or falsity of the information . . . ."[18]

The FCA also states that a claim

(A) means any request or demand, whether under a contract or otherwise, for money or property and whether or not the United States has title to the money or property, that— (i) is presented to an officer, employee, or agent of the United States; or (ii) is made to a contractor, grantee, or other recipient, if the money or property is to be spent or used on the Government's behalf or to advance a Government program or interest, and if the United States Government – (I) provides or has provided any portion of the money or property requested or demanded; or (II) will reimburse such contractor, grantee, or other recipient for any portion of the money or property which is requested or demanded . . . .[19]

If found guilty, a person is "liable to the United States Government for a civil penalty of not less than $5,000 and not more than $10,000, as adjusted by the Federal Civil Penalties Inflation Adjustment Act of 1990 (28 U.S.C. 2461 note; Public Law 104-410), plus 3 times the amount of damages which the Government sustains because of the act of that person."[20]

In this particular case, we were hired as experts for the defendant, who was sued in 2012 by a former competitor. I was tasked with analyzing the facts in the case to determine whether the government sustained financial damages, and if so, calculate the amount. I was also asked to read the opposing expert's report, and rebut any claims or assertions that were contrary to the facts produced in the case.

Upon reading the opposing expert's report, I noticed errors, omissions, and inconsistencies in his methodology. As a result, the expert altered his damage calculation at least three times through successive reports. The expert's

---

[18]FCA §3729.
[19]FCA §3729.
[20]FCA §3729.

original report asserted damages exceeding several hundred million dollars, and it was based on critical assumptions that, according to the expert, would be determined by testimony at the time of trial. He did not cite evidence or supporting documentation.

This brings up the issue of underestimating the outcome of an engagement. Some experts may make the incorrect determination that a particular case will not be going to trial in front of a judge or jury and write their report based on the hope of a large settlement number. I often wondered whether the plaintiff assumed the case would settle, and as such, the expert was simply told to do his best. As the trial setting became more imminent, it was clear certain documentation would not exist. That would explain the rationale for the statement "will be provided during trial" and "I was told" [to accept certain assumptions].

As can be seen in the rest of the story, underestimating the likelihood of trial can have dire consequences. After issuing his report, the expert was deposed and asked to defend his damage calculation and underlying assumptions. It is clear from reading the transcript of his deposition that the expert did not anticipate at the time of his writing that he would have to defend his assumptions. He claims almost 40 (!) times during his deposition that several supporting assumptions or facts would be determined at trial. He also repeated on several occasions that he relied on Counsel for numerous assumptions of facts.

Ultimately, the Defendant was exonerated in this matter, and the Plaintiff was awarded zero. As it related to the damage calculation, the decision stated that the Plaintiff's damages expert failed to provide support for the numbers he used. As stated in the appeal opinion, "Nothing in the record supports [his] valuation . . . . If the government received units of equivalent value, and thus has already enjoyed the benefit of its bargain, then the proper measure of actual damages should be zero." Additionally, the decision stated the Plaintiff damage experts, did not testify in support of the values he used. Instead he claimed he "was advised by counsel that the evidence presented in the trial will show . . . ." The expert further testified that there was no ascertainable value for the products so he could not render an opinion with respect to what the actual benefit to the United States Government would be. He claimed, "I have no expertise and – and render no opinion with respect to the actual benefit those units have to the United States Government." He concluded that the premise of his calculations was that the product was not compliant with the federal standards. Yet Defendant had certified that in fact during the damage period, it was compliant with those standards.

We have spent time addressing auditors and outside experts. What about the management of the company?

 ## MANAGEMENT AND INTERNAL AUDIT

Now, before we move on completely, remember: External auditors, expert witnesses, and fraud examiners are generally hired by management or those representing management. Any failure by those parties also has a direct impact on management. Missed deadlines, exclusions, or even a restatement can be devastating to organizations.

For this narrative, I include executive management and internal auditors as one and the same. Further, companies that have audit committees should also take note. Many companies underestimate the resource needs of those tasked with governance. Time and time again, internal audit departments cite lack of resources as their number-one risk. In fact, in my 25 years of presenting, I have never had *one* hand raised when I asked the audience, "How many of you feel adequately staffed?" I mean, not a single one. It is understandable, in that internal audit departments are cost centers, meaning they do not produce revenue. It is very difficult to ascertain the bottom-line impact of their efforts to deter fraud. It is also very difficult to measure the return on the investment in those in areas.

In 2015, the Institute of Internal Auditors published a four-part series entitled "We're Understaffed." It went into excruciating detail about the overtime hours and weekend sacrifices internal auditors make. Sadly, not much has changed since then. I recently visited with the Senior Vice President of Internal Audit for one of the world's largest banks. This is her 28th year in the profession, and the third internal organization that she has led. Without exception, she has faced extensive challenges obtaining and retaining adequate resources. She attributed this to three primary themes:

1. Management does not always appreciate the effort necessary to detect, prevent, and deter fraud, or assess and test controls. Risks assessments are ever-changing and dynamic. There are no shortcuts. They are not "one size fits all" and always subject to governmental oversight. It's not until the government takes exception to your assessments that management realizes the impact of shortcuts.
2. Talent is in short supply, and therefore expensive. Management can also have "sticker shock" when it comes time to add up the costs. While

negotiating with management, you can lose a candidate. Further, a low-ball offer can turn off a candidate, who spreads the word and deters other candidates from applying.

3. Management can also be of the belief "fraud cannot happen to us" (see Chapter 1 – Forgetting the Present and the Past). What they do not realize is that when fraud occurs, it's too late. At that stage, the company begins spending good money after losing bad.

She left me with a quote I have heard many times: "If you think compliance is expensive, try noncompliance." Her biggest advice to internal auditors included the following:

1. *Plan accordingly.* The annual audit plans should reflect those areas of the organization you can accomplish with the resources you have, not what you hope to have. Overextending can lead to poor execution as a whole.

2. *Stand your ground.* Be prepared to defend your plan and resource needs. By risk-ranking your priorities, the areas you ultimately decide to audit and the associated team needs are critical. When it comes time to explain your decisions to management, hopefully they will see the benefit of addressing such areas and share your priorities.

3. *Provide the appropriate qualifications or limitations.* There are situations in which the internal auditor may be asked to take on an assignment in which they lack the relevant expertise (similar to expert witnesses). On those occasions, the preferred response is to seek a qualified third party to assist or lead. However, if that option is not available, then inform management and the audit committee that your report and findings will be "qualified" (just as external audit) or otherwise limited.

SUMMARY

Regardless of which accounting capacity you occupy, underestimating the effort can bring on a tsunami of unwelcomed issues. Whether it's erroneously predicting the outcome of a legal matter, or the time, skill set, or resources necessary to complete a task, you are at risk of violating standards of due professional care and failing to obtain sufficient relevant data to support your conclusions.

RECOMMENDATIONS

When faced with the challenges pertaining to U – Underestimating the Effort, there is a long list of considerations:

1. *Perform a personal risk assessment.* Regardless of the assignment, each project is accompanied by a personal risk. Accepting a role brings with it certain pros and cons. For those projects that have equal, or more cons, compile a personal risk assessment, and address ways to mitigate those risks.

2. *Adhere to a system of checks and balances.* Prior to accepting a high-risk assignment, have supervisors or peers analyze the facts or the nature of the dispute to get a second opinion that you and/or your team possess the right skills.

3. *Be yourself.* Accept what you know, and what you don't. The most dangerous professionals are those that do not know what they don't know. Be honest with yourself. You have strengths and weaknesses. Own them! It is what makes you unique and a valuable learning tool to others.

4. *Seek out an objective resource and meaningful partnerships.* If you are honest in your assessment of your limitations, you will know exactly what areas need supplementation. Network with those in your industry and seek wise counsel in addressing any gaps that you expose in your skill set and core competencies.

5. *Disclose with accuracy.* Keep an accurate resume and CV. List your education background and professional experience. No one person can be all things. Your resume and CV speak on your behalf, when you are not afforded the chance. Make sure they tell the truth in your "absence."

6. *Compile flexible "budgets."* Avoid hard caps or fixed fees. Defense attorneys can assert "scope restrictions," and allude to the fact that had you been allowed to do more work, you might have reached different conclusions. Provide ranges, and communicate early and often when that range presents a risk of being inaccurate.

7. *Defend decisions.* If you find yourself in a position of having to defend an ultimate decision, explain the process you undertook to arrive at your conclusion. Hindsight being what it is, sometimes your conclusions are determined to ultimately be inaccurate. Be prepared to document how you arrived at your conclusion, why you felt the initial decision was correct, and allow yourself the opportunity to change your mind as new information is obtained.

8. *Never assume, or "underestimate," the potential outcomes of a matter.* Assuming a case will settle, that you will never be "audited,'" or that certain facts will never become known is not an effective strategy. The most prudent approach is to prepare for the worst-case scenario.

Case Study: The Accountant Who Objected to Objectivity

A Buyer and Seller have entered into an arrangement in which the Buyer agrees to pay 1.5 times revenue, plus a percentage asset value for the Seller. After paying a $1 million advance, the Buyer has 30 days to complete their due diligence in order to complete the sale. The advance will be returned if the Buyer finds material adverse information to the financial statements. Otherwise, the advance will be credited to the sales price or forfeited.

After waiting two weeks, the Buyer, who is actually a friend of yours, calls you to ask whether you can take on the assignment and complete due diligence. Although you have never completed a due diligence assignment, nor have you had any fraud training, as a sole practicing tax CPA, you feel you have a basic understanding of financial statements. You do not tell your friend that you have no experience in this area. After all, you have recently gone through a divorce and need the money. You accept the assignment and tell the friend you will meet the deadlines.

Your engagement letter between you and your friend states:

I will only perform the procedures and examine areas you specify. As such, my findings will be limited to those specific areas. Had I performed additional procedures, I may have had additional findings. Further, my report is intended solely for your use and should not be relied upon by any third party.

While the purchase price was based on a combination of revenue and asset value, your client asked that you primarily focus on revenue. This limitation was based on the fact that another CPA firm had recently completed an inventory verification as part of a bank's refinancing. While there are no "audited" financial statements, you determine this gives you a level of comfort over the largest asset, so you accept the limitation. Considering the time constraints, you decide it is unnecessary to contact the CPA firm and do not test their work.

(Continued)

(Continued)

You complete the assignment to what you believe is your best ability and only have immaterial findings, and so you "bless" the presented financial statements of the company. Still, you add the following paragraph to your report:

> This assignment has been completed in accordance with the Statement on Standards for Consulting Services promulgated by the American Institute of Certified Public Accountants and does not constitute an audit or other attestation service, the objective of which is the expression of an opinion on financial statements or a portion thereof. Accordingly, I do not express any such opinion. Further, our services did not include consideration of internal controls for the purpose of expressing an opinion on the internal controls over financial reporting. Accordingly, I express no such opinion.

It makes you happy to give your friend "good" news. Unbeknownst to you, the Buyer uses your report you obtain financing from a bank.

Within weeks of completing the purchase, the Buyer's Internal Audit Department finds fraud pertaining to both revenue and asset value.

1. Should you have accepted this engagement? Why or why or why not?
2. If "no," under what conditions would you have accepted this?
3. Despite having a limitations in your engagement letter and your report, what exposure might you face pertaining to:
   a. Lack of experience and failing to disclose it?
   b. Lack of analysis on inventory?
   c. Your reliance on another CPA?
   d. The bank's reliance on your report?
4. During the assignment, what could you have done to mitigate the exposures identified above?
5. What is the significance of: –
   a. The Buyer being your friend?
   b. Your lack of fraud training?
   c. Not having "audited" financial statements?
   d. Your definition of "good" news?
   e. The overall limitations presented in your engagement letter and your report?
6. What are some of the procedures the Buyer's internal auditor may have performed to identify fraud?

CHAPTER FIVE

D – Determining the Outcome Before the Work

Accounting Humor

Q – What do actuaries do to liven up their parties?
A – They invite an accountant. ▰

T HIS CHAPTER PROVIDES A detailed discussion on predication, professional skepticism, objectivity, bias, and due professional care.

 INTRODUCTION

Have you ever watched a thriller, and thought, "I know how this will end," as you guess your way to the climax? I do not have much time for movies, but growing up in Louisiana, I often thought of that same expression when someone boasted, "Hold my beer and watch this!" I knew exactly what to expect. I simply prayed they would not get anything on me or drag me into the disaster ahead.

In taking on an assignment, we can often fall into the trap of confirming our expectations, rather than applying an objective, healthy dose of professional skepticism. Do you expect to find fraud? Or are you certain that fraud does not exist? Are there damages in this breach-of-contract matter, or have you already determined there are no valid claims?

My first assignment with the Louisiana Legislative Auditor's Office (LLA) was in Lake Providence, Louisiana. The sheriff, Dale Rinicker, was accused of receiving bribes and kickbacks. I was given that assignment because the town was less than an hour from the farm on which I was born and raised. The rationalization was that I looked like and talked like a local, meaning I could easily blend in as we conducted surveillance. I didn't know whether to thank them or curse them! I had long retired my overalls and corncob pipe (well, not completely – I saved them for the weekends).

Lake Providence is in East Carroll Parish and had a population of 5,200 in 1995. It was a beautiful town with an oxbow lake almost six miles long, encircled by cypress trees and home to gators and possums. Not long before I was assigned to the case, Lake Providence was featured on the cover of *Time* magazine on August 15, 1994, as the poorest community in the United States. *Time* explained the town had no public parks or swimming pools, no movie theaters, no shopping malls, not even a McDonald's or a Walmart. In fact, business in Lake Providence, Louisiana, was so bad that even the pawnshop had shut down. "The only recreation we have," says a resident, "is poor people's fun: drinking, drugs, fighting, and sex." "We've got all the problems they have in New York and Chicago, but nothing to fight them with," says Mayor James W. Brown Jr. It was a shocking exposé of the poverty lurking in our own backyard, and residing under our noses.

Sheriff Rinicker was elected in 1983. He was the sheriff of East Carroll Parish. His name dominated front pages of town papers across north Louisiana almost immediately, as the man he defeated was found guilty in 1985 for plotting to kill him. Only in Louisiana! Allegations surfaced almost 10 years later that Sheriff Rinicker received bribes and kickbacks associated with a privatized prison, East Carroll Detention Center.

In 1995, prisons were paid $28 per inmate per day. The prominent, wealthy, and well-known owner of the prison was accused of paying the sheriff either under the table or for his undisclosed and hidden ownership interest. Of course, the premise was that this was in exchange for the sheriff's approval of the facilities' construction, and the transfer of inmates who could have otherwise be going to state or other local facilities. We did not know how the payments were facilitated or how the sheriff was laundering the money. We set out to find out.

I was assigned to a Senior Auditor, Maurice "Moe" Hattier. The drive from Baton Rouge to Lake Providence was almost four hours; we didn't have state vehicles, so Moe drove us up in his brand-new Acura. An hour outside of Baton Rouge, near the Mississippi state line, Mo decided to pass a slow-moving vehicle during a hilly stretch of highway. As he initiated the pass, we were met by a lady in a fast-approaching car. Within a split second, our car rolled three or four times, coming to rest upside down on its cab. Remarkably, we were unscratched, which was good, because my insurance had not even kicked in. (The lady kindly pulled over, called her husband, and made sure that we were okay. Those were the good old days when people still stopped.) We were met within 30 minutes by the LLA's Assistant Legislative Auditor Allen Brown, and General Counsel Rodger Harris. The assignment would have to wait a week, and I would drive going forward. Interestingly enough, Moe later went on to the FBI, and placed first in his class in the automotive test. Ha!

After weeks of surveillance and dozens of interviews, we received our first break when the sheriff's childhood friend and "money mule" confessed to participating in the scheme by receiving the money (in exchange for a small fee). The informant disclosed that he would go to the owner's office to receive the payments. He would then pick up the sheriff each Friday, and drive to Monroe to deposit the money. They went to a specific branch, as the sheriff's sister worked there. That enabled them to avoid the regulatory requirements involving Suspicious Activity Reports and Currency Transaction Reports, which required banks to complete forms for transactions involving large amounts of cash.

Once we received and documented the confession, we contacted the Western District of the US Attorney's Office, along with the FBI. They took part in the investigation going forward. It was truly a partnership that worked well. Eventually, we received indictments on federal charges of mail fraud, conspiracy to launder money, and money laundering. Rinicker was sentenced to five years and a $10,000 fine.

I could not have asked for a more exciting case to cut my teeth on. However, 25 years later, there is one exchange that stuck with me. At our first meeting with the sheriff, he confronted my two supervisors, Allen Brown and Daryl Purpera, the state's current Legislative Auditor. During the very first interview with Mr. Brown and Mr. Purpera, the sheriff was immediately confrontational. Certain things had already been written in the paper. The old adage – ain't no secrets in a small town – certainly applied here. The sheriff was concerned that considering the early press, he would have a difficult time denying the allegations. The sheriff barked, "You need to keep your mouth shut. If someone says I was fucking in the bushes, everyone is going to believe it whether I am or not."

That quote has remained with me all these years, not only for the absurdity of it, but for what the sheriff was attempting to do. He was attempting to challenge our objectivity. Our bias. He was accusing us of spreading falsehoods that would prevent him from receiving a fair trial. He was setting it up to claim it was a "witch hunt" (a very popular and often-tweeted word these days). I am not sure what comments the sheriff was referencing, if any, but considering our case and the facts supporting our conclusions, it would have been challenging to have slandered or libeled him. However, our words outlive us. Salacious news, such as an investigation or allegations, travels quickly. Similar to "If you do a good job, they tell their friends. If you do a bad job, they tell everyone they see."

My life-long mentor, the man who gave me my start, (and put up with more of my nonsense than anyone should!), has seen this tactic used over and over during his 40-year fraud-fighting career in Louisiana. Allen Brown practices, and preaches, the importance of lack of bias and objectivity during investigations and those charged with prosecuting the perpetrators. According to Mr. Brown, some prosecutors, not all, were reluctant to prosecute and juries were difficult as, in some cases, the fraudsters were well-liked members of the community. It could be that they had money and political power that could be brought to bear against those who did them wrong. The LLA had much success when we were able to get the matters referred to the federal authorities.

We have all heard of the O.J. Simpson murder case in 1995. Those who that are old enough to have lived through it remember being captivated by the white Ford Bronco, and the soap opera the trial became. One of the most talked-about characters of that opera was Mark Fuhrman, an LAPD detective. Mr. Fuhrman was one of the first detectives on this scene and was said to have found the "bloody glove" at the victim's estate, the site of the crime. Defense counsel alleged that Mr. Fuhrman's past was littered with racial bias and alleged misconduct. The Defense sought to go back to comments Mr. Fuhrman made in hearings 15 years prior, as well as to review records from an internal matter in 1988. The judge denied the Defense's request, however, but tapes surfaced that contradicted Mr. Fuhrman's testimony on whether he had used racial slurs. The Defense's mission was accomplished. Mr. Fuhrman's credibility had been tarnished, and it cast a long shadow of reasonable doubt with the jury. In fact, multiple media outlets reported that the Defense's success was largely due to the doubts they were able to place on Mr. Fuhrman's credibility. Fuhrman was charged with perjury, to which he pleaded no contest. He received three years' probation, and paid a $200 fine. He retired during the trial, and like many of the major figures involved, wrote a book about his experiences.

As auditors and investigators, we have to be extremely diligent in our words and actions, and be prepared to answer for them. One careless statement can result in expensive litigation and allow fraudsters to go free. It can also ruin your career and tarnish an innocent person. It can also help their defense strategy, which has become popular and effective in today's mainstream media.

In this chapter, our focus will be on interconnected concepts: objectivity, professional skepticism, bias, and due professional care, all of which pertain directly to the accountant's role as an objective party representing their profession. The lack of those principles can suggest that the accountant had already made up their mind . . . they had already determined the outcome.

We will walk through how decisions are made, including:

- Whether to conduct an investigation or more thorough analysis.
- Defending the reasons why you did not.
- Whether you, as the accountant, can demonstrate your objectivity in discharging your responsibilities during such assignments.

 ## OBJECTIVITY

Objectivity in Investigations – Predication

One concept that coincides with objectivity and professional skepticism is predication. Predication refers to the circumstances taken as a whole, that would lead a reasonable, prudent professional to believe a fraud has occurred, is occurring, or will occur. Fraud investigations should not be conducted without predication. This does not mean there must be specific allegations, but there should be sufficient information that a reasonable professional would inquire. The ACFE manuals refer to predication as "assuming there is sufficient reason." An unhealthy balance (too much or too little) can impact your ability to consider whether an investigation is warranted.

The primary way defense attorneys defend their clients is to attack the investigator: to accuse them of being biased, or pursuing these claims for political or racial motives. The old saying, "If you can't attack the message, attack the messenger" comes to mind.

Consider this. Your supervisor approaches you and explains she wants to investigate an employee for violation of the corporate computer policy, and alleges the employee shops excessively and plays fantasy sports during the day.

You conduct the investigation and the allegations prove true. The employee is terminated for violating company policy, and as a result of being terminated for cause does not receive severance. If that employee retained counsel, how would you answer the following questions you were deposed by the defense attorney:

1. How did you identify my client for this inspection?
2. Do you know whether this employee was ever told this was inappropriate?
3. We these concerns ever documented in their performance reviews?
4. How many other employee computers did you analyze?
5. How many times have you shopped or played fantasy sports on your company-issued computer?
6. Who authorized you to violate the same policy that my client was terminated for breaching?
7. Has there ever been, to your knowledge, another investigation of this nature?
8. If so, what was the outcome? If not, why?

How would you confirm that the investigation had nothing to do with the employee's age? Race? Religion? Were there allegations of sexual harassment? Was the person a whistleblower? Does this give rise to allegations against the company of discrimination or civil rights violations? Do you see just how easy it is for the attorney to rewrite the narrative? Regardless of how blatant the abuse, by not consistently enforcing policies and administering consequences to offenders, a reasonable doubt can be seeded in the jury's mind. It can also lead to litigation.

The Cost Associated with Lack of Investigating

In the above narratives, I focused on investigative abuses. There can also be enormous costs in failing to investigate. The lack of investigating can also lead to questions, and can be just as detrimental. A case I commonly reference in my teaching is MoneyGram.

On November 9, 2012, MoneyGram International Inc., a global money services business, agreed to forfeit $100 million and enter into a deferred prosecution agreement with the Justice Department. MoneyGram admitted to criminally aiding and abetting wire fraud and failing to maintain an effective anti–money laundering program. The government explained that Money-Gram had received thousands of complaints from consumers who were victims of fraud, yet MoneyGram did not terminate the suspected agents. The fraud schemes generally involved agents targeting the elderly, in which consumers received false notifications that they had won the lottery, been hired as secret shoppers, or qualified for loans. The agents convinced the consumers to set up MoneyGram accounts, and send them payments for taxes or processing fees.

Additionally, the DOJ claimed that MoneyGram's chief compliance officer failed to ensure the company followed the anti–money laundering provisions required by the Bank Secrecy Act. More specifically, the language in the Act allowed for penalties against a "partner, director, officer or employee."

Among other allegations, they accused the compliance officer of failing to:

1. File suspicious activity reports on MoneyGram agents he knew or suspected were engaged in wrongdoing.
2. Perform adequate due diligence procedures.
3. Terminate relationships with high-risk agents.

The regulators stated:

> The individual failed to take required actions designed to guard the very system he was charged with protecting, undermining the purposes of the BSA. Holding him personally accountable strengthens the compliance profession by demonstrating that behavior like this is not tolerated within the ranks of compliance professionals.

In 2017, the compliance officer agreed to a three-year injunction barring him from performing a compliance function for any money transmitter and agreed to pay a $250,000 penalty. The Financial Crimes Enforcement Network (*FinCEN*), a bureau of the United States Department of the Treasury Agency, had initially imposed a $1 million fine.

Even executives who have no fraud or compliance training can train themselves to pay attention to changing employee behaviors to prevent schemes from continuing.

In 2002, another case of a lifetime found its way to me. A large oil and gas company called me on a Friday afternoon. The CEO and General Counsel informed me that they had discovered an errant fax submittal sheet, transferring $350,000 for "taxes" from a corporate bank account that was unknown to them, to what appeared to be a personal account at the same bank. It was directed by the controller, who had been with the company almost 25 years. The controller just happened to be on vacation for a few days (which I later learned was unusual in and of itself). It was at that point I realized I would be working out of town that weekend, so I informed the family that "it has happened again." Sadly, they were used to work life taking precedence over home life (not something to be proud of). I grabbed my project manager and forensic technology professional and drove five hours at about 4 p.m. that Friday.

My first meeting was with the company's General Counsel and CEO. In the few hours since I had spoken to them, they had obtained the bank statements from the "corporate" account and determined that more than $6 million in transactions had been processed through the account in the past several years. The account had been set up by the controller, who happened to be the only signor on the account. They were stunned, as they explained that he was one of the most tenured and trusted employees in the company. Further:

1. He lived in a modest home, which was commensurate with his salary.
2. He dressed commonly, and drove an older model pick-up truck.
3. He had been married to the same spouse for over 20 years and had a teenage daughter.
4. He and his family were active in the community and the church.
5. He had been with the company almost 25 years, was loyal, and never missed a day.

They saw no red flags that would suggest he was a fraudster and were devastated. They were adamant that he was the last one they would have suspected. However, after a few long pauses and a handful of questions, I learned:

1. The controller did not socialize with other staff, and never had. He was viewed as a loner.
2. The company had recently experienced issues with the controller using the company computer for personal purposes during work hours, and reprimanded him.
   a. The controller only began using the computer on his lunch hour, with his door shut.
   b. They then noticed his web usage actually increased significantly. The controller told his superiors he was day trading. They reminded him that it was still against corporate policy, and to stop. He did not.
   c. Then, the company restricted his access. He brought in his own computer and a remote Internet connection. The company ignored it going forward.
3. They had noticed a change in his behavior. He never took lunch and recently, as mentioned, always kept his door closed.

4. And no, come to think of it, he never took vacation.
5. He had unusual hobbies for an accountant, in that he subscribed to hand-to-hand combat magazines, such as *Soldier of Fortune*, and was fond of guns and knives. He often brought them to work. The company explained, "These things did not reconcile with his observed personality." Or did they?
6. Lastly, they explained how he became defensive any time he was asked about the tax variances, yet no one checked behind him or challenged him.

How many red flags can you now count? As we imaged his hard drive and began tracing the absconded funds to his personal accounts, we found that the controller was living a secret life. Yes, he was day trading, but he was also placing adult ads to attract a certain type of companion. He was a sugar daddy for multiple women, having purchased them homes, cars, plastic surgery, and even paying for one of their children's education. He had traveled to exotic locations (claiming it was work-related, yet it was on the weekends). He had an extensive file on each woman, along with every single dollar he had given them. (That is one thing about accountants; they even balance the "second" set of books!) Each file had the lady's name, photos, sexually charged chat logs, and every single transaction between them.

As we were continuing our computer and file review in his office that Sunday afternoon, in he walked. He calmly sat down in his chair, and stared blankly at me sitting behind his desk. Bluntly, he said, "You must be the auditors." I replied, "Yes."

He responded, "And I suppose you have some questions."

Again, I replied, "Yes. I have many."

My very first question was, "How did you think this would all end?"

He explained: "I always knew I would get caught. I just figured I had another year or two to enjoy things. I know I will be going away for a while, but man, I have had one helluva time."

I could not resist the second question: "Why on earth did you keep files on each of these women?"

"One, I never wanted them to be able to extort me, or pretend that I had a contractual obligation to continue paying them. Two, I did not want anyone to claim I coerced or raped them. And three, I knew I would have to determine the exact amount I took."

He was right about one thing; he did go away for a while. I went on to learn that his "rationalization" was a strong desire to beat the system, in that he was tired of being told what to do, and the computer restrictions sent him over the edge. He was also in his late fifties, and he felt he had worked his entire life and had nothing to show for it. He want to live a different lifestyle, and this was the only way he could have afforded it.

As unique as this case was, the rationalization was not all that dissimilar to many others. The flags were in broad daylight, and had there been the least bit of skepticism, the scheme would have unraveled quickly. It does not take an accountant or an attorney to recognize odd behavior, nor does it take a specialist to identify changes in someone's behavior or lifestyle. It simply takes paying attention and exercising diligence when things do not make sense. I have called this tendency "Hey Fever" and "Yellow Fever," in that it represents the fear of simply exclaiming, "Hey, this does not make any sense. Explain."

Speaking of prosecutors, there are even times when the government watchdog's skepticism and objectivity are challenged. Government agencies can be accused of being biased, or missing certain red flags. Even lawyers.

Take for example, the R. Allen Stanford and Stanford Financial Ponzi Scheme matter. In 2009, Stanford was arrested, and in 2012, he was indicted and was ultimately found guilty of running a $7 billion Ponzi scheme. He was sentenced to 110 years in prison (although I bet he will not serve all of them). Many felt the sentence was lenient, in that he was said to have defrauded over 30,000 investors in more than 113 countries. The jury found that 29 financial accounts located abroad and worth approximately $330 million were proceeds of Stanford's fraud and should be forfeited. As a result, as part of Stanford's sentence, the court imposed a personal money judgment of $5.9 billion.

But that is only part of the story. Questions emerged as to how Stanford was able to keep the SEC away so long. In a 159-page report release in 2010, the SEC Inspector General found that the SEC examiners in Fort Worth had suspected Stanford was running a massive Ponzi scheme as early as 1997, yet no action was taken. The report claims no enforcement action was taken because of "repeated decisions by Barasch to quash the matter." Spencer Barasch was the former head of enforcement for the SEC in Fort Worth, and had gone into private practice. The report stated the Stanford investigation began "immediately" after Barasch left the agency.

An investigation by Reuters, and confirmed by the SEC's report, showed that examiners for the agency recommended investigations into Stanford in 1997, 1998, 2002, 2004, and 2005. Reuters states that in three of those instances, Mr. Barasch personally overruled those recommendations.

Mr. Barasch explained that he made those decisions because he was not sure the SEC had statutory authority to investigate the offshore entity, and that his superiors had pressured the staff to avoid overly complex matters.

However, in June 2005, Mr. Barasch sought to represent and defend Mr. Stanford, and requested permission from the SEC. The agency denied the request and told him they determined it was a conflict of interest. He asked two more times and was told "no." However, records obtained during the investigation reveal that Mr. Barasch had gone against the SEC's position, and had worked for Mr. Stanford.

When asked by the SEC Inspector General why he had chosen that path, he responded, "Every lawyer in Texas and beyond is going to get rich over this case. Okay? And I hated being on the sidelines."

As the enforcement head in the Fort Worth Office, Mr. Barasch directed a number of high-profile SEC enforcement investigations and litigation in several areas of the securities industry. Among the more noteworthy enforcement actions he oversaw were

- Major financial fraud cases involving Royal Dutch Shell, Halliburton, TV Azteca, and the Fleming Companies;
- Regulatory cases against AIM, Southwest Securities, First Command, and HD Vest;
- Significant insider trading cases involving the securities of Hispanic Broadcasting Corp., AmeriCredit, and Carreker Corp; and
- More than 50 emergency enforcement actions involving securities scams targeting inexperienced investors, recovering close to $1 billion for investors.

Barasch received a number of awards during his tenure with the Commission, including the Irving M. Pollack Award for his dedication to public service and the SEC, and his fairness and compassion in dealing with the public and the staff.

In January 2012, Mr. Barasch agreed to pay the maximum civil fine of $50,000, and was denied the privilege of appearing or practicing before the Commission as an attorney for one year from the date of the Order. Mr. Barasch transitioned his practice from the law firm in 2014.

There was never any evidence that Mr. Barasch knew of the fraud at Stanford Financial. Mr. Barasch was never accused of participating in the scheme. Nonetheless, one can see how challenges to ethical standards could arise. You can see just how a career, even one as established and exemplary as Mr. Barasch's, can be permanently damaged in a matter of hours.

OBJECTIVITY IN OTHER AREAS

The standards for CPAs are clear. Objectivity is defined as a state of mind, a quality that lends value to the accountant's services. It is a distinguishing feature of the profession. The principle of objectivity imposes the obligation to be impartial, intellectually honest, and free of conflicts of interest. A CPA in public practice should be independent in fact and appearance when providing auditing and other attestation services.

A recent case grabbed headlines when an accountant's objectivity was challenged. In 2015, the SEC instituted a proceeding against Lynn Tilton and the company she managed, Patriarch Partners. Patriarch was the collateral managers for Zohar Funds, which were collateralized loan obligation funds. A CLO fund is a securitization vehicle in which a special-purpose entity raises capital through the issuance of secured notes and uses the proceeds to acquire a portfolio of commercial loans. The SEC explained the investors made the investments in the funds in return for the promise of regular interest payments and the repayment of their principal on a specified maturity date. The collateral manager determines what loans to purchase and is generally compensated through management fees. The SEC accused Ms. Tilton of misleading investors about the value of loans, and collecting $200 million in extra management fees. The allegations also included violations of GAAP as they pertained to impairment procedures. The case concerned $2.5 billion of loan pools. Part of Ms. Tilton's defense was that she relied on the advice of outside accountants in drafting the financial statements and their compliance with GAAP. The SEC cited trial testimony in their 2017 Initial Decision: "We've [Management] always relied on [our accountant] to provide us with some guidance [on GAAP]."

During the trial, Legal 360 and the *New York Post* each provided coverage that pertained to the outside accountant for Tilton's Companies. In fact, Legal 360 exclaimed that the "accountant found himself answering questions about emails he sent telling the private equity maven to 'be gorgeous' and 'be yourself.'" Obviously, the defense attorneys were questioning the accountant's objectivity during the cross-examination. The email evidence was voluminous, and excerpts included personal notes about Ms. Tilton's daughter, thoughts about each other's appearance, and emails alluding to a dispute between Ms. Tilton and the accountant's spouse. All of that may make for good television, but it was accounting terminology that struck a chord. Professional terms used casually such as "audit," "review," and "approve" warranted extensive discussion.

During the assignments, members of management sent various emails to the accountant, asking that he "review and approve" financial information. This is significant, as a "review" in accounting terms provides a level of assurance. The accountant responded that he did not correct management's use of the terms, but that it was generally understood that he only performed "agreed-upon procedures," which has no assurance. See Table 5.1.

As you can see, there is a significant difference between a "review" and "agreed-upon procedures." Moreover, an accountant can be seen as stepping into the shoes of management when "approving" certain transactions (source).

Nonetheless, after a lengthy trial, the matter against Ms. Tilton was dismissed. But most notably, the court opined that the "reliance on accountants" defense failed. The court stated four considerations in determining whether to grant credit on this particular claim:

1. That the person made complete disclosure to counsel (or other professional),
2. Sought the advice on the legality of intended conduct,

TABLE 5.1 Assurance provided per service offerings.

Service offering	Assurance provided	Comments
Compilation	None	CPA assists management in presenting financial information in the form of financial statements.
Review	Limited	CPA provides a limited assurance: "whether CPA is aware of material modifications that should be made to the financial statements to be in accordance . . . ."
Audit	High	CPA provides a high level of assurance: "reasonable assurance that the f/s statements are free of material misstatements." Not responsible for detecting fraud through collusion.
Agreed-upon procedures	None	Client and CPA agree to certain procedures, typically provided by the client. CPA provides no opinion or conclusion, but has the anticipation that the report will be relied upon by third parties.
Consulting standards	Depends	Assignment-specific

3. Received advice that the intended conduct was legal, and
4. Relied in good faith on the advice.

The court's opinion was that the evidence failed to show the accountant was asked about the particular accounting issues to which the suit pertained, and that despite the language in the email, the accountant merely responded to specific accounting questions on various topics, and looked over draft financial statements, raising questions that occurred to him related to GAAP compliance as well as checking administrative errors.

It is also important to note that Patriarch's controller was also scrutinized during the litigation. And ultimately, the court opined that there was no evidence that showed he was asked to opine on these matters, and that he followed the historical accounting practices learned from other employees and was not involved in impairing or fair valuing loans.

Pause for a moment; can you see how this entire situation could have been avoided? Improved communication. Clarification of roles. Scoping documents. Confirmation of assignments . . . the list can go on.

 ## DUE PROFESSIONAL CARE AND SKEPTICISM

Once the decision is made to investigate, or pursue further analysis, it has to be done with professional care. The AICPA's AU Section 230, "Due Professional Care in the Performance of Work," is the third general standard. It states that the auditor must exercise due professional care in the performance of the audit and the preparation of the report. Due professional care imposes a responsibility upon each professional within an independent auditor's organization to observe the standards of fieldwork and reporting. The matter of due professional care concerns what the independent auditor does and how well he or she does it. An auditor should possess "the degree of skill commonly possessed" by other auditors and should exercise it with "reasonable care and diligence" (that is, with due professional care). Section .07 specifies that due professional care requires the auditor to exercise *professional skepticism*. This is defined as an attitude that includes a questioning mind and a critical assessment of audit evidence. The auditor uses the knowledge, skill, and ability called for by the profession of public accounting to diligently perform, in good faith and with integrity, the gathering and objective evaluation of evidence. Paragraph .09 provides further clarity. The auditor neither assumes that management is dishonest nor assumes unquestioned honesty. In exercising professional skepticism, the auditor should not be satisfied with less than persuasive evidence because of a belief that management is honest.

Internationally, there is also an increased focus on skepticism. To illustrate the importance of professional skepticism, and to emphasize it as the cornerstone of the profession, in 2015 the International Auditing and Assurance Standards Board (IAASB), the International Ethics Standards Board for Accountants (IESBA), and the International Accounting Education Standards Board (IAESB) convened a small, cross-representational working group – the Professional Skepticism Working Group – to formulate views on whether and how each of the three boards' sets of international standards could further contribute to strengthening the understanding and application of the concept of professional skepticism as it applies to an audit.

This resulting publication highlights actions of the three boards regarding professional skepticism as it relates to auditors. For other professional accountants, the question was asked whether aspects of the concepts underlying professional skepticism also have relevance. The three standard-setting boards continue to liaise with their stakeholders to better understand how to improve, and encourage support for the exercise of professional skepticism

The Risk of Bias

Bias is actually the opposite of objectivity and professional skepticism. Bias is a tendency to act in a certain way for or against a certain person or group. We like to think of ourselves as impartial, but we are not. Consider bias in our everyday life. We have an inclination to associate with those who share our interests, who are most like us. Those biases can be deep-rooted and influenced by our history, education, and experience. We also join social and professional associations to benefit from our personal preferences. Consider your choice of college. The benefits can extend far past graduation, especially if the hiring manager for a particular job is also an alumnus. At your gym (assuming you make time to go!), doesn't a particular type of workout interest you? Reading clubs? Country clubs? Religious institutions? All have a networking element involving common interests.

As accountants, bias can creep into our subconscious. I will discuss two categories of bias:

1. Conscious
2. Unconscious

Conscious Bias

Conscious biases are ones that the affected person is aware of and, as a result of the awareness, might be able to control or adjust for. However, their existence can often coincide with an appearance of a conflict of interest. Conscious biases most commonly result from one or more of the following:

- Family relationships
- Financial relationships
- Personal relationships (friends or spouses)
- Work relationships (current and former supervisors and coworkers)
- Business relationships (vendors or customers)
- Past experiences

Conscious biases are most often thought of in connection to relationships with people, but such biases can exist with respect to records and sources of information, too. For example, auditors should ask themselves:

- "Do I harbor any distrust of an electronic version of a paper document?"
- "Do I trust certain news and information sources more than others?"

Unconscious Bias

Unconscious (implicit) biases are those that the holders are not aware of at the time when the biases are affecting them (the holders might become aware of them later). Scientists say that humans have more of these unconscious biases than they would care to admit. Unconscious biases are not necessarily a bad thing. After all, the ability to make snap judgments about whether an animal is friendly or deadly, or whether another person is friend or foe, has contributed to the survival of the human species. And many of these quick judgments have been made with little or no conscious decision making.

I have been very fortunate to have been guided in my life by brilliant minds, on both the personal and professional side.

One such gentleman is David Woodcock. Mr. Woodcock is a former director of the SEC's Fort Worth Regional Office and chair of the SEC's Financial Reporting and Audit Task Force. David currently serves as the head of litigation for Jones Day's Dallas office, a leading legal institution with more than 2,500 lawyers on five continents. Mr. Woodcock has helped me on a number of panels and given me advice on how to handle serious client matters. I have heard Mr. Woodcock advise accountants many times, and one that has stuck is that *accountant's oftentimes get in trouble by succumbing to pressure by non-accountants.* He routinely cites earnings pressure, disclosures, and management estimates as areas in which even the best controls can succumb to pressure. He put special emphasis on the latter, as those controls, by their very nature, can be subjective and easily overridden.

Mr. Woodcock's quote reminds me of Walt Pavlo, a former senior manager for MCI/WorldCom. In January of 2001, Walt Pavlo received a 41-month federal prison sentence for money laundering, wire fraud, and obstruction of justice. Mr. Pavlo left behind his wife and two young sons to serve his prison sentence. However, Walt's fraud was merely a foreshadowing of what was to come, and shed light on WorldCom's toxic culture.

You may recall that WorldCom was the United States' second-largest long-distance telephone company. It filed for bankruptcy in July 2002, after their internal auditors conducted a clandestine investigation and revealed $3.8 billion worth of fraud. The investigation ultimately showed the company's assets had been inflated by as much as $11 billion. It was the largest bankruptcy in US history. WorldCom's CEO and co-founder, Bernard Ebbers, was convicted in 2005 of conspiracy, securities fraud, and filing false documents with regulators. He is currently serving a 25-year sentence at the Oakdale Federal Correctional Institution in Louisiana.

Time and time again, Mr. Pavlo revealed through interviews that he felt pressured by his bosses to commit financial statement fraud at MCI WorldCom. The pressure he faced was driven by the corporate demands to achieve aggressive earnings targets and hit or exceed forecasts. Since Mr. Pavlo managed customer payments, credits, and reconciliations of accounts, he was tasked with hiding millions of dollars of bad corporate debt from the financial statements. Walt explained: "At the time, I did not see it as excessive pressure – I saw it as opportunity."

He ultimately devised a scheme that accomplished the corporate goal, but in the process, laundered money into Cayman Islands accounts and embezzled $6 million before the fraud was discovered.

I have had the pleasure of spending time with Mr. Pavlo, and have seen, firsthand, his remarkable comeback. He currently covers white-collar crime for *Forbes*. Further, he has published a book on his story – *Stolen Without a Gun*, written with fellow Bloomberg reporter Neil Weinberg – and lectured at numerous business schools, accountancy firms, and even the FBI, to give an insight into what took place and how organizations can prevent it happening again.

In talking with Mr. Pavlo over the years, he has shared with me some of his own reflections on his poor decisions and how he relates those to business leaders. His talks are meant to better prepare leaders so that they understand what real-life situations look like and feel like. Mr. Pavlo believes that people need to know that making good choices, ethical choices, can have short-term consequences. "Nobody wants to deliver bad news," he told me, "and people need to know that doing the right thing may not feel so good at the moment." However, it is those good decisions that pay off in the long run.

Another trusted advisor is Shamoil Shipchandler, who followed Mr. Woodcock as the senior officer at the US Securities and Exchange Commission. Mr. Shipchandler also served at the US Attorney's Office for the Eastern District of Texas, where he handled significant high-profile cases and led two offices through tumultuous periods that included government shutdowns, budget reductions, and hiring freezes. As director of the SEC's Fort Worth Regional Office, Shamoil supervised all examination and enforcement activities in Texas, Oklahoma, Arkansas, and Kansas, a region that includes the second-highest concentration of *Fortune* 500 companies in the nation.

Mr. Shipchandler and I have shared the speaking stage more times than I can count. In addition to being "King of the Dad Jokes," he uses his creativity and wit to leave lasting impressions on how accountants and companies should address fraud and misconduct. One of my favorite gems from Mr. Shipchandler is "There are no risky areas; simply risky behaviors." Mr. Shipchandler explains that while each company boasts of robust policies and procedures, and of their corporate culture, often the actual behavior is not aligned. Some organizations unwittingly reward bad behavior by misplaced incentives (pay based solely on making numbers, etc.). That is the operating environment where most companies/people find themselves in trouble.

Both echo the same sentiment, in that even the best accountants and controls can be compromised under pressure and management abuses.

Management Bias

Management can also "determine the outcome" before the work. Areas that are left to management's discretion, such as financial estimates and projections, are prone to abuse. Whereas Mr. Pavlo's area dealt with bad debt and allowance for doubtful accounts, management estimates are also prevalent in forward-looking statements that investors used to make decisions.

Professional standards discuss the risk of management bias. While these risks are defined, very little is written on how to combat those risks. The areas most fraught with risks mirror those mentioned earlier – management esti-mates. The estimates make their way to prospective financial statements that present the company's expected financial position, results of operations, and cash flows.

In connection with "Determining the Outcome Before the Work," if management knows what a number "has to be," they may be prone to "fab-ricating" support for a predetermined number. Estimates manifest themselves on both the revenue and expense side in the form of reserves and accruals. It can also impact assets and liabilities. In analyzing prospective financial information, auditors are to determine whether the assumptions management used underlying the forecasts **are supported** and provide **a reasonable basis**. Little guidance is given beyond that.

In December, 2018, the Public Company Accounting Oversight Board adopted a new standard to enhance the requirements that apply when auditing accounting estimates. It emphasizes that auditors need to apply professional skepticism, including addressing potential management bias, when auditing accounting estimates. The announcement includes the following statement:

> By their nature, accounting estimates, including fair value measure-ments, generally involve subjective assumptions and measurement uncertainty, making them susceptible to management bias. Some estimates involve complex processes and methods. As a result, accounting estimates are often some of the areas of greatest risk in an audit, requiring additional audit attention and appropriate application of professional skepticism. The challenges of auditing estimates may be compounded by cognitive bias, which could lead auditors to anchor on management's estimates and inappropriately weight confirmatory over contradictory evidence.

Take for example liabilities. The definition of "liability" is fairly straightfor-ward: present obligations that have resulted from prior events, and the payment amount is known. However, contingent liabilities are different. They are obli-gations that may or may not occur in the future, and the amount is unknown. Both the likelihood of occurrence and the estimated amount are subject to management estimates. The accounting treatment of contingent liabilities is totally dependent on management's ultimate decision on the likelihood and estimate of the amount.

The likelihood of occurrence is categorized three ways: high, medium, and low. Each are treated differently in the financial statements.

A contingent is defined as "high probability" if management believes it will actually occur, and the costs can be reasonably estimated. A measure of 50% likelihood is often used. For high-probability contingent liabilities, the company must disclose the estimated amount of the potential loss and also describe the contingency in the footnotes of its financial statements.

A "medium probability" contingency is defined as one that satisfies one of the criteria above (either probable occurrence or estimable amount), but not both. These liabilities must be disclosed in the footnotes of the financial statements but not recorded in the statements.

Contingent liabilities that qualify as "low probability" where the likelihood of these contingent liabilities actually incurring a cost is very low, management is not required to report them in the financial statements or disclose them in the notes (see Figure 5.1).

Consider the impact that bias and the lack of objectivity could have on the determination of occurrence and amount. Take for example, a lawsuit that management feels is frivolous. The plaintiffs are seeking millions of dollars in damages. What sort of questions would you ask to test management's determination that it is a low-probability that they will lose and incur damages?

Keeping within the context of litigation, take for example the financial services industry. Those institutions take a more proactive approach to ensuring nondiscriminatory and nonbiased business practices. One law, the Equal Credit Opportunity Act ("ECOA"), requires such an approach. ECOA, enacted in 1974, prohibits discrimination based on race, color, religion, national origin, sex, marital status, age, source of income, or whether a person exercises rights granted under the Consumer Credit Protection Act for any credit transaction and through the life of a loan. If a lender is guilty of violating the ECOA, it can be sued in court for actual damages, punitive damages of up to **$10,000** for individual lawsuits and **$500,000** or **1%** of the creditor's net

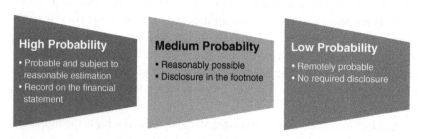

FIGURE 5.1   Treatment of contingent liabilities.

worth for class-action lawsuits. Despite being on the books for 45 years, many well-known banks are fined annually. In 2016, a large bank agreed to the following: (1) pay $25 million to a loan subsidy program; (2) pay a $5.5 million penalty; (3) spend $1 million on advertising targeted to minority neighborhoods; (4) spend $750,000 on partnerships with local minority organizations that provide assistance to residents of minority neighborhoods; (5) spend $500,000 on consumer education activities; and (6) offer banking services in minority neighborhoods and otherwise expand credit services in minority communities. The bank did not admit to any wrongdoing as part of the settlement.

With all that said, how exactly does management support an estimate? How does an auditor determine whether the number is supported and reasonable? A number that does not yet exist and may not. In testing these assumptions management used, these procedures could be used:

1. *Understanding the process.* Often, the process by which the decision is made is equally as important as the ultimate outcome. Were those closest to the number being estimated/projected involved? What input did they have?
2. *Analyzing historical trends.* This can be done for the company, and then measured against other competitors in the industry. Are the estimates used reasonable in comparison to others? Why or why not?
3. *Assessing competence.* In assessing competence, management can review prior estimates and compare them to the actual results. Are they accurate? If not, what changes were made to ensure they are achievable?

Let's apply what you have learned.

A large hospital suspected payroll fraud in their rad-tech department. Three technicians had learned to work 25 hours per day, eight days a week. You scoff at the ridiculousness of this premise; however, upon learning more of the operating environment and lack of controls, you realize it was easily susceptible to fraud.

Technicians normally worked 10- to 12-hour shifts, but had the opportunity to stay late and review charts. The technician received two hours for each chart reviewed, regardless of the length of time it took to actually complete the review. So if a technician worked a 10-hour shift and "reviewed" eight charts – boom – a 26-hour day!

1. What records could you analyze to determine whether this was feasible?
2. With such astronomical overtime, what corporate operational elements might you expect to see?

The hospital's recordkeeping system was archaic, and all of the payroll records were manual. The only supporting documentation for the chart reviews were also manual forms signed off on by the department head. Considering the lack of controls, as well as the override of what few controls were in place, it was clear the only way to resolve the matter was through interviews. These three ladies were the only ones in the entire department reviewing charts. The scope was set.

- The department head – An accomplished professional with 20 years' experience. She had been a hospital employee for approximately 10 years. She had no performance issues and no prior record.
- The department's payroll clerk – An elderly, disabled lady who had been with the hospital for almost 30 years. She also had no known employment or personal issues.
- A nurse/technician – A young lady who had been with the hospital for less than a year, but had a great resume. She was a single mom with a clean criminal history (per the background check in her human resource file).

The order in which you interview subjects is critical. Guidance suggests that you start with those likely to be the least involved, and move closer to those most suspected.

3. How would you schedule the interviews? Who would be the first? The last? Why?

I decided I would interview the nurse first, as she was least likely to have concocted the scheme. My rationale was that as she was new to the organization, and would not have known the gaps in the controls. She also had less responsibility in relation to the payroll process.

The clerk was second, as she was "a sweet old lady." She was known to have been the nicest lady. Always super-helpful and loved her job. My thought was that she had to have at least suspected something, even though she may not have been directly involved.

The last would be the department head. This was not only due to the fact that she had approved all of the overtime, but it was also reported that she had a gambling problem. She had "pressure" and "opportunity," two of the three sides of the fraud triangle.

The first interview went as expected. The nurse knew that her hours had been inflated, but did not know by how much. She did not raise concerns because she was not entirely sure how the overtime or chart reviews were calculated. She simply took what was given, as she "struggled to make ends meet." That is where the train rolled off the tracks.

The "sweet old lady" was next. And she was *anything* other than sweet. She was on edge immediately. She used attacking vulgarities and clearly did not appreciate being questioned. After clearing the air, she ultimately confessed. The pressure – her husband had recently passed away, leaving her with nothing. No life insurance. No way to pay medical bills. She was resentful. Her rationalization – she had worked for the hospital for most of her life and made less than half of what a new hire made. The opportunity was lack of controls and the fact the department head needed to fuel her gambling habit. The department head also needed friends. The clerk's plan killed two birds with one stone – we can create fictitious overtime invoices, each get more money, and all go gambling together. It's a party!

The hospital decided not to prosecute, or file a civil lawsuit. They convinced each of the employees to ultimately sign promissory notes to repay the overpayment. However, no one was prosecuted, and only one lost her job.

4. Can you guess which employee lost her job? And why?
5. What considerations must the hospital have taken to decide against legal action? Pros for and against?
6. What disclosures and estimates would be required, assuming they were publicly traded?

The hospital did not want bad press. They knew that filing either a criminal or civil complaint would have resulted in unwanted publicity, especially in a small town. Their number-one priority was recovering the funds. The department head lost her job. The hospital felt that of the three, she would have the easiest time finding a replacement job. The clerk was reassigned, and the nurse received a warning. The hospital disclosed the fraud to their board of directors and audit committee, along with remediation measures and their estimated recovery.

7. Had we not been open and adaptable during the interview process, how might our bias, our idea of who initiated the scheme, have had a negative impact on the investigation process?

SUMMARY

We all face challenges that test our objectivity and our level of professional skepticism. Those dilemmas can influence our decision to pursue an investigation, disclose certain findings, and compile meaningful numbers. Determining the outcome before the work can be detrimental and end careers, violating standards, and negating years of great work. It can destroy reputations, and can also let fraudsters and other bad actors get away scot-free, and result in expensive litigation. Accountants can mitigate their exposure by committing to remain objective, adhere to rigorous professional skepticism protocols, and discharge all assignments with due professional care.

RECOMMENDATIONS

To counteract our tendencies to D – Determine the outcome before the work, consider the following:

1. *Take inventory.* Similar to the recommendations in Chapter 4, be honest with yourself. Know your tendencies. We all have them. Who have you typically called clients? What positions have you taken when on prior assignments? When you opined on an approach? A number.
2. *Confer with a trusted advisor.* Perhaps you have a blind spot. Mentors and trusted advisors can see your tendencies through objective lenses. Ask. Listen. Address.
3. *Document and disclose.* When taking on an assignment, disclose all potential conflicts and anything that could warrant a third party's concern. The materiality of a position or relationship ultimately resides with the decision maker, not you.
4. *Consider alternative conclusions.* When completing an assignment, consider other explanations of the issues you were asked to resolve. Then, rule them out, one by one, with facts, not assumptions.
5. *Protect your reputation.* In taking on assignments, consider how they will impact future work. Consider whether your personal life conflicts with professional opinions.

Case Study: Having Faith in the Faithless

The CEO of a small, family-owned oil and gas company is a self-made millionaire. He started this company out of his home, but it has grown to a $15 million company in less than 10 years. He eventually opened a formal office in a building that also housed one of the state's most prestigious banks. The company's accounting department consists of one person, Anita Pearson. She is not a CPA and was hired with little to no experience. The CEO knew Ms. Pearson from his church, so he did not feel a background check was necessary. She did such a wonderful job, he never hired anyone else to assist her. She has served in that capacity for the past seven years. He was proud of how her employment has worked out, because Ms. Pearson had a difficult time maintaining employment previously, despite her friendly demeanor.

Ms. Pearson was very dedicated to the job. She never took vacations. And despite a modest salary, she never complained about money or asked for a raise. This was more impressive, as the CEO knew that Ms. Pearson helped her mom with her medical bills for the past five years or so.

Two weeks ago, Ms. Pearson frantically approached the CEO and told him that she needed a few days off to help her mom move into an assisted living facility. Of course the CEO approved. Ms. Pearson advised him that she had paid all the bills, deposited all the receipts, and that he was not to worry about the accounting. That was good news to him, because he hated accounting. He could not remember opening a bank statement since hiring her. Further, he had never felt the need for an audit. He simply hired a CPA to do his taxes each year. He was making money, which was most important above all else.

Within a few days of her departure, the CEO received a call from the bank. The bank informed him that a check had been drawn on a dormant, closed account. The bank asked if he could come downstairs and review. Much to the CEO's dismay, he learned the check was written to Ms. Pearson for $2,500. It contained his forged signature and was the approximate amount of her bi-weekly payroll amount. The CEO immediately asked the bank to print out all the checks written to Ms. Pearson. It seems she had been forging checks for the past five years, and had paid herself double what her employment arrangement stated.

The bank advised they did not routinely check signature cards. This was further complicated by the fact that all checks were prepared manually, and the forged checks were all cashed at a pawnshop.

The CEO felt he should sue the bank for not checking his signature card and preventing the forgery. He called you to determine the amount of fraud, and to testify against the bank on grounds they fraudulently

(Continued)

(Continued)

induced him to open the checking account by advertising nonexistent forgery controls.

1. What role did trust play in allowing this fraudulent scheme to transpire?
2. What elements contributed to this trust?
3. What red flags were missed upon her hiring?
4. Assuming Ms. Pearson could have passed a background check initially:
   a. What "pressures" may have occurred since to alter her trust-worthiness?
   b. What "opportunities" existed for her to commit fraud?
   c. How might she have "rationalized" her behavior?
5. How was this fraud discovered? By accident? By analytical procedures? By a tip? Explain.
6. How would you go about proving the CEO's case, in that the bank should have caught the fraud?
   a. How would you defend the bank?
7. What tasks could the CEO have performed to have prevented this fraud, or at least discovered it sooner?
8. How might small businesses be more susceptible to fraud than larger organizations?

CHAPTER SIX

Overcoming Barriers to Reporting Fraud and Misconduct

N THIS CHAPTER, WE discuss obstacles that may cause hesitation in accountants and their organizations in disclosing frauds they find. We also discuss the rules and regulations that require, or incentivize the disclosures, along with protections afforded to those who choose to.

INTRODUCTION

We have discussed at length the accountant's liability for not finding fraud. However, what happens when the accountant actually finds it? And discloses it? Would it surprise you to learn that there could be career-limiting consequences to disclosing fraud? And sometimes, to some, it may outweigh the incentives and exhaust their moral compass. In this chapter, and consistent with what we've discussed previously, we discuss the risks and rewards of disclosing fraud, and other barriers (pressure) that may limit professionals from doing the right thing.

If accountants have done their job and face a decision of whether or not to disclose fraud and misconduct, they must address the risk of adhering to professional standards and disclosing it, or stare down the frightening reality of the consequences they may face in disclosing their findings.

BARRIERS

There could be a number of impediments standing in the accountant's way. One barrier could be an emotional one, in which accountants may find themselves sympathizing with the perpetrator. Other obstacles include fear of consequences, such as being branded a whistleblower, or corporate fines, penalties, and sanctions.

Emotional Challenges

I've had tremendous success in obtaining confessions. I attribute this to my ability to connect with people, and obtain an avenue to penetrate their minds. Rapport. However, I often found it was much easier to get into their heads than to get out. While I would go home, pour a stiff drink to ruminate over the day's events, I was often overwhelmed with sadness. I knew exactly the impact the fraudster's actions would have on their family, as I had lived through it with mine. I knew that the time had come, that their sins would now affect those they loved far more than it affected them. That their spouses and children had no choice in the matter. I also felt despondency, imagining the helpless feeling, and desperation that had driven so many to act that way and ultimately commit fraud. (I didn't feel that way about those who simply acted out power or greed, or questioned my testicular fortitude.)

There was one case in particular that I have not been able to shake, even today some 20 years later. During a large investigation of a public entity, we ran across a situation in which a payroll clerk had clearly written herself an extra monthly check, just over $800 (yes – she made approximately $800 a month). We located her address and drove to her house. Down a long, one-laned gravel road, we arrived at her trailer. Her car was there, so we approached the house, knocked, and she invited us in. The trailer was cluttered, and we could tell she had two children; a child in elementary school and an infant. The former was in school, the latter asleep. We explained the reason for our visit, and without wasting time, showed her the check in question. She collapsed in tears. She explained that her husband had recently left, shortly after the baby was born. She couldn't make ends meet. She then went to the pantry, and brought back a receipt for nearly $600 in groceries: mainly formula and diapers. My partner began sobbing. I held back for a moment.

Once she finished her testimonial, she became quiet. She looked at me and said "The one good thing about this, is that my father won't be around to see me go through this. He died a few weeks ago. But sadly, I have a feeling he'll be able to look down and still see. He will be so disappointed in me." As I write this, I am crying just as I was then. We embraced, and I assured her that we would get through this.

I left feeling nauseous. My partner and I said very little on the ride home, but our sniffles spoke volumes. The clerk repaid the money before the next payroll cycle. I still documented the finding, along with the standard recommendation of strengthening the payroll process. I never had the courage to inquire as to whether she lost her job. And while I wasn't the one who made the poor decision, I made a vow to pursue cases that possessed a different degree of exposure going forward. I had one more career-defining assignment left in my state tenure, and was moved to Texas by an accounting firm within the next few months.

It has not always been easy. Occasionally, there is a part of me that wants to sympathize with those facing moral dilemmas. Auditors/investigators that may be conflicted over a direction to take, or whether to take one at all. Fraudsters always have a compelling rationalization for performing bad acts. However, no matter which heartstring is tugged, even though it may not have felt possible at the time, you will never gone wrong by adhering to the standards.

Fear of Consequences

Another obstacle, or even a deterrent could be the consequences and fear of being seen as a whistleblower. Perhaps no other control exists that is more important than enabling those with information to come forward. The ACFE's *Report to the Nation* states that the number-one way fraud is discovered is through tips (Figure 6.1).

Fear of Consequences – Whistleblowers

However, coming forward is not an easy decision to make for some. One of the most significant impediments comes from the natural conflict between an accountant and others tasked with "protecting the company." Consider

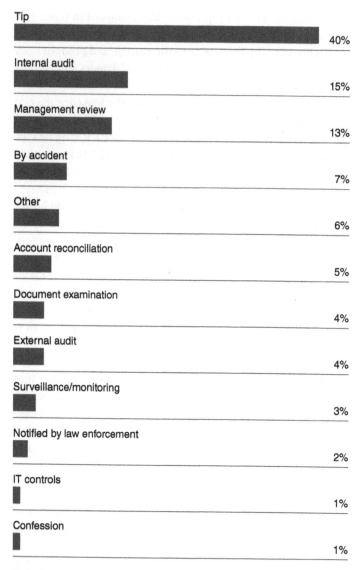

FIGURE 6.1 How is occupational fraud initially detected?

the accountant's professional obligation to disclose fraud, and the attorney's and other executive management's position as corporate advocates, and their assessment of how the disclosure will impact the company.

Many people refuse to come forward as a whistleblower for the simple fear of being branded as a whistleblower. However, there are certain protections, and even incentives, for informants to do the right thing. One protection is afforded in the Sarbanes-Oxley Act of 2002. One of the Act's provisions requires companies to have an employee hotline to confidentially report allegations of wrongdoing. Another provision prohibits companies from discriminating or retaliating against an employee because of their whistleblower activities.

The SEC took protection even further in 2010, and now offers a financial incentive to those who provide valuable information. Section 922 of the Dodd-Frank Wall Street Reform and Consumer Protection Act added Section 21F to the Securities Exchange Act of 1934 (the "Exchange Act"), which established the SEC's whistleblower program. The SEC's whistleblower reward program provides a financial incentive to informants, under certain circumstances. An informant is eligible for rewards, and the SEC may pay an award or awards to one or more whistleblowers who (1) voluntarily provide the Commission (2) with original information (3) that leads to the successful enforcement by the Commission of a federal court or administrative action (4) in which the Commission obtains monetary sanctions totaling more than $1,000,000.

The reward program has been met with concerns. Many critics of the program argue that these incentives create a conflict, in that those responsible for corporate governance will go to the Commission and circumvent the company's internal reporting process. This is a fair point. Let's discuss.

1. What advice would you give a company on how to encourage employees to report internally before going to the authorities?
2. What are the pros and cons of going internally first?
3. What positions within the company are most likely to face this decision?

The SEC also has an anti-retaliation provision that echoes the protections in Sarbanes-Oxley. To qualify for protection under the anti-retaliation provision of the Dodd-Frank Act, whistleblowers must demonstrate that they reported a potential securities law violation to the SEC, and not just internally.

Since Dodd-Frank's passage in 2010, the SEC has fined two companies for retaliation. One case was brought forward as a standalone retaliation matter. That company agreed to pay a half-million-dollar penalty for firing an employee. The employee had several years of positive performance reviews, but it was shown that he was terminated because he reported to senior management and the SEC that the company's financial statements might be distorted.

"Bringing retaliation cases, including this first stand-alone retaliation case, illustrates the high priority we place on ensuring a safe environment for whistleblowers," said Jane A. Norberg, chief of the SEC's Office of the Whistleblower. "We will continue to exercise our anti-retaliation authority when companies take reprisals for whistleblowing efforts."[1]

Since the program's inception, the SEC has ordered wrongdoers in enforcement matters to pay over $1.7 billion in total monetary sanctions, and has awarded over $326 million to 59 whistleblowers. However, that is 59 out of more than 28,000 tips. That leaves thousands of whistleblowers to still be accounted for. And as you can see, despite salacious headlines, actual payouts are rare.

Notwithstanding the Sarbanes-Oxley Certifications and the Dodd-Frank Acts mentioned earlier in this text, the profession experienced yet another watershed moment in July 2015, when the Internal Ethics Standards Board for Accountants (IESBA) issued a code of ethics. The code requires professional accountants, chief financial officers, directors, and others charged with governance to respond to Non-compliance with Laws and Regulations ("NOCLAR") and follow a specific protocol in disclosing fraud and misconduct.

Reportable NOCLAR acts consist of omissions, commissions, intentional or nonintentional, by companies or those charged with governance or those working on behalf of, or at the direction of, management. NOCLAR requires auditors and those accountants charged with governance to raise the issue with management. In certain situations, auditors and accountants, despite a likely conflict with client confidentiality and/or employment agreements, may disclose the matter to the appropriate authorities if there is an imminent breach of a law or regulation that would cause substantial harm to stakeholders, such as fraud in the financial statements (consult the appropriate laws in the jurisdiction). Additional guidance can also be found in International Standard 240.

Notwithstanding these protections, whistleblowers are often fired and almost always impacted. A 2010 study featured by the ACFE showed that 74% of the whistleblowers were fired. Another 6% were suspended and 5% were transferred against their wishes. The remaining 15% were given poor evaluations, demoted, or harassed.

In 2013, the Supreme Court of the United States ruled on *Lawson et al. v. FMR LLC et al.* In this dispute, the Supreme Court held that the whistleblower-protection provision of the Sarbanes-Oxley Act protects employees of private

---

[1]"SEC: Casino-Gaming Company Retaliated Against Whistleblower," press release, September 29, 2016, https://www.sec.gov/news/pressrelease/2016-204.html.

contractors and subcontractors just as it does employees of the public company served by the private contractors and subcontractors. Interestingly, the syllabus mentions Enron, and the fact that when employees of contractors attempted to bring allegations of misconduct to light, they encountered retaliation by their employers. The Court's interpretation went to cover every employee and contractor of every public company, as well as extending it to "outside lawyers and accountants who could have helped prevent the Enron fraud."

Similar findings were shared in a 2016 study by the Association of Chartered Certified Accountants (ACCA). The ACCA supports 178,000 members and 455,000 students in 181 countries. The study was led by The Economic and Social Research Council (ESRC), the UK's largest funder of research on the social and economic questions facing us today. *Forbes* highlighted this study. It showed that of the workers who revealed wrongdoing in their organizations, nearly all of them lost their job either by being pressured out of the organization or being dismissed. If they did stay, they suffered retaliation through bullying, demotion, isolation, or harassment while some were forced by their company to take mental health counseling. Many did crack under pressure, suffering mental illness through depression or panic attacks, or developed drinking problems.

My first, and perhaps my most significant retaliatory event came early in my career. I was conducting several small allegations at the time. Upon analyzing a general ledger of an entity, I noticed an organization's manager received reimbursements for approximately $2,500 of nonbusiness expenses. These charges included an obviously personal item, attire, and other expenses pertaining to the outing. I discussed these observations with him, and he initially "confessed." He explained his assistant had mistakenly included those items on his expense report. He attributed the lack of proper oversight to his busy schedule and told me he would pay them back immediately. Nonetheless, and despite his pleas to omit the report based on our conversation, it was my public duty and responsibility to issue a report. After all, just weeks prior I had reported various others for receiving $500 travel advances for trips they did not take. Those advances were far less than his personal trip. To make matters more precarious, the leader was of a different race from the jurors. As a professional, I knew I must avoid an appearance of bias or lack of objectivity. I advised the manager I would submit the report. That decision had consequences.

During this time, I had been offered a management role in the Department of Justice's Civil Enforcement Department. I was chosen from hundreds of candidates my senior, and had successfully endured three different background checks. Imagine the surprise that my college roommates and my high school teachers received when answering their doorbells, facing an FBI agent asking questions about me. Ha. "What the hell have you done now?!"

It was publicly known that the announcement would be made within days. I had begun transitioning my case files, and had secured my office space at the Federal building in Baton Rouge. My family and I had celebrated. One afternoon, I received a call from the target of my investigation, who stated that if I proceeded with the report, he would indict me on obstruction of justice. His idea was that by releasing the report, certain work he had done would be marginalized, resulting in failed legislation. It would be my fault, as I intentionally released the report with the knowledge this would happen. He admitted, that although the indictment would not result in a conviction, it would be enough to raise concerns at the US Attorney's Office. He told me that there was a way out; I could choose not to release the report and to turn over incriminating evidence that my bosses had abused their offices. I grabbed my recorder and asked him what he required. He rattled off a document request list. I immediately went to my supervisor's office . . . with a recording of the entire conversation. Louisiana was one-party state, meaning that only one party had to have knowledge of the recording. I was well within the law and my rights.

Within two days, our office met with the US Attorney to play the tape and explain the situation. Three of my supervisors and the office general counsel presented my case, boasted of my accomplishments. It was to no avail. I had become too hot to touch at that point and the offer was withdrawn. There have not been many points in my career lower than this one. Despite all this, I fell in love with my office all over again. Seeing state leadership stand up for someone they were losing. Hearing how proud they were of my accomplishments, despite me choosing another agency over them. It was humbling and turned into one of my most cherished moments. I still hold them in the highest regard this very day.

The fallout was immediate. Media outlets called my home and asked whether it was true that I had been fired. It was not. They asked if something happened in the background checks that caused the offer to be withdrawn. There was not. I had to put my family on notice to expect calls and advised them on how to respond. Nothing ever came of these threats. However, something did happen to me. The head of my agency went on camera in front of the state legislature and shared the story. He also asked the legislature to approve an off-cycle pay raise, which they did, to bring my salary up to the level I would have made in my new job. I gave this very little thought after that. I certainly never questioned my decision. I lost no money, simply lost a few nights of sleep. I lost some hope. However, my career actually received a boost from the publicity. And to this day, I still have a strong belief that truth prevails, and that good things generally will happen to good people.

Fear of Consequences: Whistleblowers, Corporate Sanctions, Fines, and Penalties

Companies face similar barriers in self-disclosing. Both the SEC and the DOJ have forms of cooperation credits.

The SEC's Cooperation Program was enacted in 2010, and identified four broad factors to be considered in evaluating a company's cooperation when determining appropriate charges and remedies.

1. *Assistance provided by the cooperator.* This factor includes things such as the value and nature of the cooperation provided by an individual;
2. *Importance of the underlying matter.* This factor includes things such as the type of misconduct and the danger it posed to investors;
3. *Interest in holding the individual accountable.* This factor considers, among other things, the cooperator's culpability, including culpability relative to that of other violators, and the cooperator's other efforts to remediate the harm caused by the violations; and
4. *Profile of the individual.* This factor includes things such as the individual's history of compliance, opportunity for future misconduct, and whether the individual accepts responsibility for his or her misconduct.

The SEC touts two main benefits in cooperation: considerations in charging decisions and monetary sanctions.

The Department of Justice has similar programs. In the DOJ's Principles of Prosecution, prosecutors are guided to apply the following factors in reaching a decision as to the proper treatment of a corporate target:

1. the nature and seriousness of the offense, including the risk of harm to the public, and applicable policies and priorities, if any, governing the prosecution of corporations for particular categories of crime;
2. the pervasiveness of wrongdoing within the corporation, including the complicity in, or the condoning of, the wrongdoing by corporate management;
3. the corporation's history of similar misconduct, including prior criminal, civil, and regulatory enforcement actions against it;

4. the corporation's willingness to cooperate, including as to potential wrongdoing by its agents;
5. the adequacy and effectiveness of the corporation's compliance program at the time of the offense, as well as at the time of a charging decision;
6. the corporation's timely and voluntary disclosure of wrongdoing;
7. the corporation's remedial actions, including, but not limited to, any efforts to implement an adequate and effective corporate compliance program or to improve an existing one, to replace responsible management, to discipline or terminate wrongdoers, or to pay restitution;
8. collateral consequences, including whether there is disproportionate harm to shareholders, pension holders, employees, and others not proven personally culpable, as well as impact on the public arising from the prosecution;
9. the adequacy of remedies such as civil or regulatory enforcement actions, including remedies resulting from the corporation's cooperation with relevant government agencies; and
10. the adequacy of the prosecution of individuals responsible for the corporation's malfeasance.

Pay close attention to numbers 4, 5, 6, and 7. Do you see how critical an accountant's role could be in reaching a resolution with the DOJ?

There are two cases that illustrate how the SEC and the DOJ put this into practice. In October 2001, the SEC issued a statement supporting its decision not to take enforcement action against a company it had investigated for financial statement irregularities. The report is commonly referred to as the Seaboard Report, named after the company it investigated. The SEC cites four factors in reaching their decision.

1. Self-policing prior to the discovery of the misconduct, including establishing effective compliance procedures and an appropriate tone at the top;
2. Self-reporting of misconduct when it is discovered, including conducting a thorough review of the nature, extent, origins and consequences of the misconduct, and promptly, completely and effectively disclosing the misconduct to the public, to regulatory agencies, and to self-regulatory organizations;
3. Remediation, including dismissing or appropriately disciplining wrongdoers, modifying and improving internal controls and procedures to prevent recurrence of the misconduct, and appropriately compensating those adversely affected; and

4. Cooperation with law enforcement authorities, including providing the Commission staff with all information relevant to the underlying violations and the company's remedial efforts.

A more recent example involved Ralph Lauren Corporation. In 2013, the SEC determined not to charge Ralph Lauren with violations of the FCPA, the first time that the SEC has entered a case involving FCPA misconduct. The misconduct came to light as a result of the company adopting measures to improve its worldwide internal controls and compliance efforts, including implementation of an FCPA compliance training program in Argentina. Similar to Seaboard, the SEC cited the company's prompt reporting of the violations on its own initiative, the completeness of the information it provided, and its extensive, thorough, and real-time cooperation. However, the SEC elaborated on the substantial time and resources Ralph Lauren's cooperation saved them. According to the non-prosecution agreement, Ralph Lauren Corporation's cooperation included: .

- ▥ Reporting preliminary findings of its internal investigation to the staff within two weeks of discovering the illegal payments and gifts.
- ▥ Voluntarily and expeditiously producing documents.
- ▥ Providing English language translations of documents to the staff.
- ▥ Summarizing witness interviews that the company's investigators conducted overseas.
- ▥ Making overseas witnesses available for staff interviews and bringing witnesses to the United States.

Two fascinating studies by University of Texas at Dallas Associate Professor Dr. Rebecca Files (the second of which is co-authored with Gerald Martin and Stephanie Rasmussen at American University and University of Texas at Arlington, respectively) highlight the dilemma companies' face in self-disclosure. They examined 1,162 enforcement actions for financial misrepresentation initiated by the SEC and the Department of Justice. Collectively, these studies find that self-reporting law violations to the SEC or DOJ is one of the best ways to generate "cooperation credit" from regulators. However, this and other forms of cooperation actually increase the likelihood of being sanctioned, perhaps because they improve the SEC and DOJ's ability to build a successful case against the firm. Importantly, however, both studies find that cooperation is rewarded by the SEC and DOJ through a reduction of up to $28 million in monetary penalties, with an average of $23.8 million. Dr. Files concludes that the reward for cooperation is evident through reduced fines, rather than a lack of sanctions. Moreover, Drs. Files, Martin, and Rasmussen find that cooperating with regulators can lead to significantly smaller reputation-related losses following financial misconduct. That significant reduction is evidenced by average reputation-related losses (which are defined as the cumulative loss in share value for a firm following disclosure of the financial misrepresentation and related enforcement activities to the public) that are $756 million (70%) lower for firms with cooperation credit (see Table 6.1).

Indifference, Lack of Awareness, or Simple Exhaustion

Another obstacle could be nothing more than apathy: not knowing right from wrong, and not caring. As difficult as this is to read, not everyone received ethics training or a lesson on right and wrong. In fact, this defense made national headlines in a Fort Worth, Texas, matter in 2013. A teenager and some friends stole alcohol, had a party, and chose to drive. The teenager ultimately killed four people while driving drunk. He became known as the "affluenza teen" after a psychologist suggested during his trial that growing up with money might have left him with the inability to tell right from wrong. The defense was a success, as the teen pleaded guilty to four counts of manslaughter and a juvenile court judge sentenced him to 10 years of probation. I hope I never hear or have to coin the phrase "affluenza accountant."

In their textbook, *Fraud Examination*, Albrecht, Albrecht, Albrecht, and Zimbelman provide nine factors that came together to create the "perfect fraud storm," which fostered a culture of fraudulent behavior in the early 2000s. Two factors pertained directly to ethical compromises – Decay of Moral Values and Educator Failure. The text mentioned that cheating in high school has increased substantially in recent years. This concept is further explained in the latter element, in that educators have (1) not provided sufficient ethics training to students, (2) not taught students specifically about fraud, and (3) not focused their teaching on analytical skills.

This lack of training seems to have continued. In a recent *Wall Street Journal* article, psychology professor Steven Davis states that cheating by high school students has increased from about 20% in the 1940s to 75% today. In

TABLE 6.1   Financial impact of self-disclosing in investigations

Loss category	Saved by cooperation
Reputation (share value)	756,000,000
Fines and penalties	$23,800,000

2016, the *WSJ* reported that public universities in the United States recorded 5.1 reports of alleged cheating for every 100 international students, versus 1 report per 100 domestic students. Students say cheating in high school is for grades; cheating in college is for a career.

I spent time recently with Dr. Perry Moore, director of graduate business programs and professor of accounting for Lipscomb University. He is a CPA, a Certified Internal Auditor, and a Chartered Global Management Accountant and is certified in Risk Management Assurance. He is a member of the Professional Ethics and Accounting section of the Tennessee Society of CPAs. Dr. Moore takes this even further, in that he reminds colleagues that high school students do not stop cheating when they enter college. Cheating in high school is for grades – to get into a good college. Cheating in college is for a career – to get that choice first job. Employers of new college graduates need to focus some of their in-boarding activities on that temptation to cheat. These new hires appear to have accepted cheating as a cultural norm. Each company has to assess what they are going to do to help these new hires understand the ethical expectations of the company and their career path(s) within it.

Dr. Moore advises, through various in-class discussions, that accounting professors need to initiate conversations about integrity and its role in the accounting profession. These discussions tend to be prompted by carefully selected case studies that direct each student's attention on fraud, integrity, and ethics. An unofficial motto in Dr. Moore's school is that "doing business right is the right way to do business." The first case used in his auditing classes deals with a "white lie" told by a new employee about whether she had taken the CPA exam. The resulting discussion is always rich – even if students do not agree with the direction of the conversation. He is quick to stress to students that they have to think about what they are going to do when faced with an ethical dilemma well before they are faced with it. They will face multiple professional ethical issues in their careers.

I stole a monkey when I was four years old. There. I admit it. The rubber, bathtub-toy monkey was about 6 inches tall, and was in a package hanging on a small sales rack at Buddy Bonner's General Store in Fort Necessity, Louisiana. Like most fraudsters, I started small, before I went for the big score. Each time my mom or dad took me to that store, I removed the monkey from the toy rack, and secretly opened the package a tiny bit. Over the course of a few weeks, after opening it a little more . . . a little more . . . I was finally able to take it all the way out of the package. I then hid the monkey in the rack and waited until I went back. (Apparently it was not an item in high demand.) A few days later, voilà. I had "found" the monkey in the store.

I showed my mom when I returned to the car. "Look what I found!" I remember her challenging me. Scolding me is more like it. She pulled the car over, and you know what came next. It was the seventies, and in those days, one was not spared "the rod." I was just thankful it wasn't my dad. I remember her being so disappointed in me. She dropped me off at my grandmother's house instead of allowing me to accompany her on our weekly trip to town. I cried myself to sleep on my grandmother's couch. Not from the spanking, but from the pain I had caused my mother, and the fact that as a four-year-old, I knew better. I knew what I had done was wrong. I was embarrassed. Shamed. Later that week, I returned to the store. My mother walked me to the counter and told the owner that I had "found" this monkey, but that I wished to pay for it. I paid for it with every single penny I had earned picking up pinecones. Lesson learned (Lesson – you don't make a lot of money picking up pinecones). That experience has stuck with me for 42 years now.

Imagine if I had taken something of real value? It does happen. Fast-forward to a more recent, shocking story out of Dallas, Texas, involving a contest to see childhood idol (well, a former childhood idol, as of this writing) Hannah Montana. In 2007, a six-year old girl won four tickets to a concert in New York, after penning an essay with the opening line: "My daddy died this year in Iraq."

> My daddy died this year in Iraq. I am going to give my mommy the
> Angel pendant that daddy put on mommy when she was having me.
> I had it in my jewelry box since that day. I love my mommy.

The little girl had scored big! She now had four tickets to the hottest ticket in town. However, upon further review, the Defense Department records revealed that one US soldier died on the day the essay claimed. And it was not the little girl's father.

When approached, the mother of the young girl told the contest's organizer that the father died April 17 in a roadside bombing in Iraq. However, when the spokesman asked the girl's mom if the story was true, the mother said no. "We did the essay and that's what we did to win."

"We did whatever we could do to win. But when [the competition organizer] asked me if this essay is true, I said, 'No, this essay is not true.'"

After learning of the fraud, the organizers withdrew the award and gave it to another, more deserving entrant.

Can you imagine the pain and disappointment that child felt? After all, wasn't she listening to, and learning from, the one person who has "all the answers"? They say that ethics cannot be taught, and it must be learned. Perhaps that is true. I know that I did not learn ethics and honesty on the side of the road in 1977, but I certainly received a reminder.

This is not an anomaly. Parents can be the worse enablers, by setting inappropriate examples. As of this writing, there is massive investigation underway into a scandal involving college admissions. Dozens of parents, including celebrities and well-known business executives, stand accused of paying bribes ranging from $15,000 to $6.5 million to coaches and ACT/SAT administrators at multiple, elite universities. The payments were allegedly made to help the wealthiest of families get their children into universities where they otherwise would not have been admitted.

We can only hope that these sorts of scandals put the emphasis on teaching at home, continuing education through higher learning. We must teach ethics. If not, the reminders will be far worse than the roadside assistance I received.

Last, but not least, accountants may simply be *too tired to fight*. We have chosen a difficult pursuit. Our passion is not for those with thin skin or weak stomachs. It has provided me with extreme peaks and valleys. I have celebrated victories, only to fall apart minutes later, during my drive home. Being tasked with fraud-fighting adds even more stress. Those who choose to provide these services as consultants may have it the worst. What makes the profession so challenging? Here's my list:

1. *Importance of the profession.* Auditors and accountants play critical roles in exposing fraud and maintaining faith in the financial markets. Almost everything they touch is relied upon, to some degree, for others to reach a business decision. That reliance can create exposure of the highest degree.
2. *Long hours.* It is common to work 60-hour weeks during "busy season." Most staff will argue there is no such thing as "non-busy season." The busy season for external audit professionals is the first quarter of each year, when public filings are due. For tax professions, it is the mad dash before the April 15 deadline. For corporate accountants, it can be each quarter-end close. For experts, it can be a 24/7 assignment, as new, relevant information becomes known at the very last minute.
3. *Immovable deadlines.* The deadlines accountants face are often established by regulatory agencies. Courts determine the deadlines in matters that may require expert reports and testimony. Missing a deadline can be catastrophic and cause an expert to be excluded, or your organization to face fines and penalties and market capitalization deterioration.

4. *Unrealistic expectations.* In addition to deadlines, accountants can be asked to perform accounting miracles. Hilarious phrases such as "creative accounting" and "cooking the books" are jargon used when accountants are asked to "fudge" numbers or interpret guidance loosely to make an organization's financial statements results look better. Experts hired to compute damages risk building an opinion on information that could have been intentionally limited or altered without their knowledge (or even assurances otherwise).

5. *Difficult performance measures.* How do you measure success for an accounting, internal audit, or fraud investigation unit? Is it the number of resolved issues? The number of issues received? Is it the amount of recoveries from perpetrators? Convictions? Unlike sales departments and consultants, which either hit their numbers or don't, the non–revenue producing accounting function department's success is difficult to measure.

6. *Pressure to produce.* Accountants who are external services providers face the same challenges mentioned above, as well as the added pressure of producing sales. This can cause major anxiety for accountants, who rarely are known for their sales acumen and gregarious personalities. (How many of you took a sales class in college or as a continuing education? Exactly!) This sales pressure can sometimes cause practitioners to take on assignments they otherwise would avoid. It was also cited as a large reason for Arthur Andersen's demise.

Let's dive deeper into item 6:

1. What conflict do you perceive, when analyzing the risks associated with disclosing fraud to a client and the pressure of sales?
2. What performance metrics, in addition to sales, would produce a good measure to outside accounting service providers?

The most reputable service firms address the second question in robust ways, incorporating guiding principles, corporate cultural attributes, and staff development into their performance reviews.

It is no surprise the turnover rate for accountants is the highest in the nation, and that firms consider employee retention as their biggest challenge. A recent study completed by the New York State Society of CPAs showed that accounting and auditing turnover rates were comparable to nurses, child-care workers, telemarketers, movie-theater employees, hotel and restaurant workers, and sales professionals. Think of how turnover can affect the profession: learning curves that may delay client deliverables, management's delay in disclosing the results of their operations, a manual control being overridden by someone taking advantage of inexperience. After considering the cases and professional standards contained herein, how does turnover impact:

1. Professional competency?
2. Objectivity and professional skepticism?
3. Supervision?
4. Scope? Fees?
5. Incentivizing bad behavior?

I can fill these pages with more stories of those who paid fines and penalties, and went to jail after our assignments were complete. There are clients of mine who also either won or avoided significant judgments. I am proud of the work that I've done. And while success has come at a very high price, which has included hospitalization, overexhaustion, and stress, it has also been extremely rewarding. At 40 years old, I received the highest honor in my profession: the ACFE of the Year award. However, that pales in comparison to the relationships I have made, and the love I share with my colleagues. As I embark on my next 25 years in the profession, I write and teach, hoping that others can gain confidence and comfort, based on all my starts, stops, and stumbles. And for those that are starting out, maybe I can help them save some sleep (and some hair) and maybe avoid some ulcers.

My raising was unique, to say the least. I've reflected on it almost daily to the point it has become an obsession. There have been times I have been resentful in that I did not have the "book learning" opportunities I would have had in large cities. I could not wait to leave and spread my wings. But I'm quickly reminded of the life lessons I had instead. The commitment to faith and family left me with an unusually rigid belief in right and wrong. There is no grey; only black and white. That has served me well in my career as a fraud-fighter.

However, this attitude has sometimes led to guilt and depression in my personal life. I will say, like many of you, that despite my best intentions and efforts, I have made mistakes. Without exception, I seek outside help when I feel I have failed or fallen short of my goals. My first experience with a counselor was when I was 12 years old. His assessment was that I had a tendency to "punish" myself for anything and everything that I felt I had done wrong. I had difficulty letting it go. It went beyond the belief that I had to be a perfectionist. I felt I was either "perfect" or a "complete failure." Doesn't that remind you of *Talladega Nights* – "If you ain't first, you're last"? There was never anything in between. I did not remember that diagnosis until May 2018, when another therapist, who had no connection or awareness of the first, said that exact same thing. I visited this counselor after experiencing the most difficult client in my life. While I have more experience than I ever wish on anyone dealing with adversaries, I found it particularly devastating when I encountered disrespect and abuse from a client whom I was doing my best to assist (and a job that was done very well, if I do say so myself!). Everyone has to find their own way to cope with these sorts of stresses. I find the only way for me to catch my breath is to return to the country and refresh in nature, spending time in the one place I could not wait to leave as a teenager. Doesn't life really come full circle?

As you can tell from the numerous cases I have referenced, and the thoughts I have shared, this career is challenging to say the least. But for every challenge I have shared, it has been 10 times as rewarding. Aside from providing a comfortable living to my family and those of my staff, I have seen my work result in criminals going to prison and others paying fines and penalties. I have seen companies rightfully absolved of wrongdoing. I have also traveled to far-away lands that I only knew through rumors and magazine pages. I have spent time with clients in Canada, Spain, Switzerland, London, and Italy. I have led teams working in 13 different countries at once. I have met my childhood heroes, such as playing tennis with Andre Agassi at Madison Square Garden. I shared a cocktail with Terry Bradshaw in Beverly Hills. I attended the NFL Prayer Breakfast with Drew Brees. I've ridden Harley Davidsons with Dierks Bentley. I sparred in the ring and shot a commercial with Ronda Rousey, and attended charity events that raised thousands, while shaking hands with former president George W. Bush, Emmitt Smith, Clayton Kershaw, Johnny Bench, Charles Barkley, and Bo Jackson. I have recorded a soundtrack at the famed Abbey Road Studios in London (which reinforced the opinion I should stick to writing!). I've shared special moments on our family farm with Kix Brookes. There are many others. I keep mementoes and souvenirs from those encounters – not to brag or show off. I keep them to remind myself that today's realities were yesterday's daydreams and that things I have accomplished are truly blessings, and they help me keep a healthy perspective.

Many of you have heard me say "I don't have to do this. I get to." Maybe you have a story that reminds you of just how blessed you are to have been chosen by the profession. Sometimes, we need a reminder that some of our biggest concerns are small in relation to what matters. To some, meditation helps. Others obsess over exercise. Sadly, some fall into despair and turn to drugs or alcohol. Me, well, I write. I journal. I study people and look for learning opportunities. Sometimes I find them in the unlikeliest places and from unexpected sources. However, it takes a certain level of openness and willingness. Haven't you always heard that you should listen twice as much as you talk? That's why you have two ears and one mouth? Ha.

It also takes just a little element of chance. I remember this Wednesday like no other. It was another "special" kind of day. My 8:00 a.m. flight started with a missed seat assignment, and I was the absolute last one to get on the plane. On Southwest Airlines, that means you get the seat everyone else passed up. Luckily, it was a short flight, and I knew I could survive.

It had been a stressful day. I was out of town preparing for a deposition on a matter that I had taken over from a former colleague that I knew well. The former colleague had made a number of mistakes in the damages calculation and in the report. I was in triage mode to avoid a lawsuit and to preserve the reputation of the profession. I had already agreed to write-off more than $100,000 to make things "right" on the former colleague's behalf, and also agreed to finish the case for peanuts.

The meeting finished two hours early, and I felt I had righted the ship. The clients seemed pleased. I then began to learn of all sorts of other things the colleague had said and done. I actually let it hurt me far more than it should. I reminded myself that "hurting people, hurt people." No matter how many times I thought of those words, it still stung. I was in an awful mood, but at least heading home.

I asked my administrative assistant to change my flight so that I could get home at a reasonable hour. However, unbeknownst to me, the request was not submitted in time, and the change was not made. I arrived at the airport and was unable to check in. I ended up flying standby and was able to walk onto a later flight. But it was the very last seat on the plane – the seat no one wanted . . . or was it actually saved for me?

I step off the jet bridge onto the plane, and everyone stares at me as if I'm the hold up (so you want to be popular, huh?). Two rows from the front, there is the open seat: a middle seat between two ladies. I generally like the middle seat, as I get to make two friends (yes, I am one of those). The lady occupying the aisle seat took up a lot of room, and the lady next to the window, I couldn't really tell, but I knew she was missing some teeth and looked disheveled. There was a pile of rubble in the seat between them, so I asked guardian (aisle lady) if I could take it, as "the plane appears to be full." She snaps back, very rudely, "I know there are other seats, but fine. You can sit here." She huffed and puffed and slung things around. Then I was even more determined to sit there. (I'm that kind of guy too!) But still, it was one more shot to the gut for the day.

So, the lady next to the window seemed like special-needs person. I looked closely at her, trying to ready myself for one more gut punch before takeoff. She was absolutely a mess and appeared deathly afraid of flying. Still, she looked as if she had been flying for days on end.

She offered me a breath mint, and I joked, "Well, I suppose if we are going to sit this close together, I might as well take one." She laughed . . . and laughed . . . and laughed. She slapped her knee and stomped her feet. A laugh like that is contagious. I knew, at this moment, for some strange reason, there was something special about her. I loved her immediately.

Jessica was her name, and she was from Charleston, but she explained:

Daddy was in the army, which wasn't my father. My father was from Colorado, but I lived in Plum, Texas. And did you know I graduated with eight people? We had less than 300 people in my entire school. And my schoolmate Frank, he ended up being the sheriff for the whole county! He dated my friend Stephanie, but we aren't friends now. I was engaged to a man there, and we dated for three years . . . but I decided to leave him when he wouldn't let me go to Mamma's birthday party.

So when I got in my car, my clutch broke. I wired it back together with some wire I had in my trunk, and you know what, I had to do that three more times until I got to my mamma's house . . . then Daddy fixed it.

Daddy can fix anything. It cost me $40 because I had the parts book, and he went down to the AutoZone right then and bought it. That was nine years ago and I've dated lots of men since then . . . but they all knew better than to not let me go to Mamma's birthday.

More howling and laughing. Stomping her feet and clapping her hands. I've never met a more animated storyteller. Her hands. Her laughter. I became amazed at just how "in the moment" she was. The flight attendants took notice, as if they were concerned with the disturbance. I shook and waved them off. I had tears, and we hadn't even left the gate yet. My side hurt.

I guessed she was somewhere around 30 years old, but "processed" on an 8- or 9 year-old level. I laughed to myself, because talking to her reminded me of what it must be like for people to have to talk to me on a regular basis. My apologies. She told me she was going to meet her sister and her sister's new baby in Dallas. It was so hard to follow her stories, as they jumped around between decades and states, and she used first names of people that I felt like I should have known. Every so often, she would burst out laughing to where she couldn't breathe. I loved it!

She told me that she was also going to spend time with her aunt Deb, and Aunt Deb was going to "cut off all my hair." I asked the obvious, "But why? You have beautiful hair." To wit, she laughed and responded: "Well, I have the brain cancer. And I won't ever get rid of it. I wasn't supposed to live. I'm in remission now, and have been for four years, but it is always in there somewhere. But I'm not scared of it anymore and when it comes back, I know what to do. When the doctor told me I had it, he also told me that I was going to die in six months. Do you know how many people I had to apologize to in those six months?"

She laughed so hard. More knee slaps and foot stomps. She showed me the scar on the left side of her head where "They got most of it, but I can't do math no more. Do you know, I had to learn to read and write all over again, but I still can't do math?

"I was pregnant one time, and I lost the baby. And now, look. It was a blessing that I lost that baby because I couldn't take care of it. In fact, my dog was 14 when he died. It was a few months after my surgery and I'm glad he died then because I just couldn't be sad no more.

"My daddy had just left my house when I called him to come bury my dog, and he couldn't come back so his friend Danny came over and buried the dog."

I felt like I was sitting next to the female version of Forrest Gump. Sometimes I couldn't understand her, and her stories grew harder to follow because "sometimes my brain gets tired and I shut down for a minute." Other times I sat amazed, choking back tears, much as I am while writing this. She went on and on about fishing in a Colorado stream when she was a child and remembering just how cold it was when she fell out of the boat that one time. How she worked her way up to being a supervisor, that is, when she worked.

"Now I'm on Social Security and it's really good money. Do you know, I bought my sister a Cowboys jersey last Christmas. I hate the Cowboys, so I wore my Carolina shirt for her today."

And she had it on under her jacket, and showed it to me. I've never seen anyone laugh so hard . . . and I couldn't have cried more if I had tried. Or so I thought.

I told her that I had never met a more beautiful person, and that my life was better because she was now in it. She noticed I was crying, and asked, "Why are you crying? I'm the one who's sick!" That was yet another hand-clapping shake-laugh.

She then got very serious, and said: "I remember when the doctors told me that I may not wake up from the surgery. And although I couldn't talk, or move my hands, I remember thinking, 'Oh yes I will.' I also remember when I finally could say one word or two, and when they told me I was gonna die in six months. I told them 'no' because I wasn't gonna."

"And you know something? Every day when I wake up, I smile. I smile and smile because it is another day that I wasn't supposed to have. You probably think I laugh a lot, but I laugh because I think I'm funny."

I've never quite had a feeling like I had at that moment. She was animated throughout, and wild with gestures. I don't remember if I drank anything, but she drank apple juice, and said it was "delicious." I felt ashamed for noticing her hair and guilty for being upset over my seating arrangements. I felt like a very small person, and yet, for some reason, I felt as if I had been reborn. I saw life from someone else's eyes . . . someone whom I wasn't even supposed to have met. But "someone" had other plans, didn't she?

I helped her find her baggage claim, and with that, two strangers separated. Though I know she'll never remember me, I hope I never forget her, and her laugh, and her smile and her outlook on life. It's a shame that I need reminding to be thankful from time to time. But for about 50 minutes, I couldn't imagine a better seat to have occupied. It was the "least desirable" seat on the plane, yet I would not have traded it for anything. I've replayed this in my mind a thousand times. I sat in the parking garage and journaled at that very moment. It took me two days to write it down, because I had as much trouble keeping my composure writing this as I did on the plane. Well, who am I kidding? I was a mess on the plane. It was a subtle, yet aggressive reminder that the challenges we face, although irritating, are insignificant in the grand scheme of things. I also felt thankful that all I had to "worry about" that day was whether I got home at 6 p.m., or 8 p.m. I keep that story and I have read it back to myself. My life is better because of it.

We all have tough days on the job. Not every day is good, but there is good in every day. My parting shot to you is that you are much more than your job. As passionate as we are about our profession, it is unhealthy to let it completely define you. Yes, you are an accountant. But you are also someone's son. Daughter. Uncle. Aunt. Niece or nephew. A friend. You are a colleague. Perhaps blessed to be a father or a mother. I bet someone cried tears of joy when you were born. You are so much more than your job. When you find yourself feeling unbearable pressure, facing on-the-job failures, remember, you can still be *awesome* that day at one of your other roles. And tomorrow is a brand-new opportunity to be an awesome accountant!

SUMMARY

Accountants face barriers when they identify fraud. While there are many different requirements in disclosing fraud and misconduct, there can also be perceived (and perhaps in some cases, real) repercussions in doing so. This dilemma can lead to pressure from those complicit with the bad acts and cause personal conflicts for accountants. This pressure can also lead to anxiety and personal anguish. Accountants should recognize the risk associated with remaining in such a culture and stand firm in adherence to the applicable laws and regulations.

Accountants may perform their obligations masterfully, only to face challenges when it comes time to report wrongdoing. Those challenges may consist of:

1. Sympathizing with the alleged perpetrator
2. Fear of retaliation when "blowing the whistle"
3. Prioritizing the client relationship above professional standards
4. Not fully appreciating the difference in ethical and unethical behavior

However, those who become informants do have protections against retaliation, as well as possible financial incentives. Corporations have similar incentives, in the forms of reduced sanctions and financial penalties.

Lastly, accountants may be more susceptible to exhaustion than any other profession. This can also lead to apathy, in which the accountant simply lacks the energy to fight against what seems insurmountable odds. It is very critical that accountants find healthy ways of seeking help and develop productive coping strategies.

 ## RECOMMENDATIONS

To overcome obstacles and barriers that may cause consternation when you're "doing the right thing":

1. *Find healthy coping mechanisms.* In your fraud books, and in this one, haven't you read that someone who never takes a vacation presents a fraud risk? It is also a red flag for accountants who aren't committing fraud! Working too many hours for too long can lead to burnout. When you find yourself burned out, little things become big things. It can lead to apathy in discharging your responsibilities. It can lead to carelessness. It can lead to almost every problem we've discussed in this book. While there are times in which taking a week or two off isn't practical, scheduling (and yes, I do literally mean scheduling) an hour or two each day to focus on "you" and "what makes you, you" can provide you a much-needed opportunity to catch your breath. Sometimes a barrier is nothing more than burnout wearing a disguise. The two times in my career, I sought counseling for burnout. Both times, I was told to recharge in nature. It helped! Taking a moment to catch your breath can help provide clarity, and also allow you some time to plan accordingly. Supervisors, be on the lookout for people reporting to you who may also be suffering from fatigue.

2. *Share your concerns.* As we have discussed many times in this text, nonaccountants (or those accountants who may be ethically challenged) may not fully appreciate your concerns or understand your position. Take an active approach to resolving the issue with those involved in the decision-making process.

3. *Seek independent counsel.* For high-risk situations, consult with those who have more experience in dealing with these matters. If you find that something is keeping you up at night, consult an attorney or peer. A trusted colleague can offer a fresh perspective. We can sometimes make mountains out of molehills, but that is much more preferable than failing to consider all consequences.

4. *Consider fight or flight.* Some situations warrant the ultimate decision. Should I stay or should I go now? End toxic relationships. Leave hostile

work environments. Accountants are in high demand, and life is too short, and our careers are too valuable to tolerate constant situations that threaten to compromise our ethics. After all, since you *are* keeping an accurate resume and CV, your next opportunity, client, or employer could be dying to see it.

5. *Trust your faith more than your fear.* What do you let dominate your "news-feed"? Do you spend all your time obsessing over what can go wrong, versus what can go right? Sometimes, your instincts are spot on. You are an educated professional, one who is good at your job. And if you made it this far, you are someone dedicated to being even better. Sometimes, you simply need faith in yourself and courage to stand tall in the face of adversity. And in those times, whether you feel this way at the time, you will never be alone in your convictions. You have an entire profession behind you.

This is a two-parter! Now that you have the courage to do the right thing, focus on removing barriers that may prevent others from doing the right thing, and actually encourage them to pursue the appropriate course of action, I suggest the following:

1. *Establish an employee reporting mechanism.* While this is required for publicly traded companies, and some governmental agencies, this is one of the strongest controls. Providing employees with a hotline, and ensuring only those with a need to know are alerted to the information, employees who are fearful of retaliation may have sufficient courage to come forward.

2. *Track the hotline's effectiveness.* The only hotline that truly fails is one that isn't used. Employee surveys and well as user metrics can provide insight as to whether our employees have confidence in the process. Test it! Place calls (obviously inform counsel first!) and see if the information is routed accordingly. This provides one more benchmark to assess effectiveness.

3. *Reward good behavior, just as you punish bad.* It does not have to be monetary awards. Kind and encouraging words can mean all the difference to those who faced personal risks in reaching the decision to move forward.

4. *Remove incentives that actually encourage bad behavior.* Compensation structures and promotions based entirely on financial metrics can actually encourage inappropriate actions. I don't encourage entirely ignoring financial performance, but a healthy balance between metrics and adhering to a strong set of core values is preferred.

Case Study: Whistling While You Work

Alice works for a global, publically traded manufacturing organization as the Chief Compliance Officer. She is a CPA and a CFE, and leads the company's investigative function. She has been in the role for less than one year, replacing someone who held the role for "a couple of years," before choosing early retirement.

The company is in the process of expanding in the Middle East, where the demand for their products has risen due to the increase in construction projects. The company is also in the process of building a distribution warehouse there.

Alice received a call on the whistleblower hotline. The claimant reports there are significant bribes and kickbacks on the books that are being disguised as construction variances. The caller also alleges that certain governmental contracts are "padded" to compensate the company for excessive meals, entertainment, and various expenses (such as consulting and training fees).

Alice conducts a preliminary review and determines there are excessive construction variances, and the governmental contract profit margins are much higher than those in other areas. Alice must determine whether or not to go forward with the investigation.

1. Does Alice have sufficient predication to advance the investigation? Explain.
2. In deciding whether to investigate, what might Alice's personal risk assessment include?
3. How is Alice's personal risk assessment similar, and perhaps unique, to the risk assessment the company may have completed prior to deciding to expand its footprint in the Middle East?
4. What are the costs/benefits of having an external investigative team conduct the investigation?
5. What roles do the additional accountants play in this matter, and what risks might each face:
   a. External audit
   b. Management
   c. Financial fraud expert
6. What information might the retired compliance officer provide?
7. Considering the limited facts above, what laws may have been violated?

(Continued)

8. If the company decides to investigate, what considerations must be made in advance to launching the probe?
9. If the company finds fraud, what challenges might they face in deciding whether to disclose their findings?
10. Similarly, if they do not allow Alice to move forward, assuming there is predication, what options does she have?

About the Author

Jeffrey G. Matthews is a father, a son, and a grandson. Professionally, he is an accountant, a lecturer, and a college professor. He was the 2013 Certified Fraud Examiner of the Year and has been recognized for his client service and professional collaboration on multiple occasions. He was born and raised in a small town in Louisiana. And while he has never truly left the bayou country, he finds himself celebrating his second decade of living in the Dallas/Fort Worth area.

Jeff's 25-year journey as a Certified Public Accountant and a Certified Fraud Examiner has afforded him opportunities to conduct fraud, litigation, and consulting assignments across 13 countries. These experiences have taken him in and out of courtrooms, as well as dalliances in and out of harm's way. Anchored by a strong family bond, a faith-filled constitution, and supported by colleagues spanning the globe, Jeff has experienced the intimate highs, lows, and overall price of the profession. Jeff shares his triumphs and his personal struggles to overcome his disappointments in battling personal and professional conflicts. Jeff reminds us that we will experience plenty of peaks and valleys, and that staying grounded in faith, family, and professional standards can lead to redemption.

Outside of the profession, Jeff enjoys boating, biking, and boxing. He also loves country camping trips, and exploring the world's wonders through hikes, horseback rides, or ATV drives accompanied by his three children and his handsome yellow lab, Sonny.

Acknowledgments

I HAVE LONG SAID THAT it's not that we accountants are boring; it's that we get excited over boring things. Nonetheless, this book is based entirely on my exposure to many special people, which has resulted in a very exciting journey for me. I hope I have made that evident. There is no way for me to thank and acknowledge them all, so I will cover those closest to my heart.

First, I have to acknowledge my parents. I was very fortunate to have them both in my life – a life that was not necessarily planned or a given. You see, I am here as a result of an ethical decision of the highest order. In 1973, I became the son to a 17-year-old mamma and 20-year-old daddy. That year, 25% of the teenage moms made a decision that would have resulted in me not being here, not being able to share my story and my thoughts. I do not say that to persuade my readers to ascribe to a certain belief. That is far from my intent. I am telling you this so that you can see just how the ethical decisions that you face today, and the decisions you ultimately make can, and often will, last a lifetime. They may not necessarily result in life or death, but to some it can feel like it. In my case, the ethical decision made lasted beyond my dad's lifetime. And for that, I am eternally grateful.

My relationship with my dad was complex. He was a big dreamer with wild-eyed anticipations. While he never said so, I always knew that I had altered his life's trajectory. As a child, and occasionally as an adult, I felt like an accident. I felt like a mistake. I wasn't "meant" to be here. (God had other plans. He's sneaky that way.) I felt guilty that I was the reason that my dad was forever "chained" to a small town in Louisiana, and somewhat limited by being burdened with a family at such a young age. I always tried my hardest to make it up to him by obsessively striving to achieve the only two qualities he measured – being tough and hard-working. To this day, I have not found an instruction manual or textbook informing me about how either of these are measured. It was not until his health failed and I had long moved to Texas that I began realizing I had at least made a favorable impression with him, and he let his true feelings toward me come closer into focus. I remember receiving his late-night calls from the hospital, close to the end of his time with us. He was on enough medication to tranquilize a horse, but it eased his guard, and he was able to say things that he had suppressed for decades. Sadly, those were the only "real" conversations I had ever had with the man. I have no idea if he really knew what he was sharing with me, or if he realized that it was me he was talking to. But those 2:00 and 3:00 a.m. calls are all I have to show that he felt I had proved my worth and earned his respect. When he passed, a few of his closest friends shared what he had always told them about me. At my dad's funeral, one of his closest buddies, and the man who poured the foundation on our family home, gave me a firm handshake, held me by the shoulders, and said, "You are a man today. You're ready." It took me a while to understand the depth of that comment. And while I do not always feel "ready" or "tough," I still remember the promise I made to be a man, even during those times when I do not feel like it. To this day, I occasionally find myself trying to prove myself and make him proud. It was not until I ventured into this journey that I realized how futile it is to appease a man no longer here. I realized that if I'm not careful, I can live a life for someone else. I am so very thankful that my dad stuck around for his entire life, and provided for me and my brothers and sisters. I saw many dads who fled and abandoned their families, and left them with far less than what we were blessed to enjoy. And despite the many times during our tumultuous relationship that I wished he were gone, I wish he, too, were here today – something I never thought I would say or write. Still, even to this day, I dream about him no less than once a week. That will have to suffice.

As I was writing this book, I realized that while I always sympathized with my dad, I never felt that way about my mom. Perhaps I was "fighting" for a love I never felt I had, or I deserved (my dad's) Or, maybe I was behaving in ways that I felt were more pleasing to my dad, for fear he would finally leave forever. Fleeing this small town once and for all. Nonetheless, my mamma was my rock. My one constant. She was unwavering. I never once felt she was destined to be anything other than a mommy and a nurse. During my raising, she was joyful during some very exasperating times. She never made us feel that we were a burden. Well, except for this one time that I nearly ripped my toe off wrestling with my younger brother during a "wild" Louisiana Friday night. The trip to the ER to get stitches meant she missed an episode of *Dallas*. Nothing stood in the way of her Friday night date with *Dallas*. I think she had a mind to amputate my toe and douse it with "monkey blood" while sending me to bed. The only "drug" she believed in was being "drug" to church. I digress. But imagine how terrified she must have been as an expecting 16-year-old. (I mean, I was seeing how long I could hold my hand in an ant bed when I was

16. What were you doing?) The decisions she faced. The judgment from those living in that small Baptist and Methodist town. I cannot imagine she ever dreamed of having a son attend her high school and college graduations. (Do you know, she never even got a single B in school? I, on the other hand, made up for it. I even threw in a few Cs for good measure.) She was courageous, and I like to think I inherited that from her. It reminds me of Billy Graham's quote: "Courage is contagious. When a brave man takes a stand, the spines of others are often stiffened." My mom still lives on the same plot we discussed early in this writing. She has made for an amazing grandmother, which has afforded me the opportunity to share my family history and culture with my children. Seeing my mom walk my children in the woods, sharing life lessons I have long forgotten, is one of the most cherished experiences I will ever have. Bible stories. Tree houses. Cabins in the woods. Gardening. Wildlife. Campfires. I think we would all get along better if there were a little more of that in our lives. Don't you? Every night before bed, she read me stories. My favorite story was *Where the Wild Things Are*. When I moved to Dallas from Baton Rouge, she gave me a picture with the book characters framed. On the back, she taped a note:

> When you feel overwhelmed, and the burdens of life seem like more than you can bear, take a slow deep breath. Allow your mind to wander and take you back to a faraway place. A much simpler time. One where even a little boy can be "King of All Wild Things."

I still have the picture and the note in my office, more than 20 years later (*shhhh;* we won't talk about the tattoo). For my mom always believed in me far more than she should. Far more than I ever believed in myself. I thank her for reminding me that God is always good. And I am always loved.

My uncle, Greg Matthews, was also a guiding light and enormous influence on my life. I have used him as an inspiration and still visit him every chance I get. Our talks and time together always leave me in a better place. I have leaned on him during low times, and celebrated with him during high times. He gave me hope that we can overcome most anything. "No one can ever say we had it easy." We can allow our history to confine us and define us, or we can allow it to propel us into unchartered waters. That is certainly where I feel he and I both currently find ourselves, and I'm proud to share this voyage with him. He taught me that we can succeed in spite of the most challenging of circumstances. It is the fear that our bit of success is only temporary, and that we are always one mistake away from returning to collecting bottles and cans for change, that keeps us both grounded. We share many of the same qualities, both good and bad, and I like to think we have served as good counsel for one another (well, we have been known to get each other in a lot of trouble!). Still, I cannot imagine my life without him.

I would have never graduated from college without the tutelage of my aunt, my mom's sister, Alisa Hale. She was only two years older than I was, and we were raised as siblings. I think that is why my mom was a good mamma at 16, as she has a sister the same age as her son. Ha! My aunt delayed starting college until I did, so we started and graduated together. We both majored in accounting. (She also never made anything but an A. Why didn't I inherit that gene?!) In fact, our first jobs were both with the Legislative Auditor's Office in Baton Rouge. She stayed up countless nights to help me study accounting, and introduced me to coffee. Starbucks thanks you! Whether it was working accounting problems or proctoring sample accounting tests, she was so patient with me. She was and still is a great cheerleader for me. Her dedication to seeing me through graduation is something I will never forget or take for granted. I just hope there comes a time when I can help someone along the way, as she helped me.

I could go on and on about the support of my family. My grandmothers and great-grandmothers all helped raise me, and provided a great example of our tight family bond. My brother and my sister both go out of their way to stay in touch and involve me in my nieces' and nephews' lives. Other aunts and uncles, and great-aunts and great-uncles and countless cousins make sure I know their doors and hearts are always open.

Professionally, my career started in 1995 with Mr. Allen Brown, a fellow small-town man who gave this small-town boy a chance. His family home was less than an hour from mine, in rural Louisiana. He guided me through many of the cases I have referenced, along with many that never made it to print. Along the way, he introduced me to the Association of Certified Fraud Examiners. And beginning in 1998, ACFE presidents James Ratley and Bruce Dorris gave me opportunities to share my stories and insights across the globe. Our partnership has allowed me to meet and learn from many of you. These valuable and cherished relationships helped challenge me, pushing me to continuously grow and remain curious about the profession. These relationships also led me to John Wiley & Sons and Sheck Cho. What a wonderful group to work with.

There is also the University of Texas at Arlington. In 2011, they allowed me to follow my great-grandmother and grandmother's passion for teaching. They took a chance on a graduate-level fraud examination course that I pieced together, and it has worked. Spending one night a week giving back to the profession while engaging with students has been far more rewarding than I ever could have imagined.

There is also my work team and their tireless efforts: Stephen Howard, who has stuck by me since 2000; and Veronique Chauveau and Melyana Melyana, who joined me in 2003. Those who arrived later in the game have also been a great help: Megan Martin, Katie McGee, Patricia Larabee, Gular Wiefling, David Kirk, Sunny Chu, Mai Nguyen, and Jamie Baker. (in fact, Mai, a fellow Louisianian, made us all strive to make this a special offering) They all took the time to help me research various areas included in this book. On their own time! I have always felt that it was my job to support them and their families, just as I have done with mine. I know the sacrifices it takes to be in this profession. This book is only possible because of their hard work and dedication. I would be lost without them.

And last, and certainly not least, my own family, especially Janna and the sacrifices she has made, and continues to make. See, the professional does not simply impact those working in it; it impacts all those supported by it. Being passionate about this job can lead to a degree of selfishness, and at times, misplaced priorities. It is during those times that she has shown that she is much stronger than I will ever be. My children, Caleb, Joshua, and Camryn. Caleb possessed a degree of intelligence I don't have (perhaps the straight-A thing skips a generation?). He has inherited my sense of fairness and stern belief in right or wrong. I have done nothing to deserve such a special young man. I am proud of him beyond measure. I hope never he loses his imagination. I pray he never feels alone as he embraces leaving the nest for college next year. Now, I do deserve Joshua. *Haha!* His sense of humor and adventure. He currently has purple hair (insert parental eye roll here) His love of animals and the outdoors. The support he lends his friends. His company on fishing trips, long hikes, campouts, and ATV trails. Those memories last, and I hope he always finds his way back to nature, no matter where his life leads. Speaking of last, my little spitfire Camryn. Her athleticism and energy (which led to her adorning a bright blue cast on her left arm. Ugghhh.) Her beauty. Her sense of wonder. Curiosity. She recently received the "character" award at her school, and I received a note from her teacher explaining why (those are *not* the kind of notes my parents received from my teachers!). The excitement she has for simply being alive gives me hope for a generation that sometimes appears hopeless. I love them all. Perhaps they have inherited the bit of good that I have, and can build on it far more than I have. I pray that one day, they can write about me, and recall some of the good times we have been so fortunate to have had.

Our time is so priceless and irreplaceable. It is meaningful. I am beyond appreciative that you have allowed me to borrow a little bit of yours. And I hope that I have given you something that you can take and share with others, as so many of you have done with me. Be blessed.

Index